5 50

3 50

D1222787

THE AUTHORITY
OF THE OLD TESTAMENT

THE AUTHORITY
OF THE OLD TESTAMENT

by

A. G. HEBERT

of the Society of the Sacred Mission, Kelham

FABER AND FABER LTD
24 Russell Square
London

First published in mcmxlvii
by Faber and Faber Limited
24 Russell Square London W.C.1
Second impression January mcml
Third impression April mcmlvii
Printed in Great Britain by
Latimer Trend & Co Ltd Plymouth

INTRODUCTION

It is possible to study the Bible from many different angles. It provides important material for the science of Comparative Religion. It is indispensable for the study of the ancient history of the Middle East. It gives the philologist many data for his knowledge of ancient Semitic languages and of the colloquial Greek of the Roman Empire. Read purely as literature, it contains the noblest religious poetry ever written. But in none of these cases is it being studied as 'Scripture'. It is read as 'Scripture' or as 'Bible' only when it is read in the light of the religious faith which has been held by a certain visible society, variously called Israel, the *Qahal*, the *Ecclesia*, or the Church, which has existed for more than three thousand years and still exists, and which regards it as a divinely inspired book. Therefore a treatise on the Authority of the Bible presupposes the faith of this visible society, and its main theme must be to determine what is the meaning of the term 'Bible', and the essential function of the Bible, in relation to the Tradition of the faith and the way of life of this society.

This society believes that its faith contains the essential truths which man needs to know about the meaning of his own existence in the world, and about the world itself; it believes further that this faith depends, and its own existence depends, on the historical truth of certain Events in which it is claimed that the Eternal God has revealed Himself in redeeming man; and it appeals to the Bible as giving the historical testimony to these Events. This assertion that God has acted in history, and that the story of His action is told in the Bible, demands therefore a series of historical inquiries, in order that it may be known

7

Introduction

whether the history which the Bible narrates is substantially true history, and not the product of man's wish to believe, and his power to express his religious ideas in the form of myth and of legend.

Thus in the study of the Bible theology and scientific history meet; and it is this fact that constitutes the problem of the Bible. The difficulty of the problem is felt in the conflict, still largely unresolved, which is apparent in very many books which have been written about the Bible, between the conscience of the historian, who, starting from the ordinary assumptions of scientific study, takes for granted that 'miracles do not happen', and that of the same writer as a Christian believer, desiring to make the Christian affirmations of faith. The conflict is very far-reaching; and it has involved a perplexing dilemma between a critical study of the Bible which resolves it into a composite of human utterances and robs it of its divine authority as the word of God to man, and an assertion of the divine character of the Bible which regards it as being therefore free from all possible error, and is therefore compelled to repudiate the methods and the conclusions of the critical historian. This dilemma does not affect only the professional student; it applies no less to the ordinary Christian believer, whose worship in church involves the continual use of the Bible. The result is that a paralysing uncertainty about the Bible has extremely serious results today for the Church in the fulfilment of its mission in the world.

Plainly, the difficulty centres at least to a large extent in the meaning of the words 'truth' and 'error'. There is a truth of physical fact and of the verifiable actuality of historical events. There is also a truth of the eternal meaning of man's existence, a truth of his relation to the God who made him and of the purpose of God with regard to him. Nothing but confusion can result if these different levels of truth are not distinguished. But the fundamental proclamation of the Christian Faith, that God has acted in history, implies that there these different sorts of truth meet and cross one another. No true answer can be reached by the easy assertion that the theologian and the historian work in separate and independent spheres, and need take no notice of one another's results.

Introduction

Here, then, is the problem which confronts us in this book. A book on the Authority of the Bible is primarily a theological book; but it must deal also with questions of history at every point. But historical inquiry must be carried on by historical methods, and each separate subject of historical inquiry demands a careful and specialist treatment. On these things, the theologian as such is not competent to dogmatize; he must be content to summarize what he has learnt from the historian. But the historian, for his part, is not competent to give final answers to the theological questions involved in the history; when he attempts to do so (and he often does), he is liable to err through his unconscious acceptance of unexamined theological presuppositions. Here it is the theologian's duty to examine the theological bearings of the problems of history and criticize the theological presuppositions of the historian. As theologian, he cannot pronounce on historical issues; but it is his duty to make himself at least reasonably competent on the historical questions, and know what the questions really are.

The argument of this book involves a whole series of historical problems which are the proper subject of expert historical investigation, and each of which demands for its full elucidation a special and detailed study such as would be impossible within the limits of this book, and such as, in any case, lies outside the competence of the present writer. In dealing with these subjects (see, for instance, pp. 55 and 123) he has striven to show a proper respect for the proper function of the specialist historian, while endeavouring to fulfil the theologian's duty of showing the theological bearings of the problems under discussion.

This book is concerned with the authority of the Old Testament, rather than that of the Bible as a whole. If its subject were 'the Authority of the Bible', it would have been necessary to deal with the New Testament canon on the same lines as that of the Old, and raise the whole question of the relation of the New Testament to the life of the Apostolic Church (of the gospels to the historical tradition, of the epistles to the Church's catechetical practice, and of both to its whole *via vitae*), the needs which led to the canonization of the New Testament writings, and the effects of their canonization on the Church's life.

Introduction

Nevertheless, a book which deals with the authority of the Old Testament for the Christian Church is bound to deal fairly fully with the fulfilment of the Old Testament in Christ and in the Church, and is bound also to make continual reference to the faith of the New Testament and the Church, and set that faith side by side with the faith of Old Israel. The problem of the authority of the Old Testament for the Church involves that of the theological unity of the Bible.

The *first chapter* of the book states the problem of the Bible, and particularly of the Old Testament. There is widespread uncertainty about the Bible; we have not yet resolved the dilemma between the 'conservative' doctrine of Biblical inerrancy, which accepts the Bible as being truly the word of God, but does less than justice to its human element, and fails to answer the questions raised by Biblical criticism, and the Liberal-Protestant view, which fully accepts the human character of the Bible, but is unable to assign to it a properly divine authority. Liberal-Catholicism endeavours to hold the two sides together, but fails to reconcile them. In all this, we must remind ourselves that the problem is no less acute for the ordinary Christian than for the scholar.

In the *second chapter* an answer to the problem is sought, by regarding the Bible in direct relation to the divine Purpose of Salvation worked out in history, and thus treating it as authoritative (i) as the historical record of the establishment of the Divine Kingdom; (ii) as giving us the teaching about God and the way of His spiritual service which the Israel of God learnt in the course of its history; and (iii) as declaring the End to which the Divine Purpose was moving. The principle that God has revealed Himself through human instruments makes it inevitable that there should be imperfections in the Bible.

The *third chapter* discusses the problem of Divine Revelation, and asks how far the 'conservative' view has adequately dealt with it. In the Bible, Revelation is first the personal revelation of God Himself through His redemptive action, and then the revelation of the necessary truths concerning Him and His will for man; this is illustrated by the Biblical conception of 'faith'. But in Western theology, there has been a tendency to rational-

Introduction

ize the idea of Revelation by one-sided emphasis on its second meaning; this reappears in an exaggerated form in the materialistic conception of truth that is characteristic of Fundamentalism. When, however, Revelation is rightly viewed in relation to God's action in history, the conception of the Inspiration of the Bible falls into its place; it means that God has spoken His word in and through the human record. It is thus possible to regard the Bible, as a whole, as inspired.

The *fourth chapter* asks how far the Liberal view of the Bible has put criticism in its right place, and whether it has not erred through accepting a view of history which is fundamentally secularist. When, however, the Bible is seen as the Book of the Faith, it becomes apparent that there is no opposition between Faith and Criticism. A faith which proclaims a divine action in history is bound to appeal to history; two crucial points are our Lord's resurrection and His messianic claim. The task of the Christian student is then to use critical methods to the full, while seeing the Bible always as the Book of the Faith.

These four chapters form the first part of the book, and review the theological problem. The second part consists mainly of a historical survey of the contents of the Bible, from the point of view which has been stated.

In the *fifth chapter*, the aim is to learn what the Bible is through a study of the needs which first called it into existence as 'Scripture'. It is necessary to start with the Book of Deuteronomy, and then to trace in outline the spiritual history of Israel in exile, up to the point when the Pentateuch became canonical in Ezra's Reform.

The *sixth chapter* carries on the story into the period of Judaism after Ezra, showing how the necessary emphasis now laid on Israel's exclusiveness involved a temporary obscuring of the prophetic teaching in certain respects. In this period the prophetic books became canonical; this led (paradoxically) to the rise of the doctrine of Biblical Inerrancy. Towards the close of the pre-Christian era the Canon was completed by the recognition of the 'Writings' as Scripture.

The *seventh chapter* attempts to formulate the principles of the use of the Old Testament in the New. The Purpose of God for

Introduction

Israel is proclaimed to be fulfilled in Jesus the Messiah. The legitimacy of the exegesis of the O.T. in the N.T. writers is widely questioned; but we can distinguish a 'theological' use of the O.T., in which the writers prove their points by the O.T. texts, from their use of the texts as convenient 'illustrations' of points which they believe to be true on other grounds. The N.T. theology is mostly given in terms of the concrete Old Testament imagery; but there is also the more rationalized statement of Christology in terms of the Divine Wisdom. The interpretation of the Prophecies by the N.T. writers shows how wide a view they take of the working-out of the Divine Purpose; in this respect their view of the O.T. is markedly different from that of contemporary Judaism.

The third part of the book draws the argument together in an examination of the use of the Old Testament in the Church. The *eighth chapter* deals with the 'literal sense'. It is vital to the Church's faith and life that the Bible story should be substantially true as history: that the teaching of the Old Testament about God and the way of His spiritual service should be used for edification; and that the O.T. prophecies should be accepted as truly pointing to Christ. But also in the O.T. itself we see the beginnings of a 'spiritual' interpretation of Scripture.

The *ninth chapter* seeks to draw the right line of distinction between that 'spiritual' (or 'mystical') interpretation which is of obligation for Christians, and the 'allegorical' exegesis which is of a more arbitrary character, and whose true basis is not the Scriptural texts which it expounds, but the Catholic Faith which it employs them to illustrate. This distinction follows directly from that of the 'theological' and 'illustrative' uses of the Old Testament in the New. It is the former type of spiritual interpretation that appears in the doctrinal teaching of the New Testament and the Church, and in the Church's liturgy.

The *tenth chapter* concludes the book with a rapid survey of the relation of Scripture and Tradition. The two are inseparable; it was out of the Tradition of the Faith within the Israel of God that both the O.T. and the N.T. books arose, and it was for the preservation of that Tradition in its fullness that they were canonized and used. The apostolic writings present the Chris-

Introduction

tian Tradition in its wholeness. Since that time, the assimilation by the Tradition of the Graeco-Roman and other cultures has occasioned certain distortions of the Tradition; these distortions have given rise to the schisms of Christendom, and have been also reflected in distorted views of the Bible itself. The reunion of Christendom (which must be taken to include also the return of the Jews to acknowledge their own Messiah) must depend on a progressive recovery of the fulness of the apostolic Tradition, and of the right understanding and use of the Bible.

Having completed his work, the author feels that almost every subject with which he has dealt has been treated far too briefly. Yet it was not possible for a study of the authority of the Old Testament from the point of view of the Christian use of it to evade any of the questions which are raised in these chapters. It is his hope that the questions have been asked and the problems raised in the right way, and that others will be able to make far more adequate use of the material here provided than he has been able to do.

When the manuscript of this book was complete, but not yet finally revised, I was asked by the Church Union to write a smaller book on the Bible as their Lent Book for 1947. Messrs. Faber and Faber kindly consented to this being done; I therefore laid aside this book for a few months, and set myself to express some of its main points in a popular form, with the advantage of being able to refer to this forthcoming book for a fuller justification of the positions there maintained. The smaller book was published in February 1947 by Geoffrey Bles with the title of *Scripture and the Faith*.

Kelham,
   Newark.   A. G. HEBERT, s.s.m.
March 1947.

In the second edition, the passage from St. Athanasius quoted on p. 18 is from the translation of the *De Incarnatione* by 'A Religious of C.S.M.V.', Geoffrey Bles, 1944; I have to thank Mr. Bles for his kind permission to print this.

A.G.H.

CONTENTS

Contents

Contents

But for the searching and right understanding of the Scriptures there is need of a good life and a pure soul, and for Christian virtue to guide the mind to grasp, so far as human nature can, the truth about God the Word. One cannot possibly understand the teaching of the saints unless one has a pure mind and is trying to imitate their life. Anyone who wants to look at sunlight naturally wipes his eye clear first, in order to make at any rate some approximation to the purity of that on which he looks; and a person wishing to see a city or country goes to the place in order to do so. Similarly, anyone who wishes to understand the mind of the sacred writers must first cleanse his own life, and approach the saints by copying their deeds. Thus united to them in the fellowship of life he will both understand the things revealed to them by God and, thenceforth escaping the peril that threatens sinners in the judgment, will receive that which is laid up for the saints in the kingdom of heaven. Of that reward it is written: 'Eye hath not seen nor ear heard, neither hath entered into the heart of man the things that God has prepared' for them that live a godly life and love the God and Father in Jesus Christ our Lord, through whom and with whom be to the Father himself, with the Son Himself in the Holy Spirit, honour and might and glory to ages of ages. Amen. —St. Athanasius, *The Incarnation of the Word of God*, the concluding paragraph.

CHAPTER I

A PROBLEM UNSOLVED

1. *The Authority of the Bible*

The Bible would not be the Bible if it did not speak to us with authority. But it is not so clear what precisely is the nature of its authority. To claim that it has authority is to claim that it is true; and 'truth' is very widely understood to mean in the first place the truth of demonstrable physical fact: the truth of history being that of a correct description of events as they actually happened, and the truth of ideas the verifiable correspondence of those ideas with reality. If then it is claimed that the Bible is true, is this to mean that every statement in the Bible is either an authentic record of events which happened, or an accurate expression of true beliefs about God and man? There has been the controversy between 'religion' and 'science': was the world created and made in six days of twenty-four hours each, or did it reach its present state through long ages of development out of some primaeval nebula? Was there really a man called Methuselah who lived for nine hundred and sixty-nine years and probably perished in the Flood? Certainly the Bible has traditionally been regarded as an unassailable compendium of true statements resting on the authority of God Himself; and the ordinary person to-day has a vague or clear notion that the Bible, so understood, is radically challenged by the scientific and historical knowledge which we now possess. An acute observer of the contemporary situation says that 'the real point about the Bible in the modern world is that it is a fallen oracle'.[1] Yet the ordinary person has a distinct feeling that in thus setting aside the authority of the Bible he has lost hold of something of the greatest value for human life.

[1] R. A. Edwards, *Jack, Jill and God*, Methuen 1936, p. 88.

A Problem Unsolved

This last consideration introduces another aspect of the Bible's 'authority'. In the past, European culture knew itself to be based on a tradition of living, handed down in the family and the various institutions of a civilized community, which provided men with a light to steer by, standards by which to regulate their thinking, and patterns of living on which to model their conduct; and the Bible stood at the centre of this tradition. It provided men, not only with a framework of belief, but also with a moral background; here were clear examples of right and wrong, patterns of what was honourable and what was shameful, and an authentic ideal of what human nature was meant to be. But increasingly in our day men feel that they have lost touch with this tradition of right living. They see things happening around them in the world which shock them profoundly, and make them fear that human society no longer stands on its right foundations, but is drifting away in a direction which threatens disaster. They would gladly find their way back out of the quagmire on to what they could feel to be firm ground; and they feel an envy for the men of earlier generations, in whose eyes the authority of the Bible stood unquestioned. Those men appear, indeed, to have held may opinions which are impossible for us; but at least they had a trustworthy guide to right living, and their world stood securely on its base, whereas ours is reeling and threatening to crash in ruin. Our world has left the Bible behind; but it is by no means happy with itself that it has done so. It has not replaced the Bible with something better; rather, the disappearance of the Bible from its old position of authority has left an unfilled blank.

From these difficulties and perplexities we who accept the authority of the Bible are not immune. We too belong to the confused and disordered world, and form part of it; and we have also our difficulties about the Bible itself. Ought we to say, as some among us do, that the traditional view of the Bible which our forefathers held was in all essentials right, so that the declension from it is simply a falling-away from truth into error, and that we must continue to regard the Bible as a compendium of truths vouched for by the authority of God Himself? On the other hand, this conception is radically challenged by modern

The Authority of the Bible

Biblical scholarship, which proclaims in the clearest tones that the Bible is a human book, full indeed of divinely given wisdom and insight, but by no means free from error, and characterized throughout by the human limitations of its writers. But when the Bible is presented in this way, it seems to be difficult for it to retain the position of authority which it held for our fore-fathers. It easily becomes a book of moral and religious ideals, which are valued by the religiously-minded, but whose relevance is not so apparent to the common man; and it is no longer regarded in the old way as God's book, announcing His word of truth. Thus we in the Church appear to be caught in a dilemma between the old view of it in which it held a secure divine authority, but which appears to be challenged by modern knowledge, and a modern view in which it is truly seen to be a human book, but has lost its old power. It will be our aim in this book to explore this dilemma in some detail and endeavour to find how it may be possible to see the Bible both as a truly human book written by imperfect men, and as the book of God's word to man, which tells of His mighty works in the past, and still speaks in the tones of command which ring out in our Lord's words in the gospel: 'As ye go, preach, saying, The Kingdom of Heaven is at hand.'

In one respect the Biblical writers, without exception, agree with the men of the modern world. They regard the world as a dark world, disordered and full of evil. That at least the modern man is in a position to understand. He has unlearnt the optimism of the nineteenth century, when men thought that they were embarked on a course of progress which would lead to a millennium of universal well-being. It is true that there is much wishful optimism still abroad, even among Christians; but the prevailing tone is one of profound anxiety, not so much at the amazing discoveries which our scientists continue to make, as over the power of *homo sapiens* to control these dangerous powers, in such a way as not to involve himself and his civilization in total ruin.

Here at least the Bible meets the modern man on his own ground. All flesh has corrupted its way upon the earth. The world is full of darkness and cruel habitations. Mankind as a

whole is worshipping false gods, making vain idols and becoming vain. There are the 'world-rulers of this darkness', and
'spiritual wickedness in high places'—what we now call demonic
forces. The Biblical writers do not believe in the power of man to
save himself; here they are profoundly pessimistic. Yet, though
themselves often perplexed and discouraged, they face the
world with radiant hope, because they have faith in the God to
whom the world belongs, as revealed in His own transcendent
action. Appealing to certain events in the past in which He has
intervened to constitute Israel as His chosen people, they proclaim that He is in control of His world and is working out His
purpose in it.

Hence the truth about God which we are to find in the Bible
is not a truth similar in kind to the law of gravitation, or the
law which determines the behaviour of the atom. These are
universal truths about the constitution of things, which have
been discovered by careful observation and patient research; by
applying them we can control and use the atom and the forces
of nature in general for our own purposes, beneficent or otherwise. The truth which the Biblical writers proclaim relates not
to facts of a lower order of existence than our own, but to those
of that higher order of existence from which our own existence
is derived. There is much indeed to be learnt about the ways
of God by observation and patient thought; but the key of the
matter which the Bible provides, is the revelation of God in His
own independent and sovereign action. The result of learning
such truth cannot be that man will be able to control God and
make use of Him for the furtherance of human well-being; it is
that man, at last, learns who is his Master and whose is the law
by which he himself stands to be judged.

Hence it is not a right statement of the matter to say that,
while other books deal each with its own special subject, the
Bible deals with the special subject of religion. Certainly, the
Bible is the highest of all authorities on the life of prayer and
the adoration of God; but its interests are as wide as human life,
and there is nothing in the whole activity of the gifted nation
which produced it that lies outside its scope. That which makes
the Bible different from all other books is not that it is appro-

priated to that special branch of human activity which we call religion, but that the nation, which gave it to us, was chosen by Almighty God to be in the special sense His people, and the medium of His revelation of Himself to man, that at last through it all the nations of the earth might be blessed. In the New Testament, and through the Church, we see that which had been the privilege of one nation made available for all.

2. The Conservative View

We have spoken of a dilemma, between two rival views of the Bible. On the one side there is the view which for the moment we will describe as the 'conservative' view; for it is difficult to find the right phrase for it, and impossible to fix on a single book which can be accepted as the standard and normal statement of it.[1] A review of the possible phrases which can be used to describe it will serve best to open up the subject.

That the Bible is *inspired* is acknowledged by all Christians; the problem to understand how it is inspired: that is to say, how God has spoken through the human authors. It has sometimes been maintained that the human writer is to be compared to the pen in God's hand, or to a musical instrument through which the breath of the Spirit passes; the difference in the styles of the writers is thus compared to the difference between the writing executed with different pens, or the music produced by different instruments. These comparisons can be found in some of the second-century fathers, such as Justin Martyr and Athenagoras, who use the similes of a harp or a flute,[2] or Gregory the Great, who says that since the Holy Ghost is the author of the books, it is as superfluous to inquire who is the human author as to ask what pen a man had used in writing a certain letter.[3] This notion was uncritically taken by these fathers from Philo the Alexandrian Jew of the first century, who in his compromise be-

[1] The latest book which I have been able to find, giving a full-length exposition of it with all the apparatus of scholarship, is the learned William Lee's lectures given at Dublin in 1854, *The Inspiration of Holy Scripture*.

[2] Justin, *Apol.* xxxvi, Athenagoras, *Apology* x.

[3] *Preface to the Morals on the Book of Job*. P. Thompson, *The Inspiration and Inerrancy of the Bible* (S.P.C.K., 1937), p. 16.

tween Judaism and Hellenism accepted the Greek notion of
mantikē; as the Pythian priestess, giving oracles in the name of
Apollo, passed into an ecstasy and was in no way responsible for
what she said, so Philo thought that the Old Testament writers
had been 'inspired' to speak God's word. This view is generally
rejected by orthodox writers; Lee calls it 'mechanical'; Mgr
Barry compares it to the heretical doctrine that in His human
birth the Son of God merely 'passed through' the virgin mother
and did not truly take human flesh of her;[1] and all emphasize
that in any right statement of the Inspiration of Scripture there
is a double truth to be guarded, the integrity of the human
writers, and the reality of the divine word spoken through them.
'The sacred text is wholly the work of God and wholly the work
of man, of the latter by way of instrument, of the former by way
of principal cause.'[2]

Ought we then to describe the 'conservative' view as the
doctrine of *verbal inspiration*? This means that the inspiration of
Scripture extends to its very words. The opposite view would be
that it is the writers that are inspired, rather than the words;
the written words belong to a particular age and region and are
in various ways imperfect, and the work of the Holy Ghost is to
be seen not so much in them as in the religious experience of the
writers, in the depth and truth of their experience of God. This
is the liberal-critical view, to which we shall come in the next
section.

While, however, the term 'verbal inspiration' is accepted by
all 'conservative' writers, many who dissent from the conservative view are reluctant to give it up. F. D. Maurice wrote: 'When
you speak to me of verbal inspiration, though I do not like the
phrase, though it seems to me to involve a violent, a scarcely
grammatical ellipsis, yet I subscribe most unequivocally to the
meaning which I suppose is latent in it. I have no notion of inspired thoughts which do not find for themselves a suitable
clothing of words. I can scarcely, even in my mind, separate the
language of a writer from his meaning. And I certainly find this

---

[1] Lee, op. cit., p. 23-5; W. Barry, *The Tradition of Scripture* (Westminster
Library, 1906), p. 221.

[2] The *Catholic Encyclopædia*, s.v. 'Inspiration', vol. viii, p. 48, col. *a*.

difficulty greater in studying the Bible than in studying any other book; the peculiarities of its language seem to me strangely significant.'[1]

This point may be illustrated from the partly parallel case of poetry, to which the word 'inspiration' is frequently applied. The poet has striven to express a meaning; he has known that he cannot rest till he has found exactly the right words to express what has got to find expression. Often he has felt, not so much that he has succeeded in finding the right words, as that they have been given him, and even, perhaps, that his grasp of their meaning was fleeting and transient, that they meant more to him when he wrote them than they do now as he reads them again, or that they contain a meaning beyond what his mind can comprehend. In whatever sense 'inspiration' applies to poetry, it must be an inspiration of its words, a 'verbal inspiration'; and the same must be true of the inspiration of Holy Scripture.

Should we then describe it as the *fundamentalist* view? This is a new word, which does not appear in the *Oxford English Dictionary* except in the *Supplement*; the first instance of its use is there dated 1922, with reference to certain extreme Protestant sects in America. The view which it denotes involves, as we shall show in a later chapter,[2] a peculiarly materialistic conception of the inspiration of the Bible, identifying its truth with rigid exactness in matters of physical fact. There is a distinction to be drawn between this modern doctrine of inerrancy and that which appears in the patristic and medieval tradition, prior to the scientific age; when the Bible was asserted to be in all ways free from error, the emphasis then lay on its inerrancy in teaching spiritual truth and declaring the things of God.

This last phrase, 'free from error', gives us what we want. The conservative view can rightly be defined as that of the *Inerrancy* of the Scriptures: they are inspired, God spoke through the human writers, and thereby they are guaranteed to be in all ways free from error. This includes the belief that the books were written by the authors to whom they are attributed.

[1] F. D. Maurice, *The Kingdom of Christ*, vol. ii (3rd edn., Macmillan, 1883), p. 194 f.
[2] See pp. 93–100 below.

The Problem Unsolved

The standard Roman Catholic statements of this doctrine are those of the Vatican Council and of Pope Leo XIII, in his encyclical *Providentissimus Deus* (1893): 'These books are held by the Church as sacred and canonical, not as having been composed by merely human labour and afterwards approved by her authority, nor merely because they contain revelation without error, but because, written under the inspiration of the Holy Ghost, they have God for their author, and have been transmitted to the Church as such (Concil. Vatic. Sess. III, const. dogm. de Fide, cap ii, in Denz., 1787)'; 'The Holy Ghost Himself, by His supernatural power, stirred up and impelled the Biblical writers to write, and assisted them while writing in such a manner that they conceived in their minds exactly, and determined to commit to writing faithfully, and render in exact language, with infallible truth, all that God commanded and nothing else; without that, God would not be the author of Scripture in its entirety (Encycl. *Provid. Deus*, in Denz., 1952).'[1]

We have said that there are two meanings (at least) of the word 'error', corresponding to those of the word 'truth'. If it is true that three of the sons of Benjamin were named 'Huppim, Muppim and Ard'[2] (Gen xlvi, 21), that is a truth of a very different order from the truth that the Word was made flesh. In the former sense, the word 'error' can denote a mere slip of the pen; in the latter, it is used of false teaching, and is only a slightly weaker word than 'heresy'.

That in this latter sense the Bible is the primary witness to God's truth, all Christians agree. There is no doubt that the authors of the *Westminster Confession* regarded the Bible as free from error of every kind. But the eloquent and noble words in which they describe its authority show that they are thinking first of its spiritual truth:

'The authority of the Holy Scripture, for which it ought to be

---

[1] Quoted from the *Catholic Encbclopædia*, s.v. 'Inspiration', vol viii, p. 45 f.
[2] Those who are no longer young will recollect a witty pair of tracts, *Huppim and Muppim* and *And Ard*, by the Rev. C. L. Marson, on the unintelligent teaching of the letter of Scripture in schools, with little serious effort to bring home to the children the faith for the sake of which the Scriptures were written. It is to be feared thot if in our day this particular devil has gone out, a worse set of devils has come in.

The Conservative View

believed and obeyed, dependeth not upon the Testimony of any man or church: but wholly upon God (who is Truth itself) the Author thereof: and therefore it is to be received, because it is the Word of God. We may be moved and induced by the Testimony of the Church to a high and reverent esteem of the holy Scripture. And the heavenliness of the Matter, the efficacy of the Doctrine, the majesty of the Style, the consent of all the parts, the scope of the whole (which is to give all glory to God), the full discovery it makes of the onely way of Man's Salvation, the many other incomparable excellencies, and the intire perfection thereof, are arguments whereby it doth abundantly evidence it self to be the Word of God; Yet notwithstanding, our full persuasion and assurance of the infallible Truth and Divine Authority thereof, is from the inward work of the holy Spirit, bearing witness by and with the Word in our hearts'.[1]

It was this sense of the word 'truth' rather than the other which was in Liddon's mind when he wrote to Charles Gore in 1889, about the dogmatic presuppositions of different types of Biblical exegesis:

'Criticism is an equivocal term, and is applied to very different kinds of Textual or Exegetical work. Dr. Pusey in one sense was a great critic; in another, Strauss and Bruno Bauer and Feuerbach were. What the young "experts", such as Professor Cheyne, mean by criticism now, is, I suppose, that kind of discussion of doctrines and of documents which treats the individual reason as an absolutely competent and final judge, and which has the most differentiating merit of being independent of church authority. . . . Criticism with Dr. Pusey was . . . the bringing of all that learning and thought could bring to illustrate the mind of Christian antiquity, which really guided him. All criticism, I suppose, *really* proceeds on certain principles, preliminary assumptions for the critic to go upon. The question in all cases is, Whence do these preliminary assumptions come? . . . Certainly these placita which abound in the new "Old Testament criticism" do not appear to come from the text itself; they are imposed on it from without.'[2] Clearly Liddon's concern over the

---

[1] *Westminster Confession*, ch. i.
[2] J. O. Johnston, *Life and Letters of Henry Parry Liddon*, 1904, p. 365.

A Problem Unsolved

denial of Biblical Inerrancy in Gore's essay in *Lux Mundi* went far deeper than the mere anxiety to assert that the Bible was free from error in matters of fact. We shall consider the far-reaching issues which he raises in the fourth chapter of this book.

But no orthodox Christian can agree that the witness of the Bible to the truth of God can be limited to 'spiritual truth', to matters of 'faith and morals'. So, for instance, the writer in the *Catholic Encyclopædia*, whom we have already quoted, says on this point: 'There have been (Catholic) authors . . . who maintained with more or less confidence that Inspiration was limited to moral and dogmatic teaching, excluding everything in the Bible relating to history and the natural sciences. But the Church has never ceased to protes against this attempt to restrict the inspiration of the sacred books.'[1] Most certainly it must be said that this is right in principle. The Christian Faith proclaims that God has revealed Himself in certain events in history, culminating in the crucifixion of His Son 'under Pontius Pilate' and His resurrection on the third day. Therefore the truth of the Bible must include its witness to the redemption effected in history.

The defenders of the Inerrancy of the Bible are then right in insisting that this freedom from error cannot be limited to matters of faith and morals. But how far does its inerrancy extend? If it is regarded as complete, any single proved instance of error will refute the claim that the Bible is the word of God. Hence there has been great diversity of view. The extreme position has been taken in rabbinic Judaism and certain representatives of Protestant orthodoxy,[2] who held that the Massoretic text of the Old Testament was inspired even as regards its vowel-points and the shapes of the letters; a Rabbi is quoted as saying: 'As Moses ascended the mountain, he found God making the ornamental points (Ketharim) of the letters (in the Law).'[3] Others have held that the original autographs only were inspired, thus leaving room for textual criticism; but the very

[1] *Catholic Encyclopædia*, vol. viii, p. 47, col *b*.
[2] The two Buxtorffs in the eighteenth century regarded the vowel-points as inspired: F. W. Farrar, *History of Interpretation*, 1886, p. 388.
[3] R. Joshua ben Levi, of the first generation of the Amoraim, c.A.D. 200.

impossibility, in numberless instances, of deciding with certainty which of several readings is right, besides the virtual certainty in other instances that all the manuscripts are wrong, shows that only part of the text can be guaranteed as free from error.

These extreme positions, however, are mere curiosities. The prevailing teaching is that merely material errors need not trouble us (as distinguished from 'formal' errors in which there is an intention to deceive); thus, for instance, in Matt. xxvii, 9, a prophecy relating to Judas Iscariot is wrongly attributed to Jeremiah instead of Zechariah. St. Augustine deals with this text and takes this view; he explains in the same way that there is no need to worry about differences of detail or of order in parallel Synoptic narratives, 'especially when the question of order detracts nothing from evangelical authority and truth'.[1] Here, however, Dr. Lee is more rigid than St. Augustine, but holds that wherever there are apparent discrepancies it is necessary to harmonize the accounts somehow. St. Luke tells us (xviii, 35) that as our Lord approached Jericho a blind man was healed, and St. Mark (x, 46) that as He left Jericho He healed Bartimaeus; well then, there were two blind men, and the second may have been encouraged by hearing of the healing of the first; St. Matthew combines the two stories in one summary (xx, 29 ff.), saying that He healed two blind men as He left Jericho.[2] In this last detail Dr. Lee does not notice that he has imputed error to one at least of the writers. His principle is that since the revelation given in the inspired Scripture is certainly true, it follows that there must be an explanation of every discrepancy; we can then rest satisfied if we can find an explanation which on general grounds is not improbable, or even just possible.[3] He has, however, sufficient good sense to reject the explanation given by an ingenious apologist of the arrest of the sun's motion during the battle of Beth-horon: the motion of the earth was gradually slowed down, like that of 'a steam-carriage on a railroad', so gently that no jolt was felt, as the deceleration

---

[1] *De cons. Evan.* II, xii, 28, 29. Thompson, op. cit., p. 25.
[2] Lee, op. cit., p. 393 n.
[3] Ibid., p. 387.

could well have occupied quite eighteen minutes. Dr. Lee says simply that the manner in which the miracle was effected has not been disclosed.[1]

But the position which these writers are defending is tactically unsound. It was noticed as long ago as the eleventh century by a Jew called Isaac, who was probably Isaac of Toledo, that the mention of the 'kings that reigned in the land of Edom, before there reigned any king over the children of Israel', in Gen. xxxvi, 31, implies that this chapter was written after the foundation of the Hebrew monarchy.[2] The clue to the distinguishing of the various documents was first given by Exod. vi, 3, where it is said that God was known to the patriarchs as El Shaddai and not by His Name Yahweh; yet in our Book of Genesis that Name is freely used. Then it was seen that in some places there is a stringent requirement of one sanctuary only, while throughout Judges, Samuel and most of Kings this rule is systematically ignored, as is the restriction to the Levitical priesthood of the offering of sacrifice. Thus various strata of laws were distinguished; then Deuteronomy was isolated, and identified with the law-book put in force under Josiah. This is the stage that was reached by Graf and Wellhausen. Of that great scholar Prof. MacFadyen says: 'Nothing emerges more clearly from the unresting advance of Old Testament scholarship during the last forty or fifty years than the overwhelming influence of that man of genius. The foundations he laid were well and truly laid. To him literary criticism was chiefly a means for securing an intelligible reconstruction of the history; and in their main features his criticism and his reconstruction stand.'[3]

This view of the Old Testament history involves also a revision of the account that must be given of the formation of the Canon. The old belief was that the Pentateuch was written by Moses, Judges and Samuel by Samuel, Kings by Jeremiah; while an extraordinary legend, found in 2 Esdras xiv, 40–48,

[1] Ibid., p. 414, text and note.

[2] Carpenter and Battersby, *The Hexateuch*, 1900, vol. i, p. 22. This book contains the classical account of the rise of criticism. A convenient popular summary is given in McNeile, *The Old Testament in the Christian Church*, pp. 37–49.

[3] In *The People and the Book*, ed. Peake, 1925, p. 218.

told that in the exile all the books were lost and were miraculously restored by a revelation to Ezra, and this legend persisted
till the end of the Middle Ages. In the sixteenth century there
arose a legend of the 'Great Synagogue', which was believed to
have put the whole Canon in order, under Ezra's leadership.[1]
The modern view, as we shall see in our fifth chapter, regards
Deuteronomy as the first book which became in the true sense
'scripture', and the three parts of the Hebrew Bible, the Law,
the Prophets, and the Psalms, as having been successively
canonized after the exile: the Pentateuch in Ezra's day, the
Prophets (both 'the earlier prophets', from Judges to Kings, and
'the later prophets', namely Isaiah, Jeremiah, Ezekiel, and 'the
twelve') some time between then and the third century, and
the 'Writings', substantially at least, by the first century B.C.,
though we know that it was still possible to doubt the canonicity
of Canticles and Ecclesiastes till the council of Jamnia, about
A.D. 100.

The doctrine of the Inerrancy of the Bible must then be regarded as, at least in reference to material fact, extremely vul-
nerable.[2] The fact that it persists at all is evidence that it is nevertheless witnessing to something of the first importance. The positive faith which sustains it is the conviction that the Bible is the
divine book, that the Holy Ghost speaks in it and through it
speaks to us with commanding authority. A right analysis of the
problem must separate out the permanent and indispensable
element in this traditional view from the untenable assumptions
which it makes.

3. The Liberal-Protestant View

The duty of which we have just spoken of the reconciliation of
Criticism and Faith has been the continual preoccupation of

---

[1] For this see Ryle, *The Canon of the Old Testament*, 1892, excursus A, pp.
250–83.

[2] Strictly, of course, Inerrancy can be disproved only by discrepancies,
and not by discoveries concerning the authorship and date of the documents:
as, in the Ezra-legend referred to in the last paragraph, the exact words of
the original writings are revealed to Ezra and written down by the other five
men; the books are inerrant, while not coming from their reputed authors.

A Problem Unsolved

Biblical scholars during the whole period in which the critical reconstruction of the biblical history has been taking place. The much-abused 'higher critics' have been in far the greater number of instances believing Christians, who have laboured to show that the new view of the Bible is in no way destructive of Christian faith. Nor have these labours been in vain. Sometimes they have taken the offensive, and denounced with prophetic fire the evils of a jealous and narrow bibliolatry;[1] for the new exegesis has brought a veritable rediscovery of the Hebrew Prophets, and the critic has helped the preacher to set out in stronger light the permanent and essential elements of faith in the living God.[2] Further, since our faith is based on events in history, the Church in every age needs to be served by scholars competent to carry through the appeal to history which it makes; and here very special mention needs to be made of such men as the great Cambridge trio, Lightfoot, Westcott, and Hort, in the sphere of the New Testament and Christian origins; and in the Old Testament sphere of the Presbyterian scholars such as Robertson Smith, George Adam Smith, Davidson, the monument of whose work is Hastings' *Dictionary of the Bible*, and in England above all, perhaps, the great Prof. Driver. This work has been carried on in the present century by the generation of Old Testament scholars whose names are in *The People and the Book*, edited by Dr. Peake in 1924, and *Record and Revelation*, edited by Dr. Wheeler Robinson in 1938. Parallel to the work done in this country there has been the vast labour of scholarship in the universities of the Continent.

Yet the problem of the Old Testament has not been solved. Everyone knows this, and it is being said to-day on every side. It was the underlying *motif* of the Edward Alleyn Lectures given at Dulwich in 1943, and since published with the title, *The Interpretation of the Bible*, that 'the theological study of the Bible'

---

[1] Very notably a book of American essays, *Inspiration and Inerrancy*, by Briggs, Evans, and Smith, edited with an Introduction by A. B. Bruce, London, 1891.

[2] I would emphasize that the things said here are not empty compliments. There is nowhere a better exposition of the prophecy of the Suffering Servant than that of George Adam Smith, *The Book of Isaiah*, vol. ii, pp. 336 ff.

is 'now long overdue'—with the proviso that it is essential for its solution that the results of sane Biblical Criticism be retained.[1]

Broadly, the position is this. The new view of the history throws forward the composition and canonization of most of the sacred books to a much later date, and has brought into much greater prominence the work of the great prophets from Amos to Second Isaiah. Before that time it is hard to prove the existence of a clear and definite belief that there is only one God, as distinguished from the command to worship Him alone; indeed, it has repeatedly been said that till that time the religion of Israel was practically indistinguishable from that of its heathen neighbours. True, in the dim distance there stood the figure of Moses; there had been an Exodus, of a kind, and an entry into Canaan, perhaps by several waves of Hebrew invaders, and a slow conquest of Canaan. But it is hard to make out what is history and what is legend; and it is not till the authentic documents coming from these prophets that we stand on firm ground. Indeed, since it is only now that right beliefs about God begin to emerge, we are compelled to say that it was in the mighty religious experience of these men that the Revelation of God took place. Thus a view of the Bible having the term 'religious experience' for its key-word came to be widely accepted; and this view is summed up, very conveniently for our purpose, in *The Authority of the Bible*, by C. H. Dodd, published in 1928.[2]

The book made no attempt to evade the problem set by its title. It attacked the problem of the Bible's authority along the line of 'religious experience' which is marked out in the General

[1] From the Preface, by the editor, C. W. Dugmore, p. viii. Cf. also pp. 36 and 43 below.

[2] I am most reluctant to criticize a book by so revered a teacher as Dr. Dodd. It would in any case be necessary to say something about the one book which has appeared for a very long time with a title similar to my own (this chapter was in type before Cunliffe-Jones, *The Authority of the Biblical Revelation*, appeared). A second edition came out in 1938, with some additions to the text and a new preface, which seem to me to indicate a radical change of view. But the main part of the argument was there left unaltered; and the book has lately been recommended by the Archbishop's Commission on Evangelism as 'an authoritative book on the subject' (*Towards the Conversion of England*, p. 165).

A Problem Unsolved

Introduction of the series to which it belongs.[1] 'The function of authority', says Dr. Dodd, 'is to secure assent to truth', and 'the measure of any authority which the Bible may possess lies in its direct religious value, open to discovery in experience; and . . . this value in turn will be related to the experience out of which the Scriptures came' (Preface to first edition). There is 'a religious authority in the Bible—the authority of experts in the knowledge of God, masters in the art of living; the authority of religious genius' (p. 25). So then, 'the first ground of the authority of the Bible lies in the fact that it contains within itself the utterances of men of the highest religious genius, who rise above the limitations of their age and environment, and display the authentic marks of personal inspiration' (p. 133). These are the great prophets, whose authority is 'essentially that of religious genius, which by virtue of individual "inspiration" apprehended and uttered compellingly fresh and creative ideas' (p. 165): this inspiration confers 'not inerrancy but a certain cogent persuasiveness' (p. 289). Then, in the historians and other writers, there is 'the appropriation of "inspired" ideas by a whole community, whose experience through many generations tests, confirms and revises them'(ibid.). In the psalms, for instance, 'we do not find towering individual genius, but a high level of corporate religion maintained through many generations. We are made aware of the immense range of religious experience covered by those few ruling ideas which the prophets had at last made current coin' (p. 165.). Finally, there is the life of Him who is the Wisdom of God incarnate (p. 289); and He 'was primarily concerned not with delivering "doctrine", but with making men anew, so that they could receive the revelation of Himself which God is always seeking to communicate' (p. 294). 'In a sense we might say that Jesus never told men anything about God but what they could see for themselves—when He had brought them into the right attitude for seeing Him' (p. 291).

A truth is here being asserted which it is necessary to acknowledge fully and freely. There was a religious experience of the

[1] Nisbet's *Library of Constructive Theology*. See p. 9, and compare p. vii (1928 edn.)

prophets. They were men of God. The things which the Holy
Ghost said through them were not the result of some species of
dictation, some quasi-mechanical inspiration, but were learnt
by them through waiting on God, obedience to His known will,
patience and prayer, the discipline of perseverance, the puri-
fying effect of dryness and desolation. There is danger lest we of
our generation should fail in gratitude to the Liberal scholars
for the care and thoroughness with which they learnt and expressed these all-important truths. If we criticize them, it can
only be on the ground that these positive truths which they discerned were not seen by them in right proportion to other truths.
The Hebrew prophets did indeed seek God and find Him in an
intense religious experience; but it was not the case that this
experience formed the basis of their faith. The prophets belonged to a tradition, which they had learnt from their fathers
in the faith; and the basis of that faith was, according to their
own account, that the Lord God had by His own act chosen
Israel to a position of special privilege. He had redeemed them
from bondage in Egypt and had made His Covenant with them,
that in a unique sense they might be His People and He their
God.

With one accord prophets and psalmists refer back to these
events of the remote past, as the decisive points at which God
had revealed Himself.[1] He had brought them up out of the land
of Egypt, and led them forty years in the wilderness (Amos ii, 10).
Hosea looks back on those days as an ideal time, when Yahweh
had loved Israel His child, and 'called His son out of Egypt',
and he longs for Israel to return to this first love (xi, 1; ii, 14, 15).
Micah sees Him pleading with Israel, 'O my people, what have
I done unto thee, and wherein have I wearied thee? Testify
against Me. For I brought thee out of the land of Egypt, and redeemed thee out of the house of bondage; and I sent before thee
Moses, and Aaron, and Miriam' (vi, 3-4).

A right exegesis of the Old Testament ought, then, to accept
this testimony of the Old Testament writers themselves about
the ground of their faith, unless there are very cogent reasons for

[1] See Phythian-Adams, *The Call of Israel*, 1934, pp. 11-40, for a very convenient summary of various texts from psalmists and prophets.

rejecting it as mistaken. It is, of course, true that the religion of
Israel in the period of the monarchy was deeply paganized;
digging at Lachish, Gezer and elsewhere has shown this; above
all the prophets themselves are continually insisting on it:
'according to the number of thy cities are thy gods, O Judah'
(Jer. ii, 28). But, they say, it is an apostasy; Israel did know
better. 'The ox knoweth his owner, and the ass his master's crib':
the domestic animals have a kind of covenant with man, and it
is only Yahweh's people who forget their convenant-relation
with Him (Isa. i, 3). But the difficulty of the modern student is,
that the story of the Exodus which for the prophets stood as
the firm basis of their whole faith, is told in narratives which
were written not less than five hundred years later; how then can
it be proved that these stories are not legends, or at least that the
truth of history has not been so overlaid by legend that it is impossible for us to commit ourselves to any definite assertion?
We shall attempt to deal seriously with this question in the next
chapter.[1]

A second comment can be given in Mr. Dugmore's words.
In criticism of Sanday, *Inspiration* (Bampton Lectures, 1893),
he says: 'If all that "has come down to us is Revelation, *i.e.* a
number of concrete truths contained in written books on the
subject of God and religion" (Sanday, p. 430), it is hard to see
why the particular anthology of "concrete truths about God and
religion", which we call the Bible, should not now be revised
and considerably enlarged from the writings of men in subsequent ages'.[2] Indeed it is a commonplace that many parts of the
Bible are of 'a low degree of inspiration', or are 'on a sub-
Christian level', so that it may even seem to be a matter for
regret that they are in the Bible at all, and the Bible would be
better without them. Nor can it be denied that some books
which are in the Bible compare not too favourably with books
which are outside it; thus on the whole Esther is less edifying
than Ecclesiasticus, and Jude than 1 Clement—not to speak of
St. Augustine's Confessions. This doctrine of 'degrees of inspiration' involves the abandonment of the attempt to regard the
Bible as being inspired as a whole.

[1] Pp. 53–62 below.   [2] Dugmore, *The Interpretation of the Bible*, p. viii.

Liberal Catholicism

A word must be said about the additions made to Dr. Dodd's book in the second edition, which was published in 1938. They are illustrated by what he had already written in his book, *History and the Gospel* (1935): 'The prophetic writers of the Old Testament, then, declare that a series of events in the history of their people exhibits "the mighty works of the Lord": the call of Abraham, the Exodus and the giving of the Law, the conquest of Canaan, the Kingdom of David, the Captivity and the Return. Whatever human or natural factors may enter in, the ultimate ground of this series of events is the purpose of God, who freely chose Israel to be His people, and who uses alien peoples to fulfil His designs' (p. 32–3). The additions in the second edition of *The Authority of the Bible* are all in this direction. In the second preface he speaks of the Bible as narrating a 'sacred history', which is indeed the 'inner core of all history' since it gives the key to all history's inner meaning. It is consummated in the coming of Christ, His death and resurrection; and so, while it is a finished series of events, it is 'constantly relived in the Church, in which the "saving facts" are rehearsed and through the sacrament of the Eucharist, in which the Gospel history is recapitulated' (pp. x–xii).

4. Liberal Catholicism

Finally, there have been Liberal Catholic attempts to overcome the dilemma which is set by the claim of divine authority on the one side, and the human character of the Biblical writings on the other. The difficulty here has been that it has been seemingly impossible to avoid making a juxtaposition of the two elements, with no satisfactory synthesis or reconciliation between them. This formula applies also in part to orthodox Protestant attempts to retain the traditional dogma while accepting the methods and results of Biblical Criticism; but it is seen more clearly in the Catholic writers, because here the dogmatic structure of the traditional faith and church order is more clearly defined. We have here to consider two movements in particular: the Catholic Modernism, which was condemned by Pope Pius X in the encyclical *Pascendi gregis* in 1907, and the Anglican

37

A Problem Unsolved

Liberal Catholicism which began with the publication of *Lux Mundi* in 1889, and found its fullest expression in *Essays Catholic and Critical* in 1926, and the *New Commentary* in 1928.

Catholic Modernism[1] was represented in this country chiefly by Fr. George Tyrrell, S.J., and Baron Friedrich von Hügel; but we are concerned chiefly with its Biblical side, and therefore especially with the great French scholar Alfred Loisy, whose most important works were his great commentaries on the Fourth Gospel and on the Synoptic Gospels. But the book which stirred up the controversy was his *L'Evangile et l'Eglise* (1902), a brilliant reply to Harnack's *Das Wesen des Christentums*.[2] Against Harnack's thesis that the essence of Christianity consists in the truths which our Lord taught, in the Fatherhood of God, the Brotherhood of Man, and the infinite value of the human soul, Loisy maintained with convincing force that the Gospel as it had appeared in history was the proclamation by our Lord of the Messianic Kingdom for which Israel had hoped; in so doing he laid down the lines on which modern critical study of the gospels has proceeded since. With fearless courage he set himself, while confessing himself a loyal son of the Catholic Church, to face up to Criticism in its most radical form; if then, as it seemed to him, such crucial points as the miracles of the virginal conception of Jesus and His bodily resurrection could not be justified on critical grounds, the truth must be told and the historical truth of these things abandoned. The Catholic religion, as embodied in the church tradition, was in any case an existing fact, even if it owed much to pagan elements and the orthodox accounts of its origins were in large measure legendary. Loisy's influence is seen in the manifesto issued by a group of Italian priests after their excommunication, when caution was no longer necessary: 'Faith sees a continual revelation from the Old to the New Testament, by which the divine manifests itself more and more unmistakably. It matters little to faith whether or no criticism can prove the virgin birth of Christ, His more striking miracles, or

[1] For the following, cf. Knox and Vidler, *The Development of Modern Catholicism*, 1933, pp. 161-199.

[2] English translations, *The Gospel and the Church* (Isbister, 1903) and *What is Christianity?* (Williams and Norgate, 1901).

even His resurrection; whether or no it sanctions the attribution to Christ of certain dogmas or of the direct institution of the Church. As ultra-phenomenal, these former facts evade the grasp of experimental and historical criticism, while of the latter it finds in fact no proof.'[1]

There is here a juxtaposition of the Catholic system and criticism, which is open to attack from both sides. Catholic Modernism can now be seen to have been too ready to accept the then fashionable critical opinions; while on the other side, it cut loose the affirmations of the Christian Faith from their foundations in history, and it attributed to Christian dogma only a relative value. When the Italian priests speak of the divine manifesting itself in the course of the Biblical history, they betray a doctrine of divine immanence which has lost grip of His transcendence; and similarly George Tyrrell, when he said that 'He would be a bold theologian who should affirm that such articles of belief as the Creation, or as Christ's ascent into heaven, His descent into Hell, His coming to judge the quick and the dead and many others are held to-day in substantially the same theological sense as formerly',[2] was asserting that those dogmas were, in part, untrue. The assertion that the categories of thought in which the Creeds are expressed are impossible for us nearly always veils a radical departure from the essential belief of those who framed the creeds; and so it was with Tyrrell. He made almost the same appeal to religious experience as the Liberal Protestants, the difference being that his emphasis was always on the corporate experience of the Church, while theirs was on that of certain outstanding individuals. Consequently the Pope was taking up a very strong position when he condemned the immanentism of the Modernists, even though in doing so he fastened on the Church an extreme statement of the 'conservative' views about the Bible.[3]

Anglo-Catholic Liberalism was in a position to take a far more balanced view. Thanks above all to the traditional Church

[1] *The Programme of Modernism*, pp. 132–3. Compare the position taken up more recently by Emil Brunner; see pp. 117 ff. below.

[2] Fr. G. Tyrrell, S.J., *Through Scylla and Charybdis*, 1907, p. 217.

[3] In the decree *Lamentabili*, 1907, with its syllabus of condemned propositions; Denzinger, *Enchiridion Symbolorum et Definitionum*, nos. 2001–2065.

connection of the ancient universities, the Church of England, like the Presbyterian Church in Scotland, had been able to keep the tradition of sound learning in contact with Christian faith and worship; and both at Oxford and at Cambridge there had been a splendid succession of Christian scholars. In this country, therefore, it was possible to uphold the essential Christian appeal to history, and to hold that critical study did not lead to the negative results which had been reached by most Continental scholars at the crucial point where the controversy became most acute. A great advance had thus been made towards a true solution of the problem. Liberal Anglo-Catholicism, under its great leader Bishop Gore, claimed that the appeal to history must be carried through, in faith that the Christian faith would be vindicated by it.

Yet even so the needed synthesis was not satisfactorily reached; the answer that was given still presented a juxtaposition of the Faith with Criticism, and not a true reconciliation. It is difficult for those of us who have grown up in the Liberal Catholic tradition and have grown out of it, to present a balanced criticism of it; we are liable to be lacking in gratitude for the benefits which we have received from it, while criticizing defects of which we are acutely aware. It seems plain, however, that it can justly be said that there was here a double failure, first to make a sufficiently thorough theological analysis of the problem of the Bible, and second to criticize the theological presuppositions of Criticism itself.

Somehow the Liberal Anglo-Catholics were entering into an uneasy alliance of Faith and Criticism, in which both sides were in some degree under constraint. On the one side it was rightly seen and firmly emphasized that the church dogma involves the truth of the historical facts which lie at its centre, including the virgin birth of the Lord and His bodily resurrection, and on the other that Criticism must be free. But how could the critic be free when it was necessary that he should vindicate these and other cardinal points of Christian belief? Could the scholar be content to have his conclusions dictated to him in advance? What if the evidence were found to point in a partly different direction? This at least was said by the opponents of the movement.[1] It looked as if a scholar could be a Catholic in religion, provided he were able to justify certain critical conclusions; but then, how could he urge on others, with the authority of the Church, conclusions which appeared to depend on a particular critical view of the evidence? Yet the Liberal Catholics were honourably unwilling to let go their conviction of the importance of the historical facts.

From the opposite side, too, the Liberal Catholics were reproached for what was regarded as a too great readiness to take over critical results which depended on questionable theological presuppositions. We have already had before us Liddon's penetrating criticism of the Old Testament scholars at Oxford; however untenable Liddon's own position may seem to us to have been, he was in that letter urging a positive point of real importance. The failure of the Liberal Catholic school to reach a true synthesis of Faith and Criticism can be illustrated from the *New Commentary*, of which the general criticism is that, on the one hand, conservative positions are sometimes pressed and clung to in such a way that the historian feels that his difficulties are not fairly faced (as for instance in the treatment of the critical problems of the Fourth Gospel), and on the other that the theology of the Bible is not displayed in its greatness and in its unity (in striking contrast with Kittel's *Wörterbuch*, which began to appear only four years later). In this alliance of Theology with Criticism neither the theologian nor the historical critic could feel that justice was done to him.[2]

We have seen how widely it is being said to-day that the problem of the interpretation of the Bible has not been solved; and this would not be so, if the Liberal Catholic answer were felt to be satisfactory. What is needed is not that Faith and Criticism should be felt to stand opposed to one another, in an

---

[1] Cf. the following, written with reference to the eucharistic institution: 'The genuine liberal is justified in rejecting the liberal catholic's selective treatment of the evidence as insufficiently faithful to scientific historical methods, and biased by the motive of attempting to save the essentials of the traditional theology of the sacrament from the wreck of its traditional justification.' Dom Gregory Dix, *The Shape of the Liturgy*, 1945, p. 66.

[2] Further, the *New Commentary* fails as a rule to show the way to a Christian interpretation of the liturgical texts from the Old Testament, even those

uneasy mutual toleration, but that a way should be found which both could accept with enthusiasm, and with a glad sense of having been set free to develop their energies to the utmost.

What then is required? On the one side, a better theological view of the purport of the Bible as a whole; and since the Bible is the record of God's revelation in history, this means a Christian philosophy of history, in which the events of the Redemption are seen as 'the inner core of all history', giving the key to the meaning of the rest. On the other side, a free acceptance of Criticism: not in the sense in which 'freedom' is often misunderstood, as if it signified an unlimited right of 'private judgement' on a scholar's part to hold what views he likes, but rather in the sense in which the scholar himself will claim that freedom— namely, freedom to be bound only by the exact meaning of the texts, as determined by the light which modern knowledge in many fields of study can throw upon it. The answer to this addition sum, if we have done the calculation correctly, is that the theological presuppositions which underlie the critic's work need to be derived, not from some extraneous source, but from the Faith of Israel itself. When that is the case, Faith and Criticism can live at peace.

5. The Bible and the Ordinary Christian

The problem of the Bible is one that touches the ordinary Christian very closely. It is for his sake most of all that the needed answer to the problem must be given; for while the theologian is in a position at least to state to himself what the difficulties are and find some *modus vivendi*, the layman is not. It is however plain that a more satisfactory solution than any of those now available is to be expected before long, and it is the earnest hope

---

which occur in the Holy Week services. In some instances this is admirably done, as in the commentary on Zechariah, which includes the Palm Sunday prophecy of the King coming to Zion (pp. 617–20). But this cannot be said of the notes on the Sacrifice of Isaac (p. 53), the Sacrifice of the Covenant (p. 90), and the Warrior from Bozrah (p. 480); while in the commentary on Isa. liii, there is indeed a recognition that this prophecy is fulfilled in our Lord, but no reference to His own use of it, or to the other New Testament passages in which it is quoted (pp. 470–3).

of the present writer that in this book he may be able to make some small contribution towards it. But whether that be so or not, the answer is coming; for the difficulties are being seen and the problem is being stated. Thus, for instance, Prof. R. H. Lightfoot says: 'The charge is sometimes brought against criticism that it has led to an over-emphasis of the part played by human nature in the production of Holy Scripture, and has made too little of God's word to man therein. This charge must be to a large extent admitted. For a century and more, students have been throwing light on the workmanship of the Bible and on the way in which the tools were used to fashion it. It was inevitable that they should attempt this task. . . . Had the Bible and the Bible only been excluded from this study, we should be in an evil plight to-day. . . . But this concentration undoubtedly tended to conceal for a time the message and witness of the Bible as God's revelation of Himself to man, the aspect of the Bible on which almost exclusive stress had been laid hitherto by catholics and protestants alike; and we are suffering to-day from an excessive or one-sided development.'[1]

It is not easy to give more than a quite general account of the widespread uncertainty which is felt among ordinary Christian people about the Old Testament; it seems that several different causes contribute to it. There are the historical difficulties, arising from the fact that the creation-story in Genesis does not agree with the account given by astronomy, geology and biology, and that the historical truth of many narratives is known to be called in question. There are the moral difficulties: why does the Old Testament sometimes show a fierce nationalistic spirit, and why are cruelty and vindictiveness towards enemies, as of Jael towards Sisera, and Saul's extermination of the Amalekites, represented as approved and even commanded by God? Why do some of the psalms recited in church invoke God's vengeance on enemies, in a way which seems to stand in flagrant contrast with our Lord's command to us to love them, and His own prayer for the forgiveness of those who crucified Him?

Beyond this, there is the difficulty of using the Old Testament.

[1] R. H. Lightfoot, 'The critical approach to the Bible in the nineteenth century', in *The Interpretation of the Bible*, ed. Dugmore, 1944, p. 87 f.

A Problem Unsolved

There seems to be little that is helpful in some of the narratives which are read as lessons; the prophets are usually hard to understand, and the psalms often difficult to use. Yet it is not merely a matter of obscurity of phrase or errors of translation; the correction of all such faults would not remove the difficulty. The question is rather, why is it that the Englishman to-day is expected to be so deeply interested in the successes and failures of an ancient Semitic tribe? If they were God's chosen people, does that mean that God has favourites? There is more than a tendency in some quarters for the spirit of anti-Semitism which has been running through Europe in recent years to find expression in a distaste for and a disgust with the Hebrew Scriptures.

Again, the Old Testament is admittedly imperfect, since the New Testament was needed to fulfil and complete it. Our Lord in the Sermon on the Mount contrasts the moral teaching of the Law with the higher demand of the Gospel; 'ye have heard that it was said to them of old time . . . but I say unto you. . . .' It is true that He also says that He is come not to destroy but to fulfil the Old Testament, and that everywhere in the New Testament it is treated as God's inspired word. Yet it is admitted to be imperfect; and if so, how far can it be certainly trusted? Does it represent a stage in man's spiritual development which we have left behind? If so, why should it not be allowed to drop out of use?

Then there is the difficulty, which any serious study of the Old Testament at once brings out, of reconciling the human limitations of the word spoken by the prophets with the divine authority that has been ascribed to them. The study of the prophets shows the line of development running from one prophet to another, so that each of them takes his place in the working out of a glorious hope of an ideal future; but are we not left now with the story of the development of a human messianic hope, where our forefathers believed in actual promises of God? Can we fix on any particular prophecy and say that *here* God spoke, *these* were not human words but divine?

All this is complicated by the fact that the modern person to whom the Bible message comes is himself largely ruled by fundamental assumptions about life and by standards of judgement which are at variance with those of the Bible and need to be corrected by it. In so far as this is the case, it is not the alleged or real imperfections in the Bible that cause the difficulty, but its very truth. The man in the street and behind the counter and in the schoolroom is found to be assuming that the visible is the real, because science gives us certainty here, but that religious belief is a matter of opinion and unverifiable, so that each man has a right to think as he likes; while the powerful educational influences of the newspaper, the novel, and the cinema, are steadily inculcating a view of man's nature and a pattern of conduct which are utterly different from those of the Bible and the Church. In these respects the faithful Christian is often conscious of his opposition to these standards of the world, yet at the same time he may be unconsciously ruled by them to a greater extent than he knows.

The Bible reaches the ordinary Christian primarily by means of the liturgy. The greater part both of the eucharistic liturgy up to the offertory, and of the divine office alike in the Breviary and the Book of Common Prayer, consists of Biblical material; in fact, the office consists essentially of a scheme for the regular (weekly or monthly) recitation of the psalms, and the reading of a yearly course of lessons comprising the greater part of the Bible, which is only interrupted by festivals and special seasons. The function of these services is to train up those who take part in them in the knowledge of God, of His dealings with man, and of the service which man owes to Him; and the offices both of the Breviary and the Prayer-book are intended for daily use, which is therefore in both cases enjoined, as a minimum, on all clergy. Here, then, we see the Bible being used as the Book of the Faith.

The Christian liturgical tradition goes back to that of the Synagogue; in fact, the first part of the eucharistic liturgy has come down by direct descent from the synagogue liturgy. It was from the Synagogue that the Church took over this way of using the Scriptures. Nor is it possible to doubt that the liturgical practice of the synagogue had a large part in the actual formation of the Old Testament Canon. The Bible was in its very origin the Book of the Faith.

A Problem Unsolved

It is from this point of view, then, that it demands to be seen, when it is being studied as Scripture, and as having authority for Christian faith and life. It can also be studied from the point of view of Comparative Religion, a science which must assume for the purposes of its study that all the religions stand on the same level and are comparable, and this study does indeed throw valuable light on the ritual practices described in the Bible; yet it is alien to the Bible itself, since the Biblical writers agree in declaring that the God of Israel is the one true God, and all others are no gods. It can be studied from the point of view of individual religious experience, but this point of view also is partly alien to the Bible; for the Biblical writers are almost always thinking first of His dealings with Israel, and Israel's duty to Him. But if the right point of view to approach the Bible is to see it as the Book of the Faith of Israel, such an approach should hold the promise of a right answer to the questions of its inspiration and its authority. We will then start with this line of approach in the next chapter.

CHAPTER II

THE BOOK OF THE DIVINE KINGDOM

1. The Faith of Israel

Frederick Denison Maurice had a sure instinct for seizing the essential point in a theological question; and in *The Kingdom of Christ* he goes straight to this conception when he comes to treat of the Bible. In that book he develops the thesis that there really exists in the world a divine Kingdom, spiritual in its nature and thereby distinguished from the political kingdoms of the world, and needing therefore to be set forth by means of certain outward signs. These will be universal in their application, as the Kingdom is universal, and they are, he says, six in number: Baptism, the Creed, certain traditional forms of prayer, the Eucharist, the episcopal Ministry, the Bible.[1] All these are liable to be misused and perverted by misinterpretation; but, taken in their plain meaning, they all testify to the real existence of such a Kingdom, and are means whereby men are enabled to live as citizens of it.[2]

The Bible, then, is to be seen in the context of that divine Kingdom which was consummated as the Kingdom of Christ, but which began with Abraham and the chosen family, and under Moses was extended to the chosen nation. It therefore tells the story of the Exodus, the Covenant, the Entry into Canaan, and the long period of education and discipline which was consummated in our Lord's coming, who reconstituted it in such a way that within a few years it was opening its doors to

---

[1] Cf. my book, *The Form of the Church* (1944), p. 36.
[2] See *The Kingdom of Christ*, vol. i, pp. 272–93 (3rd edn., Macmillan, 1883), for the general idea of the Kingdom, and vol. ii, pp. 178–223, for the particular treatment of the Bible.

The Book of the Divine Kingdom

men of all nations. This divine Kingdom, then, has existed in the world for some three or four thousand years, and it exists to-day; and since it regards its existence and its nature as dependent on certain historical events, it needs to have accredited documents relating the story of its foundation and subsequent history, and explaining its constitution and its present demands on men. It has and has always had its living tradition of teaching and discipline; but we can rightly demand some assurance that the teaching now given is no recent innovation, but is truly authoritative. It has such documents: they are the Scriptures.[1]

If, now, anyone has convinced himself that the claim is false and no such divine Kingdom really exists, the Bible will have no further interest for him, unless he happens to be a student of comparative religion, or of the ancient history of the middle east, or of Semitic languages. But if he believes, or hopes, that the Kingdom does in fact exist, or if he disbelieves in it and yet has reason to fear that it may exist after all, then these records are of very vital concern to him; and since they claim to tell of historical events, he must find out what is the verdict about them of the best and most thorough historical investigation—whether the result of the application of scientific tests is that the narratives dissolve away into legends, or that they vindicate themselves as trustworthy at least as regards their essential core.[2]

If the claim that the divine Kingdom has been in existence for this long period and that the account given of its foundation is substantially true, appears to justify itself, this will rest upon testimony borne to the events of its foundation and its subsequent history by honest and truthful men. But it will not add to the value of their testimony, in the eyes of our inquirer, if he is told that by special divine providence these writings alone among human writings have been preserved from all possible error; for in this case he may well be distracted from observing the true function of these men (namely, to bear witness to a divine work), by admiring their marvellous freedom from all mistakes; and he may well miss the help that he is entitled to get from realizing that as truly in their days as in his own God could

[1] Op. cit., p. 213.
[2] Ibid., p. 196.

48

call and train imperfect human beings to bear witness to Him; and then, having put the writers of the Scripture into a class by themselves, he may end by thinking of them as men belonging not to the real world, but to a fairy-story.[1]

Such a view of the Bible as the Book of the divine Kingdom appears to put the Bible in its right place in relation to other books. The assertion that the books of the Bible are inspired by the Holy Ghost does not in any way involve the truly monstrous assertion that He had nothing to do with the composition of other books on religious and on 'secular' subjects; if we believe in God the Holy Ghost, we must think that apart from Him no book could contain any truth at all. If, then, the Bible is authoritative because the Holy Ghost spoke through it, those other books should owe whatever authority they possess to the same cause. Every book is authoritative in proportion to the knowledge of its subject which it contains, and the wisdom which it embodies; the difference between the Bible and other books should then be due to their respective subject-matter. Books of history tell of the rise and fall of earthly kingdoms; but the Bible tells the story of the divine Kingdom, from its beginnings with Abraham and its foundation under Moses to its consummation in Jesus Christ. If that history is in truth the story of *God's* Kingdom, it must constitute the inner core of all history, and give the key to the inner meaning of all other events; and similarly, the Bible as the Book of the divine Kingdom, should stand in a similar relation to all other books. Having learnt to listen to the word of God spoken in it, we ought to have learnt from it a standard of judgement whereby to discern the divine truth expressed also in them.[2]

The distinction between the Bible and other books written within the Church, many of which deal with subjects akin to those discussed in some books of the Bible, will be on similar lines. The Holy Ghost has not retired into inactivity since the close of the apostolic age; and there are other writings capable of being placed side by side with Biblical writings, as in the Breviary hymns and homilies by the Fathers are used, side by

[1] Ibid., p. 198–9.
[2] Ibid., pp. 199–203.

side with the psalms and the Scripture lessons. Certainly it is not a question of value; that is not the criterion. It is by no means clear that the Second Epistle of Peter is of higher value than the Epistle to Diognetus. We must look elsewhere for the ground of the distinction; and we can find it only in the fact that the Bible relates the Sacred History, the story of the divine Kingdom.

The Bible ends at the point where Church history begins. It is not hard to see why it should end at that point. The main story with which it is occupied is the story of God's dealings with Israel, from the time when it became a nation, under Moses. Before this, we have what we may call a Preface (roughly Gen. i–xi) and an Introduction (Gen. xii–end). The Preface to the Bible places the Sacred History on the background of the history of mankind. We have therefore the story of the creation of heaven and earth, and of man in God's image; then (taking the Bible as it stands) man's duty in relation to the land, 'to dress it and to keep it' (Gen. ii, 15), to make himself a home and build a civilization. He may do what he will; only there is the prohibition to eat of one of the trees, for he is in God's world and subject to God's ordinance (ii, 17). Then comes the story of the Fall; man, as we know him, is not living under God's ordinance and at peace with God, but has chosen to 'be as God', to grow up and develop in his own way, disregarding God's law, and grabbing for himself at God's gifts. In the world as we know it, 'all flesh has corrupted its way upon the earth' (vi, 12).

Then what has God done for man His creature? In the 'Introduction' we read how God calls Abraham to make a venture of faith, and Abraham trusts God and receives His blessing. Henceforth there is to be a nucleus of men, small or large, that sets itself to acknowledge God's kingly rule. So we come to the Main Story: God delivers Israel from Egypt, makes His Covenant with them, brings them into the promised land; educates them, through many centuries, and trains them in His ways; by His prophets convicts them of sin, and brings them through the bitter suffering of the Exile to a renewed faith and a hope of a future 'messianic' order, in which they will truly be His people and He their God; when that Day comes, His Spirit will be poured out on them, and all nations will come to share in the privileges of Israel, and to know God as Israel knows Him. The announcement of the New Testament is that all this is fulfilled in the person of Jesus the Messiah. When He has come, and has re-constituted the People of God, and the Apostles have borne witness to Him, the Bible must end, because the Sacred History is now complete. The story of the Elected Nation is finished. Church History is now beginning; and Church History is the story of the works of the Holy Ghost in all the nations of the world and of the resulting conflicts. Fittingly therefore in the last book of the Bible we read how God has redeemed to Himself by the blood of Christ men of every kindred and tongue and people and nation, and has made them unto God kings and priests; and how the New Jerusalem descends from heaven, and the nations are to walk in the light of it, and the kings of the earth to bring their glory and honour into it.[1]

Thus the course of the Sacred History might be summarized in three confessions of faith, dating from roughly 850 and 550 B.C. and A.D. 50:

(i) A faithful Israelite, of the middle period of the Monarchy (we can think of one of the school which produced the J-narrative of the Pentateuch) would confess that he believed that:

Yahweh our God redeemed us out of Egypt;

He consecrated us to Himself by the Covenant at Sinai;

He brought us into the Promised Land:

We hope that we shall continue to live in peace under His blessing.

(ii) A disciple of the prophets, in exile, would assent to all this, but would add: 'We, His people, have sinned so fearfully against Yahweh that He has fearfully punished us; but now He calls us to repent, and we are promised that:

He will redeem us, from the north-country and all the countries whither He has driven us;

---

[1] This point is excellently expressed in the collect that follows the fourth of the Prophecies in the Easter Eve rite in the Roman Missal: 'O God, whose mighty works of old we perceive to shine forth also in our own day, since that which Thou wroughtest for one nation by delivering it from oppression in Egypt, Thou dost now effect for the salvation of all nations by the sacrament of Baptism: Grant that the fulness of the nations may share in sonship to Abraham and citizenship in Israel.'

He will make with us His New Covenant, and put His Spirit within us;

He will bring us again to our own land, and Himself return to dwell among us;

He will enter on His Reign, and all nations shall come to know Him as we know Him.

(iii) An Apostle of Jesus Christ would assent to all this, both the original Call of Israel and the prophetic promises, and declare that the latter had all been fulfilled:

He has redeemed us by the death and resurrection of Jesus the Christ, not from Egypt nor from Babylon, but from Satan, sin and death;

He has given us the New Covenant in His blood, and has poured out His Spirit;

He has established us in our inheritance in the New Israel, as children of the Jerusalem which is above and is free; His tabernacling Presence has dwelt among us, in the person of Jesus, and dwells now in the Temple which is His body;

He has entered on His Kingdom, and all nations are called to share in it.[1]

2. *The Authority of the Book of the Kingdom*

If then we may provisionally accept the description which we have given of the Bible, we shall regard it as having authority for us as the record of a divine Purpose worked out in history. If so, it will need to be considered in three aspects, represented by the Greek words ἀρχή, λόγος and τέλος. These words apply to any purpose or plan whatsoever, which is first conceived, then worked out, then carried into effect. We might think of some of the wonderful plans carried out during the war, such as 'Pluto', which was the scheme for laying a pipe-line across the Channel to supply oil to the armies in France in 1944. It had its ἀρχή, *principium*, or Beginning, in the first perception of the future need and the conception of the idea; the λόγος or *ratio* of it was the plan itself, as worked out in every detail with provision for

[1] I owe the idea of this threefold scheme to Dr. Phythian-Adams, in the *Church Quarterly Review*, No. cclxix (Oct. 1942), p. 3 f.; cf. his *The Way of At-one-ment*, 1944, pp. 24–6.

every contingency; it reached its τέλος, *finis*, or End, when the plan was carried into effect, the end attained, and oil supplied to the bases in France.

These three words can be applied to the divine Purpose for man, first in creation and then in redemption. They provide a formula for the Christology. They serve likewise to sum up the things that we need to know about the divine Kingdom:

(*a*) How did it begin, when was it established? The Bible should bear authoritative testimony to the historical events in which it is claimed that the Kingdom was established, when God acted in history to redeem His people and make His Covenant with them. This must apply to both Testaments: to the Old Israel and to the New. (*b*) What is the nature of the Kingdom, and what manner of service is man called to render to God in it, both under the Law and under the Gospel? (*c*) What is the end towards which God's saving purpose is directed, the fulness or completion of the Divine Kingdom in the reconciliation of man with God?

(*a*) *The Foundation of the Kingdom*

First, then, if the Bible is to be what it needs to be, it must bear authoritative testimony to the events of the Redemption. This is made very clear in the New Testament, which is substantially the book of the apostolic testimony to the Gospel. The primary function of an apostle of Jesus was that, being sent out in His Name, he should proclaim the Gospel of His Kingdom. The qualification for the man who was to fill the empty place among the Twelve was, according to Acts i, 21–2, that he should have been a disciple of the Lord Jesus during the ministry, and be a witness of His resurrection. This witness of the Apostles to the events of the life of Jesus, and above all to the resurrection, is repeatedly emphasized in the early part of Acts; they are the 'witnesses chosen before by God' (x, 41; cf. ii, 32; iii, 15; iv, 20, 33). The New Testament writings were accepted by the Church on the ground that they were believed to have been written by apostles or to embody their teaching.

There needs similarly to be valid historical evidence for believing the Exodus of Israel from Egypt to be an actual event, if the faith of Israel, which was based upon it, is to be believed to have been true. But the difficulty here is that the earliest written accounts date from centuries later; and also that the existing Book of the Exodus consists of several superimposed strata, so that the story becomes seriously confused, and it is hard for the ordinary reader to get a clear and consistent picture of it. The confusion of sources is obvious, for instance, in the narratives of the Plagues and the Crossing of the Red Sea. The historian has to decide which of three possible dates best fits the evidence of the Biblical narratives, the known chronology of the Pharaohs, the Tell-el-Amarna tablets, the excavations at Jericho, and other data; and there is at present no general agreement among scholars about the date of the Exodus, or on the question whether all or only some of the tribes took part in it. Yet the honesty and integrity of our faith depends on the historical questions being fairly faced.

The duty of applying the most thorough historical investigation is clinched by the following consideration, taken from the parallel case of the New Testament: that within a few weeks after our Lord had been put to death by that manner of execution which in the eyes of every Jew had the curse of God upon it (Gal. iii, 13), the apostles were proclaiming openly that God had reversed the sentence and had owned Him as Lord and Messiah by the resurrection, of which they were witnesses; and there seems no possible escape from the conclusion that if Caiaphas had then been in a position to confront them with a demonstration that His body lay still in the grave, the Christian preaching would have collapsed like a punctured bladder.[1] St. Paul, too, is clear that if the fact was not true, the faith of the Christians was vain, and the apostles were false witnesses of God (1 Cor. xv, 14 ff.). Thus the resurrection of Jesus Christ is proclaimed as the decisive point at which God's arm has been bared in an event of history. At this point the problems of history and those of theology meet. In proclaiming the salvation of man through Christ, the apostles point to historical facts, and their testimony becomes subject to historical tests.

[1] We shall deal later with the questions raised by this assertion: see pp. 117 ff. below.

The Authority of the Book of the Kingdom

Essentially the same principles are involved when the Old Testament writers appeal to a divine action in the Exodus, in which, they say, God redeemed Israel out of Egypt with a mighty hand and an outstretched arm. The point has thus been stated by Dr. Wheeler Robinson: 'The point of real importance is that whatever happened was interpreted by Moses as the work of Yahweh, the future God of Israel. Here we have that mingling of the event with its religious interpretation, to constitute the fact for faith, which characterizes the history of Israel as recorded in the Old Testament. Moses was doing essentially what Isaiah did in the times of Sennacherib, when he bade the people look beyond the outer deliverance to its inner meaning: "Ye looked not unto Him who had done this, neither had ye respect unto Him that fashioned it long ago" (Isa. xxii, 11). Israel's faith was created by an act of divine redemption, i.e. by the interpretation of that act as the work of Yahweh: "Israel saw the great work which Yahweh did upon the Egyptians; and the people feared Yahweh, and they had faith in Yahweh and in Moses His servant" (Ex. xiv, 31). The ancient song of Miriam (Ex. xv, 21) takes us to the heart of this faith:

Sing ye to Yahweh, for He hath triumphed gloriously;
The horse and his rider hath He thrown into the sea.

The overthrow of Egypt holds a place in the religion of Israel which may be compared with that of the victory of the Cross for the Christian. Here was that mighty act of God to which faith could ever return for its renewal. Here began the divine "election" of Israel, the consciousness of which characterizes the Old Testament from beginning to end.'[1]

It is not possible for us to embark here on an investigation of the historical problem; that is a matter for specialist inquiry, and would demand a whole book for itself. All that we can do is to lay down the main lines of the problem, and indicate the relation of the historical and the theological questions.

It is plain that in this case there is not contemporary evidence, comparable to that which is available for the story of the Second Redemption. We are dealing with an ancient tradition, which

[1] H. Wheeler Robinson, *The History of Israel*, Duckworth, 1938, pp. 34 f.

existed prior to the earliest written narratives. Probably the Song of Miriam, which has just been quoted, is the earliest literary fragment; but the Exodus-story is presupposed in all the different books. Thus when Gideon receives his call, he asks why, if Yahweh is with them, the present evils have befallen them: 'and where be all His wondrous works which our fathers told us of, saying, Did not Yahweh bring us up out of Egypt?' (Judges vi, 13). It is appealed to by the writing prophets, from Amos onwards; it appears in many psalms of various dates. It is presupposed by the traditions concerning the Passover, the Ark, the Tent of Meeting. Further, for the historian, the fact that the written narratives can be analysed into various sources constitutes evidence far stronger than would be that of one single narrative.

The content of the tradition, again, inspires confidence. The Israelites believed about themselves that they had been bondmen in Egypt before they were free nomads in the desert; they told how far their fathers had been from consistent obedience to the divine call, and how they had desired more than once to return to bondage. Above all, the tradition of the crossing of the Red Sea, and of the sight of their enemies dead on the sea shore, appears to be an authentic memory which had stamped itself on the minds of those who had witnessed it, and had been handed down from father to son. With this must be put the tradition of the events at Sinai or Horeb, and of the Covenant with Yahweh which was regarded by them as marking the beginning of their existence as a nation. To quote Dr. Wheeler Robinson again: 'In the light of this conviction ("I will take you to Me for a people, and I will be to you a God", Exod. vi, 7) we gain our surest clue to the ultimate distinction of the religion of Israel from all its contemporary religions, such as Moab's faith in Kemosh. Yahweh is no nature-God, like those Baalim of Canaan whom He will ultimately overcome, though He thunders from Sinai and can come in storm to the help of His hard-pressed people. From the outset of His historical relation to Israel, He is characterized by this initial choice of them, which is a moral act. Here is the germ of that unique correlation of religion and morality which was to bear its noble fruit in the prophets. Here is the secret of their strange ability to re-interpret even national disaster in terms of a divine purpose. In this sense, Moses is the human founder of the religion of Israel. He taught that Yahweh had chosen this group of tribes by delivering them from Egypt, and Yahweh was henceforth to be the only God of Israel. By the side of this primary contribution, all others that he may have made to moral and religious legislation are secondary.'[1]

While then the details of the great events of the Plagues of Egypt, the Passover, the Crossing of the Red Sea, and the Covenant at Horeb must remain in large measure uncertain, it is possible to affirm with much confidence that the core of the tradition is substantially sound. The line that we are following is not at all what the late Prof. R. G. Collingwood called the 'scissors-and-paste' method of writing history:[2] namely, to proceed by the methods of literary criticism to distinguish the earlier and presumably better narrative sources from the later and less reliable, and then go cautiously forward to a provisional re-construction of the story on the basis of the oldest narratives. It was in this way that most of the nineteenth-century 'Lives of Jesus' were written, on the basis of the identification of Mark and Q. as the primary gospel-sources, and the assumption that their general historical reliability made it possible to proceed at once to write the history from them, while at the same time the Christological beliefs of the writers, and the *Sitz im Leben* of the anecdotes as narrated in the Church, could for the historian's purposes be discounted, and the story be told much as in a modern biography. But the modern student of the gospels realizes that as the story was first told from the point of view of the faith that Jesus had been Messiah and Saviour, so the historian can only be truly scientific if he studies the narratives in the light of that faith, and then endeavours to account for its origin.

With regard to the Exodus-narratives, the 'scissors-and-paste' method labours under the initial difficulty that the earliest narrative is four, five, or even six centuries later than the events

[1] Ibid., p. 35.
[2] See his *Autobiography* (1939), ch. viii.

described. More than this, it is radically unsound, because it misconceives the relation between the history and its theological meaning. It is necessary, therefore, to study in the first place the tradition itself, as the tradition of the faith by which Israel lived, concerning the facts on which Israel believed that its own existence rested.

To the present writer it seems that Dr. Phythian-Adams, in his book *The Call of Israel*, presents an account of the course of the events which may well be right; the volcanic and seismic theory certainly co-ordinates in a remarkable way the phenomena which the narratives relate. Perhaps, however, the greatest contribution which that book makes lies in the distinction which it draws between the core of the traditions of the Exodus and the Wilderness-period, and various episodes which may have become attached to the central core in the course of the later history, in the time of David, perhaps, or of Rehoboam. But the core of the tradition, consisting of the tale of the events on which Israel's existence as a nation was believed to rest, must be distinguished from these narratives, as being the central nucleus round which they gathered, and which took then and always a central place in Israel's faith, as the death and resurrection of Jesus Christ have always taken a central place in the Christian faith.

Such is the argument. Phythian-Adams notes a variety of points in the story which raise questions: the two water-miracles, in Exod. xvii and Num. xx, and the location of the latter at Kadesh in Num. xxvii, 14;[1] the visit of Jethro in Exod. xviii, and the fact that he there proposes a judicial system which cuts across the tribal divisions;[2] then the stories of the Golden Calf, of the Breaking of the Tables of Stone and their replacement, and the disgrace of Aaron,[3] seen in connection with the loss of the Ark to the Philistines in Eli's day, its presumed desecration by them, and its recovery by David, and the fall of the priesthood of which Abiathar was the last representative and its replacement by that of the sons of Zadok.[4]

Here, it would seem, we have items in the tradition which

[1] *The Call of Israel*, p. 65 ff.   [3] Ibid., p. 104 ff.
[2] Ibid., p. 72 ff.   [4] Ibid., p. 85 ff.

can be approximately dated, and which partly interrupt the main story itself; thus a valid distinction between the accretions and the central core appears to establish itself.

The structure of the argument remains unaffected if the details of these supposed accretions are in some instances open to criticism. Thus the correlation of the provision of new Tables of Stone by Moses with the presumed provision of new Sacred Stones by David when he brought the Ark to Jerusalem is an attractive theory, and one that may well be substantially right; but it is difficult to defend it against the criticism that it is insufficiently proved. Yet an ample sufficiency of instances remains. It is impossible to doubt that there is some close connection between the story of Aaron's Golden Calf and those at Bethel and Dan, which are bitterly criticized in 1 Kings xii, 28: Jeroboam makes two calves, and says of them, 'Behold thy gods' O Israel, which brought thee up out of the land of Egypt', using the exact words attributed to Aaron in Exod. xxxii, 4 (repeated in v. 8).[1] Jethro's advice to appoint rulers of thousands, of hundreds, of fifties, and of tens (Exod. xviii, 21), reminds us of the description of Solomon's reign given in advance by Samuel in 1 Sam. viii; there in v. 12 it is said that a tyrannical king may appoint captains of thousands and captains of fifties, and this corresponds with the later descriptions of a census, of taxation, and labour gangs sent to Lebanon (2 Sam. xxiv; 1 Kings v, 13 ff.; xii, 18).

Of these additions to the main story, Dr. Phythian-Adams says that they 'are in no sense the Tradition itself: very frequently they are not even embellishments of it: they are Sacred Stories (ἱεροὶ λόγοι) designed for specific purposes: and in no one absolutely clear instance is the purpose to be recognized as what *we* should call historical'. But 'however much they may embellish the facts, or even obscure them in the interests of their particular purpose, at the heart of their narrative these facts remain as a solid, resistant core, the indestructible nucleus of

---

[1] *The Call of Israel*, pp. 108–111. All commentators agree that Exod. xxxii shows signs of being composite; the command to the Levites to slay the people in vv. 25 ff. is recognized to have originally belonged to a different story.

historical reality, without which there would have been neither Scripture, nor symbolism, nor Inspiration. In a word, the facts are *there*, though they may not be by any means recognizable in the *form* in which they are presented; they are there, but we shall not discover them until we have penetrated behind the immediate purpose of the individual writer and the garb in which he has clothed it.'[1]

This can be well illustrated from the 'priestly' writers, who elaborate the simple 'tent of meeting' of the old tradition into their magnificent Tabernacle, which is in fact a portable Temple, transferred bodily into the wilderness, but just half its dimensions. Certain it is that the authors of these narratives and descriptions were not writing history in our sense of the word, having persuaded themselves that these things had actually happened in just this way a thousand years before. But if that be so, neither were they falsifying history. In putting back the pattern of their Temple into the wilderness-period, they were saying through the only medium available to them that the worship offered to God at their Temple was one thing with the ancient religion of the wilderness, and rested on the Covenant for its sanction. There was a continuity. The regulations about the Tabernacle must therefore be inserted into the tradition of the events at Sinai, because those events were not episodes in a story (as was for instance the victory over Sihon), but were the crucial events on which the very existence of Israel depended, events whose effects continued into the present, events comparable only to that later series which the New Testament scholar calls 'eschatological events'.

If this distinction between the core of the tradition and its elaboration is a sound one, it is no more legitimate to argue that the unhistorical character of the additions casts doubt on the central events themselves, than it would be to argue that our Lord probably did not die on a cross because some early medieval crucifixes represent the Crucified as robed and crowned, or because some Italian painters put the Crucifixion on the background of a Tuscan landscape, or because Dorothy Sayers gives St. Matthew a cockney accent. The crucifixion of the Son of

---

[1] Ibid., p. 64.

The Authority of the Book of the Kingdom

God is an 'eschatological event'; it took place in history, yet must be realized as ever newly present by every generation in its turn. Each Good Friday in the liturgy the people hear themselves accused as sinners, as from the Cross: 'O My people, what have I done unto thee, and wherein have I wearied thee? Testify against Me.' In the same way, Israelites in every generation went back in thought to the events on which Israel's existence depended, and saw those events come back to them, out of the past into the present. 'Thou shalt remember that thou wast a bondman in Egypt, and the Lord thy God brought thee out thence by a mighty hand and a stretched-out arm: therefore the Lord thy God commanded thee to keep the Sabbath day' (Deut. v, 15). As the historical fact that our Lord was crucified is in no way endangered by the various ways in which Christians through the ages have expressed their devotion to the Passion, so the diversity of the documents in which the Israelites told the story of the events of the Exodus and the Covenant only throws into stronger relief the historical actuality of those events.

It is on such lines that the historical investigation of the Exodus-story needs to be carried through. It is not sufficient to go back to the earliest sources, and make the best of them; it is necessary to go back behind the written sources to the tradition as it was handed down in the living faith of Israel, which appears fully formed in the written narratives, and the exhortations in Deuteronomy. It is then necessary to ask whether such a faith can seriously be believed to have created its own object. Such a hypothesis becomes more and more difficult in proportion as the faith of Israel in Yahweh is seen to have been different in kind from that of the surrounding tribes, in bearing stamped upon it the mark of objectivity and reality. It depends on a tradition of a God great and terrible, who has shown His power in His mighty works:

'I will sing unto Yahweh, for He hath triumphed gloriously;
The horse and his rider hath He thrown into the sea . . .
Who is like unto Thee, O Yahweh, among the gods?
Who is like Thee, glorious in holiness,
Fearful in praises, doing wonders?'

(Exod. xv, 1, 11.)

The Book of the Divine Kingdom

'For ask now of the days that are past, which were before thee, since the day that God created man upon the earth, and from the one end of heaven unto the other, whether there hath been any such thing as this great thing is, or hath been heard like it. Did ever people hear the voice of God speaking out of the midst of the fire, as thou hast heard, and live? Or hath God assayed to go and take to Himself a nation out of the midst of another nation, by temptations, by signs, and by wonders, and by war, and by a mighty hand, and by a stretched-out arm, according to all that Yahweh your God did for you in Egypt before your eyes? Unto thee it was showed, that thou mightest know that Yahweh He is God: there is none else beside Him' (Deut. iv, 32–5).

The Biblical narratives which tell of the divine Acts of Redemption demand of their very nature to be submitted to historical tests. Yet the events in question in being asserted to be *divine* acts, are thereby asserted to be different from the ordinary events in the ordinary run of history. If there really have been such events, they must inevitably be misjudged if the tradition which describes them is not studied in the light of the faith which inspired the tradition. It will be necessary for us to return in the next chapter but one to the delicate problems which are here involved. But we have seen enough to make it permissible to argue that the discussion of the history itself has in certain instances been seriously vitiated by the assumption that all that was distinctive in the religion of Israel began with Amos, and that therefore the truth or falsehood of the 'Exodus-legend' is really irrelevant. The origins of Israel's religion must, in any case, have been such as to make its later developments possible.

This, then, is the first sense in which the Bible is claimed to be authoritative. In it we get the official testimonies concerning its origins which the Israel of God preserved because it believed that in the Events there recorded the King of the universe has taken action to claim the obedience of men by setting up His Kingdom over them, that they may be His People and He their God.

The Authority of the Book of the Kingdom

(b) The Spiritual Education of Israel

It is claimed in the second place that the Bible is authoritative in its λόγος, in its revelation concerning God's nature and His ways and His will for man. In the New Testament, the Son of God Himself is presented as the *logos:* God is revealed in the person of the only-begotten Son, who hath declared Him. The Gospel *is* Jesus Himself; He is no mere bearer of a message from God, like the prophets; it is His person that makes the message what it is. In Colossians, the 'mystery of God' is more than a teaching which finds its centre in Jesus: ultimately it is Jesus Himself (i, 27; ii, 2).[1] The way of life for the Christian is to be a disciple of Jesus, to be transformed according to His likeness by the Holy Ghost.

In the Old Testament His way is prepared by the divine education of Israel in the primary and fundamental lessons which needed then, and still need, to be learnt. After Israel had been constituted as the People of God, it had to learn what that privilege involved and what it cost. To give an account of these lessons, it would be necessary to give an exposition of the entire contents of the Old Testament, and a history of Israel's whole spiritual development. Here we can mention only some of the salient points.

The Exodus is a work of redemption. But it is characteristic of the Faith that it holds in a just balance the doctrine of God as Redeemer and as Creator; this is very beautifully expressed in Ps. cxxxvi, which after praising God for creating sun, moon and stars ('for His mercy endureth for ever'), goes on to praise Him for 'smiting Egypt with their first-born'. This psalm belongs to the wisdom-literature, in which detailed studies are made of the revelation of God's glory in the created order. The truth that God is the creator is evidently one that was learnt by degrees, and was not included in the original *datum* of His redemptive action, since monolatry precedes monotheism: the prohibition of the worship of other gods belongs to an earlier stage than the explicit recognition that one God alone exists. That later stage was reached before the Exile. Amos is clear about it: Yahweh is 'He that formeth the mountains and createth the wind', and He it is

[1] See p. 78 f. below.

63

who brought up the Philistines from Caphtor and the Syrians from Kir, as well as Israel from Egypt (iv, 13; ix, 7). But behind both monolatry and monotheism lies the prior belief in Him as *real*.

Always His relation to Israel is conceived as personal; His personal presence in the midst of His people, His favour and displeasure, are described with a simplicity and directness and in a matter-of-fact way, which belies the modern notion that all language used about deity should be 'numinous'. For this reason again, it is repeatedly said in the prophetical books that sacrifices may not be regarded as transactions in which men settle up their accounts with God, much as they clear up debts by a money payment; when men think they can sin and then buy God's favour by offering sacrifice, they are denying the truth about His personal relation to them. Or again, the power of the king can never be absolute when behind the earthly ruler stands the divine Overlord. When David lusts after a pretty woman and brings about her husband's death in order to make her his wife, as any oriental king might do, the historian comments, 'But the thing that David had done displeased Yahweh', and goes on to relate how a prophet came and extracted from him the confession that he had sinned.

The essential point, shown here and elsewhere in the history, is that the Israelite monarchy stood upon a divine *foundation*, not that it was to be upheld by certain divine *sanctions*. It was not that the king, desiring to behave as if he had unlimited power, but knowing this to be impossible, therefore sought to buttress his throne by making use of the fears which men have of an Invisible King; but that he confessed himself to be actually subject to and responsible to that Invisible King. Here is the root of the whole conflict between idolatry in Israel and the acknowledgement of the One God. For the one purpose, any worship would doubtless serve; if only the required effect were produced, any god made in man's image would suffice, and there would be no need to be too particular. But the opposite conception depended on belief in the real God, who is therefore the jealous God, because He is intolerant of all falsehood.[1]

[1] This paragraph is from F. D. Maurice, *Prophets and Kings of the Old Testament*, 1853, Sermon vi, p. 98 f.

The Authority of the Book of the Kingdom

The moral and religious teaching is very largely given by means of precepts; but it is also given, very characteristically, by means of stories, whose value lies in the atmosphere which they breathe and the presuppositions which they take for granted. G. E. Phillips tells a story of a lady missionary in India who returned one day after a long afternoon in the zenanas with an Indian Bible-woman, who had been telling Old Testament stories in the dullest possible way; but when she expressed to an Indian Christian graduate, who was staying in her house, her impression that it had all been sheer waste of time, he took the matter up warmly and assured her that she, a European, could never fully realize the difference of atmosphere between those Bible stories and that of the Hindu myths; that to those women it was an utterly new thing to hear stories which rested on the belief that there was a God who really cared about human life: 'whether they know it or not, as they come to know these Bible stories their whole outlook, the climate of their spirits, is slowly being changed', and even the clumsy telling of the stories does not rob them of their power.[1]

It is assumed throughout that there is a divine goodwill and blessing resting on the people, on their homes, their family life, their land, their work in the fields with the oxen; that there is a worth-whileness in the ordinary simple things of daily life, depending on the direct relation of the people and the land to Yahweh. When idolatry is condemned as the worst of sins, as in the first two commandments of the decalogue, and it is insisted that Yahweh is a jealous God, it is because to forsake Him is to deny the basis on which rightly ordered human life rests. Hence the authority which the Bible teaching had for the ancient Israelite, and has for us, is largely that of a formative and educative influence: 'These words which I command thee this day shall be upon thine heart; and thou shalt teach them diligently unto thy children, and shalt talk of them when thou sittest in thine house, and when thou walkest by the way, and when thou liest down and when thou risest up' (Deut. vi, 6–7). Here has lain the authority of the Old Testament stories for us who have been brought up on them; they have been a formative influence

[1] G. E. Phillips, *The Old Testament in the World Church*, p. 113.

by which our thinking and our standards of judgement have been moulded. It was for this end that the Church, after its separation from the Synagogue, continued to use the old synagogue service, with psalms, scripture, preaching and prayer; and always the Christian liturgical forms have been written in Biblical language. In this way the Church has always used the Old Testament. The psalter, above all, has been the staple of Christian devotion; the psalms of praise providing the texts for the adoration of God in His glory, the penitential psalms setting for us the pattern of true contrition, and the psalter as a whole a model for meditation on God's dealings with man, and on human life as seen in relation to Him. There can be no more thorough acknowledgement of the authority of the Old Testament than that the Church throughout the centuries should send her children to school with it, to learn to think its thoughts and share its outlook.

(c) The Fulness of the Kingdom

The revelation of the divine Purpose includes also the τέλος or End to which the Purpose is moving. In the New Testament, that Purpose is declared to have been completed, so far as the course of this world is concerned, by the advent of the Messiah and His redemptive work: He came to announce and to set up the Kingly Rule of God among men. The Church exists to proclaim that the Christ reigns as the true King of men, and to be the primary means whereby that Reign of God is actualized in the world. Yet since history still goes on, and the men who are citizens of the Kingdom on earth are still immature in their spiritual growth, and there are still tares among the wheat, the New Testament and the Church look forward to the final perfection of the Kingdom in the Second Advent, when His Kingly Rule shall be consummated under the conditions of that heavenly existence on which He has already entered by His resurrection and ascension.

In the Old Testament the earthly process is still incomplete. The End to which it is moving is proclaimed in the messianic prophecies. These prophecies have always been regarded both in the New Testament and in the Church as inspired and

The Authority of the Book of the Kingdom

authoritative; and necessarily so, for to confess that Jesus is the Christ and the Son of Man and the Servant of the Lord, is not only to acknowledge Him to have been sent from God, but also to accept the Old Testament prophecies as having been divinely ordered. The difficulty here is that of equating human hopes with divine promises. It existed for the New Testament writers, who were aware of the imperfect and fragmentary character of the prophets' knowledge:[1] it is more serious for the modern student, whose comparative study of the prophets in their historical development makes him acutely aware of the extent to which their messianic prophecies reflect in each case their personal character and outlook; how then can he identify any one prophecy with the very truth of God, and call it a divine promise? This is one instance of the general problem of the relation of the word of God and the word of man.

The crucial period of the development of the messianic hope is that of the Exile. Yet it is obvious that in the days of the Monarchy the faithful Israelite must have had some conception of the future purpose of Yahweh with His people. In the time of Amos there was an optimistic hope of a Day of Yahweh, in which He would intervene to provide for His people a Golden Age of unbounded joy and blessing;[2] Amos tears this optimism in pieces, declaring that the Day of Yahweh will be a terrible day of judgement on the nation's sin (v. 18, 20). This message of judgement is the burden of the following prophets for two centuries. If the 'messianic' prophecies of Isaiah ii-xi can be accepted as the work of Isaiah of Jerusalem, this means that he did indeed look forward to a Golden Age, but only after a fearful judgement in which the remnant that should escape would be purified as by fire (ii, 3, 4; vi, 13; x, 22,) and the King who should reign would rule in righteousness (ix, 7; xi, 2-5).

The predictions of disaster came to pass; the cup was drunk to the dregs. But the faithful remnant, taught by Jerimiah and Ezekiel, accepted the punishment of Jerusalem as Yahweh's most

---

[1] Heb. i, 1, God spoke through the prophets in diverse fragmentary ways; 1 Pet. i, 10-11, the prophets were straining to discern the mystery of redemption through suffering.

[2] See Oesterley, *Evolution of the Messianic Idea* (1908), esp. pp. 246-9.

just judgement on their sin, and could therefore look to Him in hope, pray to Him, and believe that He was with them still. It was only on the basis of a most thorough penitence that the hope of a future Salvation, which these prophets proclaimed, took shape. Penitent Israel would be delivered by Yahweh in a new Exodus, be united to Him by a new Covenant, receive the outpouring of His Spirit, see His glorious Presence return to dwell in their midst; to this we must add that all nations would then come to share in the glorious knowledge of the one true God, the God of Israel.

Such is the pattern of the messianic hope. But when we come to details, there is much that is far from clear. Who could tell from the Old Testament alone, whether the authentic messianic expectation was that there should be a temporal king reigning in Jerusalem, or a descent of God Himself to rule over them in person: whether the Gentiles were to be in political subjection to Israel, or to have free access to the restored sanctuary and come to pray and offer sacrifice: whether this world-order were to continue, or be replaced by a 'new heaven and a new earth': whether only the generation living on earth at the 'Day of the Lord' would share in the Kingdom, or the saints of the past would rise from the dead to enter into it? Certainly the New Testament writers understand that One alone had been able to read the riddle, give a new and creative interpretation of the prophecies, and show their true proportion.

The New Testament does not endorse the expectation which seems to have been the common opinion of the Pharisees in our Lord's day,[1] that there was to be a temporal King reigning in Jerusalem, and exercising political domination over the Gentiles; and the gospels plainly attribute to Jesus Himself the rejection of this answer to the problem. On the Mount of the Temptation He refuses to seek 'the kingdoms of this world and the glory of them'; in the ministry that follows He takes no steps to realize such an aim, and significantly substitutes other designations for the title 'Christ'. Yet He is as far as possible from rejecting the idea of a Kingdom: He proclaims the Kingdom of God, with Himself as its central figure, but not the popular

[1] Ryle and James, *The Psalms of Solomon*, p. lvii.

68

notion of it. He enters Jerusalem as King, but in the sense of the peaceful King of Zech. ix, 9–10, who was to come to Zion riding on an ass and not on a war-horse, and break the battle-bow from Ephraim and speak peace to the nations: King, but 'come not to be ministered unto but to minister, and to give Himself as a ransom for many': King, but also the Servant of Yahweh: King in the sense of John xviii, 36–7, having no police nor standing army, but come to bear witness to the Truth.

God had spoken by the prophets, but 'in many manners and many fragments' (Heb. i, 1); each prophet's vision was partial, and therefore liable by itself to wrong emphasis and balance; no prophet's vision could be taken as expressing the fulness of what God purposed. Yet the core of the messianic hope stands firm. There was to be a messianic King, under whom Israel would truly come into its own, as the People of Yahweh, with Him reigning over it as its God. But how it was all to work out in detail could not be known till He came who alone could fit the various elements together, being Himself the Wisdom of God.

We thus reach a result remarkably parallel to that which emerged when we were seeking to justify the authoritative witness of the Bible to the facts of the Redemption. In the predictions of the Messiah, as in the narratives of the Exodus, there is no such thing as 'inerrancy'; but there is a core of truth lying behind both, to which the writers in either case bear witness with a knowledge and an insight which are real but limited. Consequently, as we are justified in accepting the historical testimony of the ancient traditions, so we can affirm the true inspiration of the prophecies of the Messiah, even though we cannot completely equate any particular prophecy with the divine promise and say that *these* verses of *this* chapter have the absolute and infallible truth of a divine oracle.

3. The Divine and the Human Elements in the Bible

The conception which we found in Maurice of the Bible as the Book of the divine Kingdom, as being the record of the Sacred History in which God's Purpose of Salvation for man was worked out, compels us to view the Bible as a whole, and interpret the meaning of the various parts of it in relation to the whole. At the same time it compels us to acknowledge the imperfection of the human writers; they were pupils in the divine School, engaged in learning lessons which He had to teach. We are not to regard that imperfection as something which we must explain or explain away as best we can, nor indulge a secret wish that certain parts of the Bible were not there; they all belong to the history, and the history is the story of God's Purpose as it was actually worked out. Further, the fact that the Old Testament contains the messianic prophecies means that the End towards which the Purpose is moving confessedly lies outside the Old Testament. The New Testament writers announce that in Jesus Christ the Purpose has reached its fulfilment; they supply, therefore, that which was needed to complete the Old Testament. The Christian Bible must consist of two Testaments. The Old Testament is incomplete apart from the New; and Christians, in accepting it as divine, are accepting it as fulfilled in the New, and in their practical use of it must necessarily read back New Testament meanings into it.

We may hope, then, that we are on the track of a right solution of the dilemma with which we started. Either, it seemed the Bible, as being God's Book, must be free from all error, and it became difficult or impossible to do justice to its truly human character; or, when the greatness and the imperfection of its human authors were freely recognized, it became difficult or impossible to ascribe to their writings a truly divine authority. But it is otherwise when we start with the conception of a divine Purpose of Salvation for man, in which God has made human nature, imperfect though it is, the instrument of His revelation, and has consummated that revelation in the Incarnation of His Son in true manhood. This Biblical principle of the revelation of God through human nature provides the true key to the problem raised by the Inspiration of the Bible on the one hand, and its truly human character on the other.

The definition of the 'Inspiration of the Bible' is that in it God has spoken His word. Plainly, the word which God had to speak cannot be simply equated with that truth which Isaiah, or Jeremiah, was able to apprehend and to express; it is heard in its completeness only in Him who personally is the Word of God. Yet the fact that He and the Apostles who are His witnesses constantly appeal to the Law and the Prophets means that through them God's word had been spoken; He came not to destroy but to fulfil. The word which is incompletely spoken in the Old Testament is thus illuminated by its fulfilment in the New.

To say that the word of God spoken in the Old Testament is to be understood in the light of the New does not at all exclude, but on the contrary demands, the exact investigation of the literal and original meaning of the prophecies. The Gospel is the proclamation that God's messianic Purpose has been fulfilled in history; it looks back therefore to the previous working out of that Purpose in the history of Israel. It is not, therefore, that the literal sense of the Old Testament is to be abandoned, and interpretations consonant with the New Testament fulfilment forced upon the writers; it is that the genuine historical continuity of the Old Testament and the New is to be traced. When this is done, it is claimed that the Old Testament truly leads up to the New, and then the texts receive a fuller meaning in the light of that messianic Day which prophets and kings had desired to see, and which the disciples of Jesus saw (Luke x, 23-4).

Hence the Inspiration of the Bible, which consists in God's word spoken in it, must apply to it as a whole, and not to the various writings taken separately and in isolation from the whole and from one another. It is this isolation of the writers from one another that constitutes the misleading element in the notion that we are to attribute to them 'degrees of inspiration'. It is obvious, indeed, that they differ from one another. But Inspiration properly describes the word which God was speaking through the writer, not that which the writer himself was able to grasp and to express. The error then lies in the treatment of the writers as individuals, and the laying of the emphasis on the particular word which each spoke and on the 'religious experience' which lay behind it. But Inspiration is a theological term. It refers not to the prophet's human word, taken by itself, but to the divine truth which was finding imperfect expression through its human instruments, till in the fulness of time *the* Word was made flesh.[1]

The relation of the imperfect moral ideas expressed by various persons in the story and by the writers of the books, to the truth which the Lord God intended to teach, may be illustrated by a brief consideration of the attitude which is taken towards the enemies of Israel; and this belongs to the wider theme of the conflict with evil, which runs through the whole Bible.

In the earlier stages of Israel's history, which correspond to that of adolescence in the individual, it is only to be expected that crude moral ideas should find expression; everyone knows that boys are often thoughtlessly cruel. In the early period, the enemies of the Lord are identified with the enemies of Israel. Jael strikes Sisera down (though here the probably contemporary ballad in Judges v does not attribute to her the cold-blooded violation of the laws of hospitality which appears in the prose narrative of Judges iv: in the ballad, it seems that the brave woman strikes him down with the mallet while he is on his knees with the drinking-vessel raised to his lips); Saul is commanded to exterminate the Amalekites. But as time goes on, this simple equation of the Lord's enemies with Israel's enemies becomes impossible. The prophets accuse Israel of sin, and declare that He Himself is sending their enemies against them for their chastisement. From this time onwards, the question who really are the Lord's enemies is difficult to answer. Is it Israel itself which by its sin is provoking His wrath? or is it the sinners in Israel? From Jeremiah onwards, there is a continual conflict between the faithful remnant and the 'ungodly', which finds expression in many psalms. On the one hand there is the sharp line drawn between the 'righteous' and the 'wicked'; on the other, the fact that a prophet such as Jeremiah who denounces the nation's sin himself shares the suffering which comes as the chastisement for that sin. Correspondingly, there are expressions of corporate penitence for the common guilt. In such acts of

---

[1] We shall return to this question of the Inspiration of the Bible in the last section of the next chapter, in its connection with the idea of Revelation; see pp. 100-6 below.

The Divine and the Human Elements in the Bible

contrition as the penitential psalms the sinner who accuses himself of sin declares that thereby he has done evil in God's sight and incurred blood-guiltiness (Ps. li, 4, 14); thereby he has ranged himself with the Lord's enemies.

It is only when the issue is raised in the acutest possible form in the Gospel story that the problem is finally cleared up. The Messiah when He comes accuses the righteous Pharisees of hypocrisy, that is, profane godlessness, seeing in them a self-righteousness which is worse than the sin of the publicans and harlots; yet His mission is to gather together the people of Israel like a hen gathering her chickens under her wings, and its climax is His offering of Himself as a ransom for many, as the sacrifice for sin. His enemies were not the blinded sinners whom He had come to gather into the divine Kingdom, among whom were found even His own disciples, who all forsook Him and fled. The enemies against whom His battle is fought are 'not flesh and blood, but the principalities and powers, the world-rulers of this darkness, the spiritual hosts of wickedness in the heavenly places' (Eph. vi, 12); for when St. Paul, in this passage, calls upon the Christians to arm themselves for this battle, he bids them 'take up the whole armour of God': that armour which God took on Him when He came in person to fight His own battle against evil, as is clear from the Old Testament texts which are here quoted.[1] It is 'the prince of this world' whom the Christ overcomes by His cross and resurrection (John xii, 31–2).

Such is the final issue. Yet there is a continuity in the whole conflict; and in the New Testament and in the church liturgy the Old Testament texts are freely used to describe the Lord's victory over the powers of evil which have held man in bondage. Even for the ordinary Englishman, David's conflict with Goliath stands as a type of the battle of the champion of the right against insolent and boastful powers of evil, far superior in brute strength; and in the Church, the regular interpretation of the psalter in the daily office is that it is used as the prayer of Christ

---

[1] 'Take unto you the whole armour of God', Wisd. v, 17 ff.; but the primary passage is Isa. lix, 17 f., 'He put on righteousness as a breastplate', and there are reminiscences also of the Davidic King, Isa. xi, 4 f., the Servant of Yahweh whose mouth is a sharp sword, Isa. xlix, 2, and the messengers of the Good Tidings of peace, Isa. lii, 7. Robinson, *Ephesians*, pp. 133–5.

and of the many members of the Church which is His body, in the age-long battle with the evil in the world. Thus the Old Testament texts, whose original reference was to the struggle of the believing Remnant of Israel to maintain the Faith against the 'ungodly', receive a wider meaning when they are seen in the context of the whole conflict with evil which runs through the Bible and finds its consummation in the victory of the Christ.

Thus it is right to speak of the Bible as the Book of the Church, since the Church is Israel, the direct heir of the Old Israel in which the Old Testament Scriptures were written. They come to us as from within the life of faith and common worship lived by the Israel of God; within that environment they were written, for believing and worshipping Israel to read and to use. We shall see later how important a part was played by the Synagogue in the actual formation of the Old Testament Canon; and the Church carried on the tradition of synagogue worship in the psalmody, Scripture-lessons, preaching and prayer which still forms the first part of the eucharistic liturgy, and further developed the same elements in the Breviary offices. In its forms of liturgy the Church teaches us to interpret the Bible. Its texts are still to us, as they were to Old Israel, the staple forms by which the tradition of faith and of worship and of the way of God's service is transmitted, and is imprinted on the minds of the People of God to-day. The Bible is the Book of the Faith, the Book of the divine Kingdom.

CHAPTER III

REVELATION

The strength of the conservative view of the Bible has always lain in the firmness with which its divine authority has been proclaimed; that of the liberal view, in the courage with which the methods and results of critical study have been accepted. The failure of each side to do justice to that which the other affirms is evident to all, and enough has been said about it already. We must go on next to the strange fact that both sides fail as seriously, and more dangerously, at the point where they are strongest: the conservative view, in its conception of Revelation and of Truth, and the liberal view, in its acceptance of Criticism.

We must begin, in deference to the authority of the Bible, by going to the Bible to find what its view of Revelation is; in such a case it is plainly necessary to begin with the New Testament. We are not concerned for the moment with the question *how* the revelation comes, but with the question *what* it is that is revealed: is it in the first place truths about God, or is it God Himself? The familiar illustration of this point is, that it is one thing when from a dinner which I eat I learn various truths about the capabilities and tastes of the cook, and quite another thing when I am introduced to her. We shall find that both these meanings are found in the Biblical usage, and are there inseparable. But the primary fact is God's personal revelation of Himself, and it is just this that the theological statements of the doctrine of revelation have often tended to lose.

1. The Biblical Idea of Revelation

The idea with which we are concerned is represented in the

Revelation

New Testament not only by the word 'revelation' (ἀποκάλυψις), but also by the words 'mystery', 'gospel', and 'word'.

The Latin *revelatio* is the translation of the Greek ἀποκάλυψις, 'unveiling'. This noun, with its verb, is used (*a*) of individual revelations, by visions or otherwise, several times in the New Testament.[1] The verb and noun are more often used (*b*) of the revealing of the Son of Man at His Advent; this will be an unveiling of the 'Glory', of the Judgement, of the nature of each man's work, and of the sons of God, who will then be known for what they truly are, when all that is now covered is brought to light.[2] (*c*) Yet the First Advent of the Son of Man is no less an 'eschatological' reality than the Second. That which is thus revealed in the coming of the Gospel had hitherto been hidden because the time for the revealing of God's Righteousness and His Wrath had not yet come; so to St. Paul, at his conversion, the Son of God had been revealed.[3] (*d*) Yet also, the Truth of God had been hidden from men for another reason: because of the blindness of their own hearts, in the self-sufficiency of their own wisdom; but it is revealed to babes, and St. Paul prays that it may be revealed to the Christians to whom he writes.[4] In the New Testament, however, this word 'revelation' or 'unveiling' never seems to become a technical term, as do 'mystery', 'gospel' and 'word'.

---

[1] 1 Cor. xiv, 6, 26, 30; 2 Cor. xii, 1, 7; Rev. i, 1, and presumably Gal. ii, 2.

[2] Christ at the Parousia, Luke xvii, 30; 1 Cor. i, 7; 2 Thess. i, 7; 1 Pet. i, 7, 13;
The Glory, Rom. viii, 18; 1 Pet. iv, 13, v. 1;
Salvation, 1 Pet. i, 5;
Judgement, Rom. ii, 5; the nature of each man's work, 1 Cor. iii, 13;
The sons of God, Rom. viii, 19;
All that is covered, Matt. x, 26=Luke xii, 2; cf. Luke ii, 35.
Cf. the revealing of the Man of Sin, 2 Thess. ii, 3, 6, 8.

[3] 'Faith' revealed, Gal. iii, 23;
God's Righteousness and His Wrath, Rom. i, 17, 18;
The Son of God to St. Paul, Gal. i, 12, 16.

[4] Truths revealed to babes, Matt. xi, 25, 27=Luke x, 21, 22;
to St. Peter by the Father, Matt. xvi, 17;
to the Philippians, Phil. iii, 15;
The revelation of the mystery of God's Purpose in Christ, Eph. iii, 3, 5, cf. i, 17;
of the 'arm of the Lord', John xii, 38, quoting Isa. liii, 1.

The Biblical Idea of Revelation

The noun 'mystery', or 'secret' ($\mu\nu\sigma\tau\acute{\eta}\rho\iota\sigma\nu$) is constantly used with the verb 'reveal'. It is used in the *LXX* of Daniel (ii, 17 ff. and elsewhere) of a 'secret', as of the dream which Nebuchadnezzar has forgotten; but the translators avoid it elsewhere, even in Amos iii, 7, 'the Lord God will do nothing but He revealeth His secret unto His servants the prophets' (but it is used in Rev. x, 7, where there is a reminiscence of this text) and Deut. xxix, 29: 'the secret things belong unto the Lord our God; but the things that are revealed belong to us and to our children, for ever, that we may observe to do according to all the words of this law'. These two texts illustrate well the use of the word in the New Testament.

The Gospel message itself is the great 'secret' in Mark iv, 11: 'to you is given the mystery of the Kingdom of God'; and in 1 Cor. ii, 1, 2, where St. Paul says he came to Corinth preaching the 'mystery of God', namely 'Jesus Christ and Him crucified', and this 'secret' was hidden from the rulers of this world who crucified Him (ii, 7). The mystery of the divine Purpose extends, in Rom. xi, 25–36, to that truth which had proved a stumbling-block to Israel, and might be so to the Gentile Christians also if they became wise in their own conceits (v. 25): namely that the law-abiding Pharisee was as much a sinner as the Gentile, and 'God hath shut up all unto disobedience that He might have mercy upon all' (v. 32). This is the mystery which has been 'kept in silence from times eternal, but now is manifested, and through the scriptures of the prophets according to the commandment of the eternal God is made known unto all the nations, unto obedience of faith' (xvi, 25-6).[1]

This is the regular use in Ephesians and Colossians. It does seem that St. Paul[2] here uses from time to time phrases reminis-

[1] In other places the word 'mystery' is used of secret meanings revealed, as by prophecy, 1 Cor. xiii, 2; xiv, 2; xv, 51 (the change in our bodies at the Advent); 2 Thess. ii, 7; Rev. i, 20; xvii, 5, 7. But it is never used in N.T. of sacramental rites; in 1 Cor. iv, 1, the apostles are stewards of the mysteries of God, i.e. of the Gospel; in Eph. v, 32, it is not the marriage-rite but the Bridegroom-bride relation of Christ and the Church that is the 'great mystery'. Similarly 1 Tim. iii, 9, 16.

[2] I take it that 'Ephesians' is Pauline, because the personal names in 'Colossians' are mainly the same as in 'Philemon', and 'Ephesians' and 'Colossians' are closely parallel; but still more, because 'Ephesians' takes up

cent of the pagan mysteries; but the meaning he attaches to the word μυστήριον is the same as in Corinthians and Romans. It is the Purpose of God's will, the divine Secret which was in former ages not made known, but is now revealed to apostles and prophets (Eph. iii, 5); it is the Purpose according to Selection (Rom. ix, 11) of Isaac and not Ishmael, Jacob and not Esau; it is consummated in the Messiah, through whom men of all nations have equal access to God, the wall of partition being done away. But since the great Secret can be hidden from men also by hardening of their hearts, his great prayer for the readers of 'Ephesians' is that they may come to true knowledge and understanding of their Christian calling (i, 15 ff.; iii, 14-21).

Thus the Christian meaning of the word 'mystery' excludes altogether the idea of an esoterical lore, a theosophy of the kind which in more than one period of history has been greedily absorbed by persons who take delight in long words imperfectly understood. St. Paul is well aware of this danger, and satirizes in 1 Cor. xiii, 2, the intellectual pride which delights to have the gift of prophecy and know all mysteries and all knowledge, without the one thing needful, which is the renunciation of the self. The Christian Mystery demands of all who receive it the denial of the heathen way of life, the putting off of the old Adam, and the becoming identified with Christ in His resurrection and in His ascension (Eph. ii, 1-6; Col. iii, 1-11).

While then the Mystery which is revealed is primarily the Secret of God's purpose which is consummated in Christ, in the last resort the content of it *is* Christ Himself. The Mystery, St. Paul says in so many words, '*is* Christ in you, the hope of glory' (Col. i, 27); and again, the Mystery *is* 'Christ, in whom are all the treasures of wisdom and knowledge hidden' (ii, 2-3).[1] The

---

many characteristically Pauline phrases, and its theology represents a direct and continuous development of his thought from that of his earlier epistles. See Prof. L. Cerfaux's admirable and excellent book, *La théologie de l'Église suivant Saint Paul* (Les Editions du Cerf, Paris, 1942), esp. pp. 250-2.

[1] The text is notoriously uncertain. Yet it seems that the R.V. text and rendering can be accepted with some confidence, since the very difficulty of the idea which St. Paul is expressing seems to have caused the confusion in the texts, and this reading best explains the variants. Cf. Radford, *Colossians*, pp. 215-6.

Mystery which has been unveiled is the Person of Christ. The revelation consists of the Son of God manifested in the flesh, as He in whom all history finds its fulfilment, and by whom it is brought to the attainment of its End, 'to the praise of His glory'.

The word 'mystery' leads naturally on to two other words, 'Gospel' and 'Word'. The making-known of the Mystery is the proclaiming of the Gospel (Eph. iii, 6, 8), and 'the Gospel', particularly in St. Mark, is not merely the Good Tidings which Jesus announced, nor yet which others announced about Him; in the last resort it *is* Himself. In the Old Testament, the idea expressed in the noun *evangelion* 'is connected with the Advent of the Salvation of God, with His Mercy, with Remission of Sins, with the Peace of God and the coming of His Righteousness, with the Acceptable Year of the Lord, with the Justification of the Poor, with the emergence of Zion as the centre of the world where the Action of God would take place. This Old Testament background with its hope of the future and supreme action of God is clearly presumed in the title of Mark's book and in the summary with which he announces and introduces the ministry of Jesus.'[1] As we go on, in two passages we hear Him speak of the breaking of worldly ties and the losing of life itself 'for My sake and the Gospel's' (Mark viii, 35; x, 29). 'So close a connection between Jesus and the Gospel suggests that . . . "the Gospel" is for Mark an all-embracing term which gives a peculiar significance to his narrative of Jesus of Nazareth, His Teaching, His Actions, and finally His Death and Resurrection' (p. 118). 'Jesus both announces the Good News and is Himself the Good News. Hence Mark portrays Him throughout as bearing witness to Himself, not merely in His teaching, but even and indeed primarily by His actions. The interest of the narrative is fixed upon the question whether men and women will recognize in Jesus the Gospel of God, and will accept the witness which He bears to Himself' (p. 120).

There is then from this point of view no novelty in St. John's

---

[1] Hoskyns and Davey, *The Riddle of the New Testament*, pp. 116–7. References are given to Isa. xl, 9; lii, 7–10; lx, 6; lxi, 1; Joel ii, 32; Ps. xcvi, 2; Nah. i, 15; Ps. xl, 9.

identification of Jesus with the Word of God. In His Person, God whom no man hath seen at any time has been revealed (i, 18). The Life and Light of the eternal Word were there to be seen in the Grace and Truth of the Word made flesh (i, 4, 14). St. Philip ought to have understood that to see Him was to see the Father, or at the least have so believed 'for the very works' sake' (xiv, 9–11); for the Father abiding in Him did the works (v. 10), and He whom God sent spoke the words of God (iii, 34). All things that the Father hath are His, and the Spirit's work is to take of His and show it to them (xvi, 15).

Enough has been said to show that while the idea of 'revelation' in the New Testament includes the disclosing of truths to individuals, its most fundamental meaning is that of God's action in making Himself known to mankind in His Son. But the New Testament in no way justifies the notion, widely held to-day, that God is revealed in Jesus as in an isolated figure, separated from the Old Testament background on the one hand, and from His body the Church on the other. Prof. William Manson provides the needed corrective, when he says: 'Strictly speaking, there is not within the frontiers of the Synoptic tradition any presentation of the person of Jesus which does not keep throughout to his functional significance as Messiah, Son of God and Son of Man.'[1]

Everything in the synoptic gospels has relation to the Gospel of the Kingdom of God; that is the setting in which the Christology comes. Precisely parallel is St. Paul's teaching about the Mystery of the divine Purpose which is brought to its completion in Christ. The personal revelation of God in His Son is the consummation of the Purpose which began with the creation and is fulfilled in the Church which is His body.

In the Old Testament we find the same double conception of Revelation, as the revelation of God Himself, and of truths concerning Him. Continually God is represented as speaking His word to individuals, from the very beginnings of the narrative, and He 'reveals His secret to His servants the prophets' (Amos iii, 7). Indeed, the fact that we owe the historical books mainly to the prophetic schools may account for the frequent occurrence

[1] W. Manson, *Jesus the Messiah* (1943), p. 94.

of this conception of prophetic revelation of divine truths; and this prophetic revelation has come to be very widely taken as the type of all revelation. It may, however, be pointed out that for the prophets themselves there existed a problem which the modern theologian has not always faced: there were false 'revelations' as well as true. Did Yahweh speak through Micaiah the son of Imlah, or through Zedekiah? through Jeremiah, or through Hananiah? Deuteronomy gives one test of the false prophet: 'if the thing come not to pass' (xviii, 21 f.). Jeremiah, however, makes a far more searching analysis of the matter (xxiii, 15–40): the false prophet is the man who has not stood in God's council (v. 32) and so mistakes his own dreams for the true word of God.

To Israel as a whole He made Himself known, when He called them to be His people and made His covenant with them. Everything here is set out in such concrete and personal terms that it is more than a little difficult to define the idea of 'revelation'. Most characteristic of all in this connection is the idea of the making-known of His 'Name', and the presence of His 'Name' with them.

Driver gives this note on the meaning of the word 'name':

'The name with the Hebrews is the expression of the nature . . . "the 'name of Jehovah' is the compendious expression of His character and attributes as He has revealed them to men" (Kirkpatrick on Ps. v, 11); to act "for His name's sake" is to act in such a manner as not to belie His revealed nature. Jehovah's revealed nature is especially associated with His people Israel, and with His sanctuary in their midst; hence He will not forsake His people, for when Israel suffers contumely or reproach, it is His own name which is profaned; and the sanctuary is the place of Jehovah's "name" because He there vouchsafes the special tokens of His presence, and graciously responds to His servants' devotion.'[1]

The making known of the Name is connected in two of our sources directly with the Exodus. According to J., indeed, the Name had been known from the beginning. But the Elohist

[1] Driver, *Deuteronomy*, p. 141.

makes it clear throughout Exod. iii that the God of Abraham, Isaac and Jacob first revealed His Name Yahweh at the Burning Bush, the famous interpretation of the four letters, J.H.V.H., being given in v. 14; and the Priestly author says expressly that 'God spake unto Moses, and said unto him, I am Yahweh; and I appeared unto Abraham, unto Isaac, and unto Jacob, as *El Shaddai*, but by My Name Yahweh I was not made known unto them. And I have also established My Covenant with them.... Wherefore say unto the children of Israel, I am Yahweh, and I will bring you out from under the burdens of the Egyptians, and I will rid you out of their bondage, and I will redeem you with a stretched-out arm and with great judgements; and I will take you to Me for a people, and I will be to you a God; and ye shall know that I am Yahweh your God, which bringeth you out from under the burdens of the Egyptians' (Exod. vi, 2–7).

It is in this concrete fashion that the Eternal is declared to have revealed Himself to Israel. The Sacred Name is not a designation, not an abstract term, but a proper name. True, Moab had its Chemosh and Syria its Rimmon, and these were proper names; do we then say that the Eternal was revealed in every tribal deity? No, for this the Old Testament itself is continually denying, by the assertion of the essential difference which marks off Israel's worship from all others. Phrases are often used which have led many scholars to doubt whether those who used them were really monotheists, such as that which we use daily: 'The Lord is a great God, and a great King above all gods' (Ps. xcv, 3). But nothing is further from the psalmist's mind than the philosophical notion, such as a Greek might have asserted of Zeus Olympios, that there is a plurality of divine beings of whom Yahweh is the greatest; but rather that He is *real*, emphatically not one among many, and His worship far excels all other worships. Dr. Gavin wrote that there has never been such a thing as a systematic theological formulation of Israel's belief, nor any historical theology of Judaism, produced by any Jewish scholar. 'The one attempt made by a non-Jewish scholar, Dr. Weber (*Die Lehren des Talmud*) ... has been levied upon by all subsequent non-Jewish students, who, often to their sorrow, too easily trust the superimposed framework of the author as if it

were really knit up with the content.'[1] Throughout, the Old
Testament uses personal and concrete language. He is the
Husband to whom Israel has been continually unfaithful. He is
the Shepherd of Israel; He is its true King. It is in such terms
that the revelation of the Eternal to Israel is set forth.

Thus, when we look behind the word Revelation in both
Testaments to its underlying idea, we find at the centre the
thought of the living God made known in His personal action.
Thereby also truths about Him are made known; as when, in
knowing a friend we come to know a great deal about him, and
progressively as our friendship continues. But to learn many
true facts about a man at second-hand is an entirely different
thing from meeting him and knowing him personally. So, when
God is revealed, not as an abstraction or hypothesis, but as the
living God, that means of necessity that much is revealed about
Him by His acts in history and in His dealings with men. Most
is known by those who know Him best. But what is primary is
the action of God in history, whereby He makes and renews
His Covenant with Israel and establishes His Kingdom.

2. The Biblical Idea of Faith

Much light is thrown on the Old Testament conception of
God's revelation of Himself by the remarkable word used for
'to believe', which, in a way difficult to reproduce in our
language, throws back the emphasis from man's act of faith on
to God who is the Object of faith.[2] It is not uncommon for a
phrase in Biblical Hebrew to defy all efforts to measure it with
the cold precision of our logic; an instance might be Ps. cxliii, 9,
'I flee unto Thee to hide me', where the literal rendering is,
'Unto Thee have I hidden'. A similar idea of *movement* seems to
be conveyed by the word for 'to believe'. Yet that which it expresses is far different from the act of an investor who, after cal-
culating all the contingencies, decides to put his money in a

[1] F. Gavin, *The Jewish Antecedents of the Christian Sacraments*, 1928, pp. 5–6.
[2] The words are *'aman*, to confirm, support; the causative *he'emin*, to
believe; *'emunah*, firmness, steadfastness, fidelity; cf. *'emeth*, firmness, faithfulness, truth. See the *Oxford Hebrew Lexicon*, pp. 52–4; B. B. Warfield in
H.D.B. i, 827 ff.; Dodd, *The Bible and the Greeks*, 1935, pp. 65–75; and cf.
Hoskyns and Davey, *The Riddle of the New Testament*, on ἀλήθεια, pp. 35–43.

particular 'security'; it is rather the thought of m[...] aware of his own weakness and the transitoriness o[...] life, and of his own moral instability and the fickle[...] wayward heart, and so throwing himself upon God, t[...] refuge in His mightiness, hiding under the shadow of His wing The Hebrew for 'to believe' comes from a root meaning stead-fast, reliable, firm; and this applies above all to God:

> '*Thy loving kindness, O Lord, is in the heavens,*
> *Thy faithfulness reacheth unto the skies.*
> *Thy righteousness is like the mountains of God;*
> *Thy judgements are a great deep;*
> *O Lord, Thou preservest man and beast.*'
>
> (Ps. xxxvi, 5–6, R.V.)[1]

God's 'faithfulness' is thus almost the synonym of His eternality: 'I the Lord change not: therefore ye, O sons of Jacob, are not consumed' (Mal. iii, 6). Consequently he who 'believes' becomes firm and rock-like in his turn, unlike the weak king Ahaz, whose 'heart was moved, and the heart of his people, as the trees of the forest are moved with the wind', at the threat of an invasion; and Isaiah says to him, 'If ye will not believe, ye shall not be established'.[2]

But the two great texts of the Old Testament about Faith are those which St. Paul uses. First, Abraham 'believed in the Lord, and He counted it to him for righteousness' (Gen. xv, 6). The emphasis throughout the story of Abraham is on a Call of God heard, promises of God believed, a command to offer up the promised son obeyed, a blessing bestowed; and it is no new blessing that is given to Isaac and to Jacob, but Abraham's blessing that is continued.[3]

---

[1] In v. 5 the word 'faithfulness' is of course '*emunah*.

[2] Isa. vii, 2 and 9. In the latter verse the word '*aman* occurs twice; cf. 2 Chron. xx, 20: 'Believe in the Lord your God, so shall ye be established; believe His prophets, so shall ye prosper.'

[3] References: The call, Gen. xii, 1 ff.; the promises, xii, 2; xiii, 14–17; xv, 4–5; xviii, 10, 17 ff.; xxii, 16–18; the command, xxii, 2; the blessing, xii, 2; xxii, 17; xxiv, 1; Isaac, xxvi, 3, 24; Jacob xxviii, 3, 13 f.; xxxi, 42; xxxii, 9. All these are from J.E. (except Gen. xxviii, 3). What is added by P. is chiefly the covenant of circumcision in ch. xvii. See Pedersen, *Israel I-II* (1926), p. 190 f., on Abraham's 'blessing'.

The Biblical Idea of Faith

In all this it is God who acts, in revealing Himself; Abraham obeys the call, holds the divine word to be true, does what is commanded, receives the blessing. But his part is not one of co-operation, but wholly of response; that is what makes him the man of faith.

The other great text is Hab. ii, 4, 'The just shall live by faith' ('*emur̄ah*). Here the *Oxford Hebrew Lexicon* renders, 'A righteous man by his faithfulness liveth'; and this is in itself a right meaning. But 'faithfulness' is made possible by 'faith': Warfield's comment is, 'The point of this passage is the sharp contrast which is drawn between arrogant self-sufficiency and faithful dependence upon God'—between the insolent self-assertion of the Chaldeans, and the Israelites who are set forth by contrast 'not as men of integrity and steadfast faithfulness, but as men who look in faith to God and trustingly depend on His arm'. This is the one place where the noun 'faith' occurs in the English versions of the Old Testament; 'but on this its sole occurrence it rises to the full height of its most pregnant meaning'.[1]

The phrase 'to believe that' occurs only three times in the Old Testament.[2] This does not mean that the Hebrew faith in God does not involve a very definite dogmatic conception of His personality and nature. But part at least of the reason why the phrase is so rare, in contrast with its frequent occurrence in the New Testament, is that the question *whether* Yahweh is the God of Israel and has redeemed Israel out of Egypt in the ordinary way does not arise; the thing that is doubtful is whether Israel will obey, and do its known duty. But the question does come up once, at the very beginning of the story, in Exod. iv, 5, when Moses doubts whether the Israelites in Egypt will *believe that* Yahweh has appeared to him. There is scarcely another instance where this point is raised, except Elijah's controversy on Mt. Carmel against the rival worship of the Tyrian Baal: 'If Yahweh be God, then follow Him; but if Baal, then follow him' (1 Kings xviii, 21). But it is otherwise in the New Testament, where those who disbelieve in our Lord must necessarily deny *that* He is risen from the dead and is Messiah; thus the Jews ac-

---

[1] *H.D.B.*, i, 827, col. *b*.
[2] Exod. iv, 5; Job. ix, 16; Lam. iv, 12.

counted for the empty tomb by asserting that the disciples came and stole the body while men slept (Matt. xxviii, 13–15). Hence there have always been Christian forms of belief, beginning with the form of words about the Resurrection which St. Paul quotes in 1 Cor. xv, 3 ff., and taking shape in the baptismal confession of faith. But even so, the creed is always cast not in the form 'I believe that . . .' but 'I believe in . . . who. . . .'

While in the New Testament, therefore, the form 'believe that' occurs with some frequency, the conception of faith is on similar lines to that of the Old Testament. It is not indeed quite uniform. In James ii, 19, it is used exceptionally of belief which is purely intellectual: 'the devils believe (that there is one God) and tremble'. In Hebrews the idea of faith has a perceptibly more intellectual cast than in St. Paul. In chapter xi the object of faith is not so much the personal God as the realities of the eternal world, which faith discerns, like an eye of the soul beholding the things unseen, or like the pilgrims gaining a view of the Heavenly City from the Delectable Mountains. Faith, moreover, has a distinct flavour of 'faithfulness', as when he speaks of 'those who through faith and patience inherit the promises' (vi, 12).

In the rest of the New Testament, however, the conception varies little. The object of faith is ordinarily the personal God, or it is Christ. In the Synoptic gospels, faith is regularly demanded of those who seek bodily healing; there must be an entire concentration of mind towards Jesus, as able to heal, as in the case of the father of the epileptic boy, Mark ix, 23–4. So necessary is this faith, that in three instances[1] He says, 'Thy faith hath saved thee'; but that the patient's faith is not regarded as the operating cause of the cure is shown by the fact that in one of these cases 'Jesus immediately knew in Himself that power had gone out of Him' (Mark v, 30), while in another the benefit conferred is the absolution of sins (Luke vii, 50). Other instances are of faith in God's providence or this present action, as when in the storm on the lake the result of not having faith is to be frightened (Mark iv, 40), and when He calls for faith in praying to God over difficulties which seem insurmountable, having

[1] Mark v, 34 and x, 52 (and parallels); Luke vii, 50.

taken full stock of the situation, but believing that the thing asked for is coming to pass (Mark xi, 22–4).

Faith, with St. Paul, is normally and regularly used of that personal faith in Christ through which a man is justified; thus it is as good as identical with the Synoptic usage. Neither in that instance nor in this is there any notion that it is through the psychological earnestness and sincerity of a man's faith that he is justified.[1] It is by the blood of Christ, or by the grace of God that he is justified, and there is only one place where faith is regarded as something in itself without reference to its object: and that is 1 Cor. xiii, 2, 'Though I have all faith, so that I could remove mountains, but have not love, I am nothing', where with bitter irony he characterizes a false attitude in which the Biblical meaning of faith has been perverted into its precise opposite. Thus St. Paul's conception of faith is thoroughly in accord with the regular Biblical pattern, and indeed the Hebrew word is sometimes clearly discernible in his Greek, as in Rom. iii, 3, where πίστις is used of the faithfulness of God.[2]

[1] The worst heresy of our time is the substitution of belief in 'religion' for belief in God; and the awful pitfall besets the expositor of St. Paul, of making 'faith' into a rival species of merit to 'works'. So N. P. Williams speaks of St. Paul's 'great thesis that "Justification", or the state of being free from guilt in the eyes of God, can only be won by Faith, and not by "legal works" ' (in the *New Commentary*, on Rom. iv, p. 459). From all such false doctrine the Biblical conception of Faith brings complete deliverance.

[2] Perhaps there are other places where *'emunah* throws light on πίστις. Rom. i, 17, 'God's righteousness is revealed from faith to faith', might then mean 'from (God's) faithfulness to (man's) faithfulness', which, as regularly in O.T., is the result of his 'faith'. In Rev. iii, 14, Christ is 'the Amen, the Faithful and True'; we may compare 2 Cor. i, 20–22, where it is said that He is the Yes to all God's promises, and therefore through Him is the Amen (the making sure); and it is God who confirm s(βεβαιοω='aman) us with you in the Anointed One, and has anointed us. Further, if πίστις can be used in Rom. iii, 3, of the faithfulness of God, why not of that of Christ? In Christ the Righteousness of God is revealed (Rom. iii, 21; cf. 1 Cor. i, 30, and see Dr. Goudge's excellent exegesis of the word in the *New Commentary*, pp. 409 and 429 ff.); and if πίστις represents *'emunah*, we ought surely to translate Rom. iii, 22: 'the Righteousness of God through the Faithfulness of Jesus Christ unto all them that believe'; for if διὰ πίστεως ἰησοῦ χριστοῦ means 'through *our* faith *in* Jesus Christ' the words that follow become redundant. A similar phrase comes in Gal. ii, 16 (cf. ii. 20), Eph. iii, 12, Phil. iii, 9. The very fact that in Hebrew one word covers both 'faithfulness' and 'faith' should warn us, in interpreting the Hebrew-minded St. Paul, not to assume that his πίστις

St. John avoids the noun πίστις as he avoids the noun γνῶσις. No doubt for the same reason in each case, that he may avoid any suggestion that either faith or knowledge can be regarded as a personal and meritorious quality, he uses the verbs 'to believe' and 'to know', which show the activity of the soul directed towards God or Christ. Faith is distinguished from Love in being the outgoing of the whole mind—not merely of the analytical reason which assents to propositions, but of the thinking man—whereas Love is the outgoing of the Will. Thus it is that 'to believe' becomes the comprehensive term to describe man's response to God, so that the sin of the world is described in xvi, 9, as 'not to believe in Me' (but to remain self-centred); and St. Thomas's act of adoration, 'My Lord and my God' is described as an act of 'believing' (xx, 29).

3. The Danger of Rationalism

All who are living their lives by the light of the Christian Gospel know what 'faith' means. However much they may fail through imperfection of knowledge, through weakness of confidence in God, or unfaithfulness to the light which they have received, they nevertheless know the meaning of faith as their response to God's call and their acceptance of His revealed word. But it is another matter when they try to express its meaning in rational terms, particularly if it is necessary to explain it to those who are not Christians. Hence in the world to-day there are strange confusions about the Christian meaning of faith. In ordinary usage 'faith' or 'belief' denotes a degree of sureness which is greater than 'opinion' and less than 'knowledge'. Christian faith, therefore, is supposed to be contrary to reason; by it we are thought to hold firmly to views which are really only opinions, but are vouched for by the authority of the Church or the Bible, regarded as infallible and inerrant. Or there is thought to be a right of private judgement, at least in

---

is the same as the Latin *fides*. Perhaps even in Heb. xi, 1 πίστις means *'emunah*, since ὑπόστασις is predicated of it. Similarly throughout ch. xi and in xii, 2. Cf. the comment on Eph. iii, 12, in Hoskyns and Davey, *The Riddle of the New Testament*, p. 227.

religious matters; faith is each man's opinion about these things, and each man has a right to think as he chooses.

It would be easy to multiply illustrations. It is plain what has happened. The attempt is being made to explain Christian faith in rational and universally valid terms, apart from the revealed God who in the Biblical use is the proper Object of faith, and from whose unique character the word derives its special meaning. The Biblical use of the word is what is described in our modern jargon as 'existential thinking', as opposed to 'rational thinking', which is, according to the ordinary assumptions of logic, valid for every human or other intelligence. Certainly there is a contrast between the rationalism of Western theology and the concrete, eschatological presentation which the Bible gives of the action of the living God. We shall be much occupied in the later chapters of this book with the Biblical imagery, both as it is given in the sacred books themselves and as it reappears in the Christian liturgy.

On the one side, we are confronted with the Biblical teaching of a God living and active, judging men and punishing them, intervening in history, coming to save, promising to come again at a Last Day, and with the sacraments of grace, instruments of His present action. The Eucharist 'may be regarded as a dramatization of the Advent of the Lord, which is *at once* His remembered coming in humiliation and His desired coming in glory, both realized in His true presence in the Sacrament. In the Eucharist therefore the Church perpetually reconstitutes the crisis in which the Kingdom of God came in history. It never gets beyond this. At each Eucharist we are *there*—we are in the night in which He was betrayed, at Golgotha, before the empty tomb on Easter Day, and in the upper room where He appeared; *and* we are at the moment of His coming with angels and archangels and all the company of heaven, in the twinkling of an eye, at the last trump.'[1]

On the other side, there is our attempt to live with this terrifying thing in the visible church, with liturgies and ceremonial, services, sermons, classes, guilds, and the whole apparatus of teaching in parish, school and university, of biblical scholar-

[1] C. H. Dodd, *The Apostolic Preaching and its Developments*, 1936, pp. 234-5.

ship and exegesis, of systematic and pastoral theology. Sometimes the Gospel is found translated into terms of personal religion, and we get Pietism in its Catholic or its Protestant form;
sometimes it is seen as a programme for the common life, and
then we get at best 'Christian Social Action', or at worst the
'Social Gospel'. In the one case the eschatological element is
rendered as 'conversion', in the latter as 'the social revolution'.
In innumerable instances there is the liability to blunt the edge
of the sharp sword of the word of God. And always there is the
question how far this is a matter of our human limitation, and
how far of our sin: how far it is involved in the duty which lies
upon us to interpret the word of God in our own language, and
how far our performance of this duty bears the marks of des-
perate efforts to avoid the unpleasant fact that we ourselves
stand under God's judgement. It is recorded of the first man
and woman that after they had disobeyed they tried to hide
their nakedness among the trees of the Garden. In the methods
of this evasive action, man has become amazingly clever and re-
sourceful as he has evolved and has become civilized; and next
time man found his God in a garden he knew better what to do
with Him.[1]

But quite apart from man's sinful endeavour to escape from
God, there remains always the tension between the revelation of
God Himself and man's doctrines about Him, between the
Object of faith and man's statements of belief. There is no escape from this tension. We need to have the Biblical epic of the
creating and making of the heavens and the earth by the Lord
God of Israel, and side by side with this a Natural Theology,
with its metaphysical expositions of the idea of God in relation
to the world as its First Cause, as the Absolute Being who is
the ground of all contingent being, as the Pure Actuality presupposed by beings existing in a state of potentiality. But *these
two are not the same*. The first is a tale told in sublime language

---

[1] 'It is written that when Adam (Hebrew for Man) and Eve heard the
Voice of God walking in the garden in the cool of the day, they ran for it.
However, they learnt something which they used; for next time men found
God in a garden, they crucified Him in sheer desperation. What else could
they do?'—H. H. Kelly, *The Gospel of God*, p. 112.

about the personal action of the living God; the second is a commentary, a sort of *midrash*, upon it, helping to relate it to the rest of our thinking. When we hear the creation-story read, it can rightly stir up in our minds these philosophical thoughts.

We need the Biblical eschatology, with its conception of the breaking-in of the heavenly world into the world of time, in the Incarnation, the sacramental coming, the Advent. On the other hand St. Thomas sets out a metaphysic of Time and Eternity, defining the former as the measure of movement and change, and the latter as that which is outside all movement and change, because It is present in Its totality in each moment of time, and gathers up in Its one and single moment that whole manifoldness which unrolls itself in the whole course of time. The tenth Question of the *Summa Theologica*, Part I, is a magnificent rendering in philosophical language of the eschatological idea; and all is well when it is thus viewed in the light of the Biblical doctrine and of the sacramental rite in which the heavenly reality is present in the visible sign *sub specie aeternitatis*. But all is not well when it is separated from its Christian context, and is handed over to the philosophers to dispute whether the Absolute thus discerned by reason is the All or the Nothing.

The fault came when the two were identified: when the Biblical doctrine of God was regarded as being re-stated in philosophical language; when the metaphysical proofs of God's existence were regarded as *reaching the same point* as the revealed datum of the creation of the world by God. St. Thomas seems to be aware of this difference when in the very first article of the *Summa Theologica* he explains that a revealed doctrine of God is necessary, because God, who is the last end of man, surpasses human reason, and it is necessary for man to know Him. But he is on more doubtful ground when he continues that even in the case of those truths concerning God which can be investigated by natural reason, revelation was necessary, because the truth about God thus investigated could come to man only from a few philosophers and after a long time and with the admixture of many errors; yet on the knowledge of this truth man's salvation depended. Therefore it was necessary, in order that salvation might come to man in a more fitting way and with greater certainty, that there should be revelation to instruct him (*S.T.* I, i, 1).

Here, assuredly, is something to which St. Paul and St. John would never have assented. Assent to a demonstration by a philosopher-theologian of the real existence of a Supreme Being is by no means the same thing as the faith with which Israel received the word of the living God, the mighty, the terrible, the jealous God. It is true indeed that there is one God only to whom the metaphysician's thought is directed, and in whose Name the prophet speaks. But there is a world of difference between the two. The philosopher is straining the resources of his mind to think rightly about Him. With a St. Anselm the metaphysical analysis blends into meditation; the ontological argument in the *Proslogion* is all addressed to God, as *Thou*. Here man is setting himself to think of God and speak to God aright. But the prophet is setting himself to hear God speak: conscious of his own littleness and inadequacy, he tends to be reckless of any anthropomorphism or other crudity which may appear in his words, provided only that no hindrance is put in the way of the urgent divine message being heard, and so heard that it may be obeyed.

Assuredly both are necessary, and both are found in the Bible: but chiefly the action of God, His revelation, His command. Both are necessary, and the tension between them must always be there, because human thought is not commensurable with the reality of God. Whenever the tension is lost, it means that man's thought has lost sight of the Biblical element. It is the Bible's primary function to bear witness to the direct action of God.

It would be absurd to blame the medievals for seeking a synthesis between the forms of the Biblical revelation and those of rational thought; some sort of a synthesis is a necessity of life. We, too, in our disordered and unharmonized age, are bound to seek a synthesis, or at least a *modus vivendi*. The disaster of the Middle Ages was that they succeeded only too well, and came near to thinking that the infinite reality or truth of the living and acting God could be equated with a series of theological statements about Him.

Fundamentalism and Materialism

The vital thing is that the Bible in the Church should be allowed to stand side by side with the tradition of theology and teaching, and not become merged into it; and it is precisely at this point that the notion that revelation is primarily of truths about God becomes really dangerous. The form which the danger takes is somewhat as follows. The statements of the Bible are often obscure and impossible to reconcile with one another; it is difficult to say, on many points, what the teaching of the Bible really is. But the church doctrine is far clearer and more explicit; for it is the function of the theologians to present formulated and orderly statements of doctrine, and in popular teaching to state just what a Christian needs to know and believe to his soul's health. The result has been that in countless Catholic books the authority to whom appeal is most often made is St. Thomas Aquinas, while the Bible is little quoted except for an occasional proof-text. Then again, since the man who has drawn the conclusion implied in the premises of a syllogism actually knows more than the man who has not drawn the conclusion, it is hard not to admit that an increase of enlightenment and of clarity of rational statement is actually an increase of revelation. Thus the notion that revelation is primarily of truths about God leads straight to the notion of a 'development of doctrine', such that a later age which possesses a fuller formulation of doctrine will be thought to enjoy a fuller revelation of divine truth than the Apostles.

Such a notion, as soon as it is stated, is seen to be contrary to the fundamental notion of the authority of the Apostles, and of the Bible, as witnessing to the finality of the Revelation once for all given in Christ. But that notion is the direct result of the conception that Revelation is primarily the making known of truths about God; and it is this conception which underlies the interpretation of the Inspiration of the Bible as consisting in its inerrancy.

4. Fundamentalism and Materialism

The Eastern Orthodox criticize the theological outlook of the West as being rationalistic and materialistic; and this criticism applies even more to Protestant than to Catholic thought, since

Revelation

Protestantism can only be understood in the light of the late medievalism out of which it sprang. A modern Orthodox writer says: 'A dualist philosophy which for three hundred years and perhaps more makes a radical separation between matter and spirit, body and soul, sense and intellect, is doubtless responsible for the attitude which instinctively makes us place God on the spiritual side and oppose Him thus to the corporeal world . . . (this) often leads us to forget that for Christian theology there is another supremely significant separation, viz., the separation which opposes Uncreated Being, God, and Created Being, the world created from nothing together with all the spiritual and corporeal entities which go to make up its entirety. Is God merely the God of spirits, or is He not rather the God of all flesh also? For the Cartesian conception of God the Mathematician, the answer is obvious: He is a God of spirits, a God of intelligences; but for God the Trinity dwelling in inaccessible light and penetrating by means of His energies the created world, the world of pure spirits as well as the world of corporeal beings, it is not the same: He is at the same time as removed from and as close to intelligences as He is to senses.'[1]

The traditional view of the Bible has been profoundly modified in the last four centuries by the rise of the scientific spirit, and the acceptance by the ordinary man of the truth of physical fact as the norm of all truth. Hence the statements of the Bible must, if the Bible is the word of God, be true statements of physical fact. On the other hand, if they can be proved not to be true, then the Bible is not the word of God. This change of mind was already far advanced by the seventeenth century, when English churchmen 'retained a literal belief in the Bible, yet did not pause to ask whether they were using words in a manner different from that of their forefathers. Fundamentalism may

[1] From an article by V. Lossky, *La Théologie de la Lumière chez Saint Grégoire de Thessalonique*, in *Dieu Vivant*, no. 1,; translation from a lecture on St. Gregory Palamas by Dom Clement Lialine, in *Eastern Churches Quarterly*, vol. vi, Jan. 1946. To what extent the Easterns have grasped the Biblical meaning of Faith, and to what extent their criticism of our Western rationalism is based on other grounds than those of a truly Biblical theology, are questions which the present writer is unable to answer, but which are evidently of great importance.

Fundamentalism and Materialism

claim the Bible for its mother, but it has Hobbes for its father. A blend of materialism and Christianity became characteristic of English thought, and the universality of the concepts of material science was unquestioned.'[1]

In the Middle Ages the modern Fundamentalism was not possible, for the scientific view of the world had not yet appeared; physics formed part of a world-outlook which saw all life and experience as comprehended within a vast scheme of which the doctrine of God formed the apex. No conflict existed then between 'religion' and 'science'; the four-element theory 'gave an account of the facts of chemistry which was at the same time an allegorical picture of the realities of the spirit. The relations of earth, air, fire and water, it seemed, corresponded in some way to the relations of body, spirit, intellect, and love.'[2] Even Kepler in his first book 'saw the universe as an image of the Trinity: the sun at the centre of all things was God the Father; the heavenly bodies, God the Son; and the intervening ether . . . the Holy Spirit';[3] but a note in the second edition said, 'Formerly I believed that the force which moves the planets was really a soul. But when I reflected that this motive force decreased at a greater distance, I concluded that it must be corporeal.'[4]

Here we see an induction from observed facts. The metaphysical theory of the heavens, based on Aristotle, was now confronted with the comets, new stars, and sunspots seen through Galileo's telescope; and Galileo was sure that knowledge so gained was 'far more certain than any deduction from purely rational premises'. This was far from obvious then. It was not a bishop but the Professor of Philosophy at Padua who refused to look through Galileo's telescope; and his colleague at Pisa tried, as Galileo said, by means of logical arguments to 'charm the planets from the sky'.[5]

Thus, says Roberts, Hobbes by 'restricting philosophy to the

[1] Michael Roberts, *The Modern Mind*, 1937, p. 86.
[2] Ibiid., p. 40 f.
[3] Ibid., p. 48 f.
[4] Ibd., p. 51.
[5] From B. Willey, *The Seventeenth-century Background*, 1934, p. 20; quotations from Galileo, *Mathematical Collections and Translations*, 1661.

study of the evidence of the senses, and rejecting introspection, made it impossible to demonstrate the necessity of religion'; for religion uses language to depict the things unseen, and its appeal cannot be made if language is restricted to describing the evidence of the senses. Hence the crucial charge against Hobbes is that he was blind to poetry: 'not that he denied its existence, but rather that he regarded it as trivial: it had no essential place in his scheme; there were no things which needed to be said which could only be said through the poetic use of language. Understanding only the scientific use of language, he interpreted theological doctrine as if it were scientific.'[1] Consequently, we find a Christian philosopher like Locke half a century later speaking of our knowledge of the existence of a God as 'the most obvious truth that reason discovers', and the evidence for it as 'equal to mathematical certainty'.[2] 'The highest testimonial he can give to a religious belief is that it has the same degree of evidence as a geometrical proof.'[3] As for rhetorical and poetical language, 'if we would speak of things as they are,' said Locke, 'we must allow that all the art of rhetoric, besides order and clearness, all the artificial and figurative application of words eloquence hath invented, are for nothing else but to insinuate wrong ideas, move the passions, and thereby mislead the judgement.'[4]

'There is no doubt that the lack of serious consideration of Christianity by men like Bentham and Mill was due largely to the progressive narrowing of the conception of verbal meaning in the eighteenth century. Taken directly, as description of scientific fact, the doctrines of Christianity were opposed to those of science. The material truth of many scientific doctrines could be demonstrated, and the rest were logically coherent. Therefore the doctrines of science were true; and those of Christianity were false, except in some figurative or symbolic sense which was felt to be less "real" and less important than the direct sense of science.'[5]

[1] Roberts, p. 101.
[2] Willey, op. cit., p. 278.
[3] Ibid., p. 281.
[4] Roberts, p. 125, quotation from Locke, *Human Understanding*, iii, 34.
[5] Roberts, op. cit., p. 156.

Fundamentalism and Materialism

Prof. T. W. Manson has lately pointed out how the theology of Liberal Protestantism has been based on presuppositions derived from Kant, and others taken from 'the vigorous, swiftly moving, and very confident scientific thought of the nineteenth century: in particular, the doctrines of the universal reign of natural law and of biological evolution'; and he quotes Harnack as saying, 'We are firmly convinced that what happens in space and time is subject to the general laws of motion, and that in this sense, as an interruption of the order of Nature, there can be no such things as "miracles".' 'The effect of this', Dr. Manson goes on, 'is to establish a thick plate-glass window between God and the world. The eye of faith can see through the window and observe that there is a God and that he appears to be benevolently disposed towards men; but nothing more substantial than signs of paternal affection and filial trust and obedience can get through.' Similarly the effect of the evolutionary idea was to remove the focus of interest from theology proper to the history of religion, so that Christianity is seen, in Bousset's words, as 'the highest point which religious development has reached'; but evolution abhors finality. Here then theology in general and the exposition of the Gospel are subordinated to presuppositions derived from natural law and biology.[1]

But it is not only German Ritschlian theology that shows the influence of these tendencies; they are felt everywhere, even among orthodox circles. In an age which is dominated by the resounding successes of natural science and of technical achievement, but is feeble in its grasp of philosophical principles, the truth of the Bible is judged by its reliability in matters of historical and physical fact. The ordinary modern reader of a biblical narrative wants chiefly to know what exactly it was that happened, or what a trained observer would have seen if he had been there; and he thinks that this is the real truth of the matter. Would our Lord's Transfiguration, for instance, be quite real if it was not such an event as the ordinary passer-by would have

[1] T. W. Manson, essay on 'The Failure of Liberalism to interpret the Bible as the word of God', in *The Interpretation of the Bible*, pp. 93–4. Quotations from Harnack, *What is Christianity?* 2nd edn., 1901, p. 28 f, and Bousset, *What is Religion?* p. 265.

been able to see? St. Mark's gospel, having been recognized to be the earliest gospel, has often been treated as if it were simply a photographic picture of the events, something like a transcript from a diary. In the Old Testament, many people feel most at home with the narratives which bear on their face the marks of historical authenticity, such as the stories of David and Absalom.

It is this attitude of ours towards the narratives that constitutes the problem. Such an attitude was alien to the Middle Ages, when our modern sensitiveness to accuracy of physical fact was unknown, and men's interests were centred much more on the moral and symbolical meanings of the narratives; and it was alien to the Biblical writers themselves. The evangelists, as the modern scholar knows very well, were not writing 'biographies of Jesus', in our sense of the word, but were announcing the Gospel which had been enacted in that series of events. Similarly in the Old Testament, the 'historical' books from Joshua to Kings stand in the Hebrew Bible as 'the earlier prophets'. There was a tradition of the history, but the interest of the writers was very different from that of the modern critical historian.

Hence the Inerrancy of the Bible, as it is understood to-day, is a new doctrine, and the modern fundamentalist is asserting something that no previous age has understood in anything like the modern sense. 'When the atheist to-day denies that he has a Father in Heaven, he is denying something which his ancestors never asserted; for he is interpreting in terms of physical time and space and matter words which were first used with no thought of such interpretation.'[1]

When divine Revelation has been understood in a materialistic way, and it has been argued that because the Bible is the word of God everything in it must be taken as 'literally' true, the discovery that many things in it are not literally true leads to the inference that it is not the word of God; and without doubt this inference is very widely drawn to-day. The Bible stories are thought of as fairy-stories. We hear people speak of 'the Christian myth', with the implication that the Christian Gospel is a mythology, which is beautiful and moving, but not

[1] Michael Roberts, *The Modern Mind*, 1937, pp. 94-5.

true in the sense in which the atomic theory is true. The Christmas festival retains its popularity on the religious as well as on the social side; but how many people take seriously the pretty angels on the Christmas cards? When nativity-plays are presented, the actors in them are believing Christians who hold it to be really true that the Son of God was made man for our salvation; but, for many who see them, there is little relation between the scenes there enacted and the hard realities of life. Similarly, the Old Testament stories, not only those of Adam and Eve, but the rest of the Old Testament also in so far as it is understood at all, are not seen as having any real relevance to the life of the modern world.

That which needs to be recovered is in part a right view of poetry and art, as being vehicles of a truth of a higher order than the truth of natural science. It needs to be seen that natural science is a departmental study of one aspect of human experience: important, because it is the study of God's created order, but limited in its scope, because it is limited to the truth of physical events. There are higher levels of truth, concerned with man's own life as a personal being and the meaning of his existence; and the Christian Gospel is concerned with the meaning of his life in relation to God, who is the Alpha and Omega, the ἀρχή, λόγος and τέλος of all created existence.

Therefore in such a recovery of a sense of a 'spiritual' truth, the Christian Faith and the Bible must take a central place. The Christmas story has not only a 'poetical' truth, in the meaning now commonly given to poetry. Its truth is not that of a myth, but rather of an epic, in the sense in which we can speak of the 'epic' of the advance of the Eighth Army from El Alamein to Tunis and Italy in 1943-4. At its centre there is a claim to truth of material fact, because it is the essence of the Christian Gospel that God has redeemed man through a series of events in history; we shall examine this claim in the next chapter, on 'Faith and Criticism'. Therefore also it is directly related to the hard facts of life in our dark and sinful world; and it was doubtless a deep sense of this relation which led the Church to commemorate the murders of the St. Stephen and of the Holy Innocents within the octave of the Christmas festival.

Revelation

Similarly the Sacred History as a whole must be treated as history. It has been through a history and by means of human nature that God has revealed Himself. In chapter viii of this book we shall therefore deal with the general question of the Bible as history. That is not to say that there is not myth and fable in it; the writer of the stories of Adam and Eve was deliberately using the language of myth, as the only possible medium in which he could express the primary facts about man's place in God's created order, and the Book of Jonah is a fable. But the Sacred History must be substantially true as history, if it is true that in it God has revealed Himself.

Therefore Fundamentalism was in a sense right in insisting that the truth of the Bible cannot be confined to matters of spiritual truth, but that it must also be historically true. The fault has been that the relation of spiritual and material truth has not been rightly grasped, and that it has not been sufficiently understood that the word of God in the Bible has been spoken through imperfect human instruments.

5. Revelation and Inspiration

We set out in the last chapter the thesis that the authority of the Bible, as the Book of the divine Kingdom, is seen both in its testimony to God's saving action in the past and in the future, and in its expression of the truths concerning Him and the way of His service which Israel was set to learn; and this corresponds closely with what we have seen in this chapter of the Biblical idea of Revelation, as being both the personal revelation of God Himself in His mighty acts, and the revealing of the necessary truths about His nature and man's duty. The difficulty that has arisen over the conception of Revelation in the western tradition of Christendom has been due to the rationalizing of the idea. Where the Bible gives us concrete eschatological imagery and existential thinking, western thought has tended first to a philosophical mode of rationalization, whereby imagery has been systematized into doctrines, and faith has been treated as assent to doctrines, and then to a scientific mode of rationalization, which envisages only the 'literal' truth of natural science and history. In both cases, Inspiration is necessarily rendered as Inerrancy. In the one case, the inspired Scripture is incorporated into a theological system; in the other, it is understood as an infallible record of events. The alternative view, when this breaks down, is to treat Inspiration psychologically, as denoting the religious experience of inspired individuals, who are subject to 'degrees of inspiration'.

The 'conservative' view, both in its Catholic and its Protestant forms, always refuses—in our view, rightly—to accept the notion of 'degrees of inspiration'. Yet it is obvious that there are degrees of *something:* not indeed of Inspiration, if Inspiration is co-extensive with Canonicity; but degrees of revelation, or of prophecy.

St. Thomas is explicit on this point in his treatment of Prophecy. The prophets, he says, do not behold the Primal Truth (*prima veritas*) Itself; 'hence it is not necessary that they should know all things, but each of them knows some things, according as this or that is specially revealed to him'.[1] 'Prophecy is as it were an imperfect thing, in the order of divine revelation; hence it is said in 1 Cor. xiii, 8, that "prophecies shall be done away", and "we prophesy in part", that is, imperfectly'; and the perfection of revelation will be in the hereafter.[2]

Again: 'The end of prophecy is the making-known (*manifestatio*) of some truth that is above man. In proportion as this is more excellent (*potior*), prophecy becomes higher (*dignior*). A making-known of divine truth through open contemplation of the truth itself is more excellent than that which is given through a likeness drawn from bodily things, since it approaches more nearly to the vision in the hereafter (*in patria*), by which the truth of God is beheld in its essence. Hence that prophecy by which some supernatural truth is discerned by intellectual vision is higher than that in which a supernatural truth is made known by a likeness of bodily things, in imaginative vision.'[3]

There are then degrees of revelation and of prophecy. As Fr. Thompson says, interpreting St. Thomas, the inspiration of a

[1] St. Thomas Aquinas, *Summa Theologica*, iia–iiae, clxxi, 4.
[2] Ibid., *ad 2*.
[3] Ibid., lxxiv, 2.

prophet means that his mind is 'divinely exalted to advert to divine things', and prophetic revelation that his mind is 'divinely lit up to perceive and estimate the divine things which are shown him; this prophetic inspiration comes first, but Biblical inspiration comes after, and its purpose is to sustain his attention to the truths already revealed to him, or to another, for so long as he is engaged in writing them down for the benefit of his readers'.[1]

Similarly Lee understands by Revelation a direct communication from God to man of such knowledge as man could not of himself attain to, as in the case of 'the prophetical announcements of the future, and the peculiar doctrines of Christianity', or of information which might have been gained in the ordinary way but was not; while Inspiration is 'that actuating energy of the Holy Spirit . . . guided by which the human agents chosen by God have officially proclaimed His will by word of mouth, or have committed to writing the several portions of the Bible'. Thus 'the *Revelation* of the Law from Sinai and the *facts* concerning the wanderings of the Israelites were alike recorded under the influence of inspiration'. 'The Patriarchs enjoyed revelations, but were not inspired to record them; the writer of the Acts of the Apostles was inspired for his task, but we are not told that he ever enjoyed a revelation.' 'Revelation and Inspiration are also to be distinguished by the sources from which they come: Revelation being the peculiar function of the Eternal Word, Inspiration the result of the agency of the Spirit.'[2]

In their main purport these two statements agree closely; but the medieval writer is freer than the nineteenth-century writer from the materialistic notion of truth, and he at least speaks plainly of 'degrees of prophecy'.[3] Since there was certainly a development in the apprehension by Israel of divine truth, it might seem that we are not far from the notion of 'progressive revelation' dear to many nineteenth-century theologians, who saw here an opportunity to bring the idea of revelation itself under evolutionary categories. But it is possible that this con-

[1] P. J. Thompson, *Inspiration and Inerrancy* (S.P.C.K., 1938), p. 13.

[2] Lee, *Inspiration*, pp. 27 f., 28 *n*, 30, 29.

[3] The term 'gradus prophetiae' occurs in S. T. iia–iiae, clxxiv, 3.

nection was not particularly illuminating, since in regard to spiritual insight the later parts of the Old Testament are by no means necessarily on a higher level than the earlier.

The distinction thus made between Revelation and Inspiration justifies itself by the close connection made by 'conservative' writers between Inspiration and Canonicity. It is true that this connection was made to justify the Inerrancy of the Bible at all points, and we have said that this is to be discounted; yet it was substantially sound, because it was an assertion that the Bible as a whole is inspired; and this, as we have seen, is necessary when the Bible is viewed as the Book of the divine Kingdom. When the Bible is so viewed, it becomes possible to assert both that the Bible as a whole is inspired, as being the record of the Sacred History which is consummated in Christ, and at the same time freely to recognize the imperfection of the human recipients of the revelation; by distinguishing the truth which God was teaching through the writers from that measure of His truth which they themselves understood, we can keep the idea of divine Inspiration for that which God Himself intended to teach, and refuse the false psychological view of Inspiration which ends by making Inspiration not something properly divine, but something human, and substituting for the doctrine of the word of God a notion of many words of men.

A virtual identification of Revelation and Inspiration is, however, made in the typically Liberal view, which tends to treat each writer as an individual, and therefore inevitably speaks of 'degrees of inspiration'. Thus Dr. Orr, who took on the whole a 'conservative' view, though with a large admixture of 'liberal' elements, criticizes Dr. Lee's view of revelation as too exclusively doctrinal; here, no doubt, he is justified.[1] He goes on to quote part of a passage from A. M. Fairbairn, who reverses the two terms, saying that 'if God is by nature spirit, it will be to Him a matter of nature to reveal Himself. But if He speaks to man, it will be through men; and those who hear best will be those most possessed of God. This possession is termed "inspiration". God inspires, man reveals: inspiration is the process by which God gives; revelation is the mode or form—word, character, or institution—in which man embodies what he has received. The terms, though not equivalent, are co-extensive, the one denoting the process on its inner side, the other on its outer. According to the quantity of the inspiration will be the quality of the revelation.'[1] The fact that the order of the two terms can be thus reversed shows that the distinction between them has been lost. It makes little difference whether we say that God reveals His truth to men in religious experience, and then inspires them to write down what they have thus learnt, or say that inspiration applies properly to their religious experience itself, and their writings reveal to us its content.

That is possible and inevitable when Inspiration is taken as essentially a psychological fact: it refers to the writers rather than to the writings; they are known to be inspired by the fact they are found to be inspiring; and they are inspiring because of the freshness of their apprehension of the things which have been 'revealed' to them, or 'discovered' by them in their religious experience. Since, however, there are some parts of the Bible which we do not find very inspiring, it is not uncommon to find expressions of regret that certain books, particularly Esther and Ecclesiastes, are in the Bible at all. It thus becomes impossible to think that the Bible *as a whole* is inspired and is the word of God. Only the 'best' parts of it are inspired.

It is otherwise when we start with the conception that God has acted in history, revealing Himself personally by redeeming His people and making His Covenant with them, and further revealing the necessary truths about His nature and His will, as they were able to learn. The apprehension by men of God's revelation has been partial and imperfect; yet through His imperfect human instruments His word has been spoken. The Scripture, too, is inspired, and is imperfect; inspired because it is divine, and imperfect because it is also human.

The books of Esther and Ecclesiastes have been mentioned, and a word must be said about each. Esther certainly has its imperfections. It is not history, but a romance, in which the Jews, threatened with pogroms throughout the Persian Empire, not only escape this danger but execute wholesale massacres of

[1] Fairbairn, *Christ in Modern Theology*, 1898, p. 496.

their would-be persecutors. Here, no doubt, is seen the unlovely nationalism of the later Judaism. Yet there is another side to the matter; and perhaps the wisest words that have been written about this book are those of Bishop Gore: 'The divinest element in the book is perhaps to be found in the profound sense of the indestructibility of Israel, and the duty of an Israelite to maintain the cause of his people at whatever risk (see especially iv, 14). It was this probably that caused its final inclusion in the O.T. Canon.'[1] All who love Israel will wish to make these words their own.

Ecclesiastes too must be read not as an isolated book, but in its place in the Canon. In our Bible it follows Psalms and Proverbs; here is its context. It was written within Israel, under the shadow of Temple and Synagogue. Its author is an honest man, who tries to see life whole, and he will have none of those pious but shallow explanations of difficulties which constitute a besetting sin of the godly. Round him, he sees the solemn but rather stupid piety of the *Chasidim*, and the somewhat commonplace moralism of the Book of Proverbs. He, too, has tried the way of 'righteousness', as he has tried the way of carnal pleasure, and he has found them both to be 'vanity'. Certainly he has not found the answer to the problem of life; but he does not pretend that he has when he has not; and his greatness is, that he is one of the chief witnesses in the Old Testament to that truth which the Messiah, when He came, forced to the surface: that there is no 'justification', no peace with God, to be found in the performance of the works of the Law. Saul the Pharisee was to make the same discovery later, and to be given the answer. For Ecclesiastes the answer was not yet available. But is it not his perception of the negative truth that justifies the inclusion of his book in the Canon?

We trust that we have shown that the traditional distinction of Revelation and Inspiration is fundamentally sound, provided that Revelation is not wrongly understood. God has revealed Himself by His personal action in His mighty acts of redemption,

---

[1] In the New Commentary, p. 305 n. Esther iv, 14, contains the words: 'Who knoweth whether thou art not come to the kingdom for such a time as this?'

and has revealed 'by various modes and in many fragments' in the Old Testament books the necessary truths concerning Himself, till at last He should speak His word, once for all and inclusively, in His Son. Of the acts of God in the Second Redemption, the Apostle is the chosen witness; but an evangelist like St. Luke, who was not an eye-witness, stands in essentially the same relation to the tradition of the events as the authors of the J. and E. narratives of the Exodus, who write down the tradition as they have received it. The revelation of the truths about God and the way of His service come to us from those who apprehend them; there are degrees of revelation and of prophecy, and in the Bible some books hold a more honourable, some a less honourable place. The Inspiration of the Bible is seen in the fact that through these books God has spoken to us His word, in the written record of the Sacred History.

In thus refusing to identify Inspiration with the personal insight of each writer, and attributing it to the Canon as a whole, we are laying a great weight on the Canon, and asserting a providential guidance in the formation of the canon. This, like other assertions, needs to be historically justified; we must therefore devote a special inquiry to this point. In chapters v and vi we shall study the question how the canon was formed; what it meant when certain books were first set apart as authoritative, and regarded as 'scripture'; what *is* this Scripture, to which as a whole divine Inspiration attaches? But we have first to consider the big question which we have still left over, that of Faith and Criticism. We said at the beginning of this chapter that both the conservative and the liberal views fail most dangerously at the point where they seem to be strongest, the former over the doctrine of Revelation, and the latter over its use of Criticism. This latter assertion must next be examined.

CHAPTER IV

FAITH AND CRITICISM

1. The Real Conflict

When the right clue to a problem has been found, it is a fact of experience that elements in the problem which had hitherto caused difficulty drop easily into their place. This appears to be the case with regard to Biblical Criticism; we have seen already that it is necessarily demanded, when the Bible is viewed as the Book of the divine Kingdom. It is asserted that God has established His Kingdom by redeeming His people through a series of historical events; it is necessary therefore that there should be a Book containing the testimony to those events, and that it should be subjected to strict historical examination. We need to know whether the narratives are in general reliable, or whether on the other hand they fall to pieces when examined, and show that the assertion of a direct action of God in history rests on a later interpretation imposed subsequently on events which, according to the earliest records of them, were originally believed to have been a series of quite ordinary happenings. If this were to be demonstrated beyond all reasonable doubt—as for instance it is proved beyond all doubt that Moses did not write the Pentateuch—then the Gospel of the divine Kingdom would have been refuted. St. Paul is quite clear on this point. 'If Christ hath not been raised,' he says to the Corinthians, 'your faith is vain; ye are yet in your sins' (1 Cor. xv, 17), since the forgiveness of sins is part of the New Covenant promised by Jeremiah, and if the Messiah has not been raised up from death, no such messianic deliverance has taken place; and we apostles, who have witnessed of God that He raised up Christ, are found to be 'false witnesses of God' (v. 15). The appeal is to the facts; if the facts are untrue, the Gospel is untrue. The historical truth of the facts must therefore be tested by critical inquiry.

Yet there has been for a long time an opposition, varying between suspicion and open hostility, between the representatives of the traditional Church doctrine and those of Biblical criticism. There have indeed been generations of Christian scholars who have laboured to bridge the gap, and show that the full acceptance of the critical methods is entirely compatible with the Christian Faith; it is as good as agreed on all hands that the challenge of Biblical Criticism is one that the Church must take up, and meet it on its own ground. But it must not be forgotten how acute the conflict has been in the past, between the traditional orthodoxy which regarded itself as committed to maintaining the complete inerrancy of the Bible, and the critics who in attacking that doctrine as untrue seemed to be denying the orthodox dogma, and in many cases had to strive hard to clear themselves from the imputation of heresy. Even now, the suspicion still remains that acceptance of the church dogma means that certain critical questions have in effect been decided in advance, and so research is not free; orthodox Christians may take up with Biblical criticism, provided they accept only 'safe' opinions and the results reached by 'conservative criticism'.

But in our day the situation has cleared up in a remarkable way. With the break-up of the accommodation between Christianity and society which was reached in the Victorian age, and with the emergence of political ideals and programmes which are directly opposed to Christian standards, it becomes plain that the real conflict is that of the Christian view of life and the secularist view; of the Church and paganism: of the Biblical assertion of an existing Kingdom of God, and an anti-Christian belief in a Kingdom of Man. The former asserts the actual and present lordship of God over His world, and that man, denying that lordship, is in a state of Original Sin, and the world is a dark and sinful world; and it goes on to proclaim, in terms of the Bible teaching and the Church doctrine, how God has taken in hand a purpose of Salvation for sinful mankind. It follows that the problems of human society cannot be rightly solved except when it is acknowledged that man is under law to God. But the latter assumes that the kingdom belongs to man; Original Sin is denied, and man's need is declared to be not conversion but enlightenment, progress, the advance of scientific knowledge, and man's emancipation from superstition and all that impedes his advance towards earthly well-being and the realization of his dominion over the world.

If this be the case, it is plain where the conflict really lies. There is no conflict between Faith and Criticism as such, but only a tension between two elements which are both necessary if man is to render to God a rational obedience. The conflict lies between two rival views of the world and of man. The representatives of either view can be equally well equipped with the apparatus of learning, and can be, on the basis of their respective presuppositions, equally open minded. Faith is in no way opposed, in the last resort, to Reason, or to Criticism; it is radically opposed to a view of the world which leaves no place for God.

Liberalism however has thoroughly confused this issue. Its roots go back to the Renaissance of the late Middle Ages and the Enlightenment of the eighteenth century. It attempted a synthesis of a modified Christian belief and of Christian moral standards, with an anthropocentric attitude of mind. Reacting against the remains of medieval Christianity, as represented by orthodox Catholicism on the one side and orthodox Protestantism on the other, it attempted to harmonize a 'reduced Christianity' with the fundamental Renaissance assumptions about man. The Christian tradition was re-interpreted in evolutionary, immanentist and pelagian terms; a strong resentment was felt against the traditional dogma and church order, which were labelled 'reactionary'. Orthodoxy was treated as synonymous with ignorance, and 'heretical' became a laudatory epithet.

But the Liberal synthesis is now falling to pieces; and with its disappearance a right answer to the problem of the Bible becomes possible, since the Biblical view of life can now more readily be taken at its own valuation.[1] There remains, as we have

[1] There is an admirable treatment of the questions raised in this chapter in *Christian Apologetics*, by Alan Richardson (S.C.M., 1947).

said, a tension between Faith and Criticism, between Biblical eschatology and our rationalizations of it, between God's Revelation and man's response to it. But these are the necessary tensions which must always exist within an integral Christianity. As in the sphere of conduct the tension between God's will and man's endeavours to solve his problems of practical ethics is resolved in the surrender of man's will, in his effort, in the Johannine phrase, to 'do the truth', and his discovery that God's service is perfect freedom, so in the sphere of Biblical study the exercise of the critical faculties is seen as necessarily demanded by the acceptance of the Bible as the Book of God's Kingdom. When it is believed that all truth is God's truth, the Christian scholar cannot think of his studies as the finding of reasons for conclusions prescribed in advance by the orthodox dogma; the object of his study is the way in which God has chosen to act in history. It is this conviction that has sustained Christian scholars in their acceptance of critical methods; they have believed that there is no ultimate conflict between Faith and Criticism, however difficult and exacting they have found the tension to be.

2. The Liberal Confusion of the Issue

The glory of Liberalism in the realm of scholarship has been that it has striven to the utmost of its power to be entirely honest and impartial in seeking the truth and learning what the facts really are. In the study of the Bible it has endeavoured to go back to the literal and original meaning of the text, and find out what it was that the writers actually intended to say. This vindication of the literal sense has been the outstanding and permanent contribution of Liberal scholarship to Biblical study.

Here the Liberal scholars were standing on orthodox ground. The primacy of the literal sense, though often obscured by fanciful allegorical interpretations, has been asserted by the best Catholic theologians; in Dr. Darwell Stone's words, 'The usual opinion of theologians has been that the mystical sense, however valuable it may be to illustrate or enforce truth otherwise known, cannot rightly be used to supply arguments for the

The Liberal Confusion of the Issue

proof of doctrine.'[1] The present Pope, in his very interesting *Encyclical* on the Bible, has reaffirmed the primacy of the literal sense: 'Well equipped, then, with a knowledge of ancient languages and with the aids afforded by the critical art, the Catholic exegete must approach the most important of the tasks imposed upon him: that of discovering and expounding the genuine sense of the Sacred Books. In discharging this function, interpreters must bear in mind that their chief aim must be to discern and determine what is known as the literal sense of the words of the Bible, "from which alone", as Aquinas excellently observes, "an argument can be drawn" (*S.T.* I, i, 10 *ad* 1). This literal meaning they must investigate with every care by means of their knowledge of languages, using the help also of the context and of comparison with parallel passages—aids which are commonly employed also in the interpretation of profane writings for the clearer understanding of the author's meaning.'[2]

It is necessary to go to the Bible and learn exactly what it says: and it is astonishing how much light modern scholarship is able to throw on the meaning of the text. But it is the very success and fruitfulness of Biblical scholarship that has led to its undoing. It has seemed that it is here that the one indispensable key to the right understanding of the Bible is to be found. Exact knowledge has opened a thousand doors in all regions of study, and has given man an amazing power of control over the forces of nature. Whether man himself is spiritually and morally fit to be in possession of such powers is another question, which the events of recent years have made exceedingly acute. But twenty years ago the prevailing tone was strongly optimistic; and in a book published in 1924 Dr. Israel Abrahams wrote, in a context where he had been describing the work done on the Bible by Jewish and Christian scholars: 'Exegesis of the Hebrew Bible deserves and requires a limiting denominational epithet when it is at its second, not at its first best; when it is apologetic, dog-

[1] Darwell Stone, in the *New Commentary*, O.T., p. 696.
[2] Pope Pius XII, in the encyclical *Divino afflante*, 10th Oct. 1943 (E.T. Catholic Truth Society, 1944, p. 18). The passage referred to from St. Thomas is cited at length on p. 268 f. below. I am indebted to the courtesy of Canon G. D. Smith for permission to quote from his translation of the Encyclical this passage and that on p. 264 f. below.

matic, controversial, and to a minor degree traditional—not when it is scientific, objective, unprejudiced, and free.'[1] This was to accept very thoroughly the view that science holds the key to progress.

From this point of view, the thing seems self-evident. The scholar's first duty is to truth; he must view the evidence through the untinted pane; he must gain an objective, disinterested, dispassionate view of the events. The Old Testament historians saw the story from the point of view of Israel; but we can read the Moabite Stone,[2] and see how things looked to Mesha, king of Moab, who worshipped his god Chemosh as the Israelites worshipped Yahweh. Comparative Religion shows us the religion of Israel in its place among the religions of the world. (Here again it must be acknowledged, from the orthodox side, that it is highly salutary for those whose chief concern is with Israel according to the spirit to get this view of Israel according to the flesh.)

The study of the Bible by the methods of scientific history forms one department of the general investigation of human history, natural history, and all the other spheres of scientific research. So wonderful has been the advance of knowledge that there can be dreams of something like the medieval *summae theologicae*, a compendium of all human knowledge; only, this time it will be rather a *summa historica*. The dream can never be fully realized, because the front is continually advancing with amazing rapidity; but the ideal is there, and it is tempting to represent it pictorially, somewhat thus: We can study the geography of our home county in one of the beautiful contour maps that are on sale, and then picture some forty or fifty of these maps laid out in order, till the whole of England is spread out before us; then we can add, in imagination, similar maps of the rest of the world, and then extend the picture in several different directions, backwards through history, outwards into the study of an immense variety of flora and fauna, till we have a view of our planet swimming in space, surrounded at vast

---

[1] I. Abrahams, in *The People and the Book*, p. 404.
[2] See e.g. *H.D.B.*, iii, pp. 404 ff. cf;. 2 Kings iii, 4–27, which describes the same events.

distances by the stellar universe, and of man himself who has made his home upon it, with his animal body, his queer psychology, his wonderful mind, his art and poetry expressing the meanings which he has seen in the civilization which he has built up through long centuries. In so far as it is possible for us to do this, we are, it seems, getting a TRUE picture of our life in relation to the world around us. There comes an ideal of a universal human knowledge: Professor's Lods' book *Israel* is a volume in a big series entitled 'The History of Civilization: a complete history of mankind from prehistoric times to the present day, in numerous volumes designed to form a complete library of social evolution'.

Into this scheme, then, the Bible is expected to fit. But the question is, whether that is possible, or if in being fitted into the scheme the Bible will break it in pieces. For the Biblical comment on our ideal of universal knowledge might be to ask *where* this whole view of world history actually exists? It does not exist in any one human mind, for no such mind is of sufficient capacity to take it in. It exists in many minds, in unharmonized fragments. It is shared to some extent by many students, chiefly through the circulation of books; but those who read the books and thus acquire knowledge at second-hand never know the facts and possess the knowledge as fully as does the man who has given his life to that study. And then again: however diligent our would-be encyclopædist may have been throughout a lifetime of study, that lifetime will come to an end; and when the breath of man goeth forth he shall turn again to his earth, and then all his thoughts perish, at least so far as the advance of human knowledge is concerned.

Man, when all is said and done, is not in a position to make a survey of all existence from a vantage-point commanding a view of the whole. That position belongs to God alone, the maker and owner of the universe. Man, His small creature, is situated in the midst of the flux of things; and though he is made in God's image, he is not able to comprehend universes. 'What is man that Thou art mindful of him?' says the psalmist: how insignificant in comparison with the whole universe of being! And yet what wonderful gifts he has: 'For Thou hast made him but little lower than God, and crownest him with glory and honour.'[1] Man, seeing himself in right proportion to God and the rest of the created order—this is what humility means—is privileged to be God's child. But when man sets himself up to be something in himself apart from God, then the judgement of the Bible on this self-sufficient human knowledge is that 'the wisdom of the world is foolishness with God'; and the central point of conflict is the cross of Christ, which to the Jew is a stumbling-block, but to the Greek with his wisdom seems nonsense. Yes, says the apostle, and it is God's nonsense, whereby human self-sufficiency is shown to be hollow and vain, till man finds deliverance from his own unreality and falsehood in the Christ, whom he has derided, but who is in truth the power of God and the wisdom of God.[2]

There is then a conflict between the 'scientific' view of history and that of the Biblical writers. Nor can it be assumed that the conflict will be found to have been overcome in books on the Bible written by Christian scholars. For them, too, the presuppositions of scientific history make a difficulty from which it is hard to escape. What is the historian of the Israelite nation to do when in tracing the course of the history he comes to Jesus of Nazareth, whom the high priest Caiaphas caused to be executed as an accursed blasphemer, in order to blot out from Israel's history His name, His influence and His Gospel, but whom the Christian Church ever since has believed to have been raised from the dead by the hand of Almighty God and thereby vindicated as the true Messiah of Israel and King of all mankind? Should he, being a Christian, assert at this point the truth of the Christian belief? But it is a question whether it comes within his province, as a historian, to do so. It is a 'denominational' belief; it is denied by many to-day, as it was denied by the unbelieving Jews of that time; it demands not only a judgement on facts of history, but also a personal confession of faith. The expedient that is therefore adopted in the second volume of Oesterley and Robinson's *History of Israel* is to omit all mention of Jesus of Nazareth, though two pages are devoted to Pontius Pilate. It is impossible not to think that the decision to do this

[1] Ps. viii, 4, 5.   [2] 1 Cor. i, 18-31.

must have been a very difficult one; for the very act of passing over such a series of events in silence might seem to imply a negative answer to the question of religious faith which they raise, and also to involve a falsification of the history by the omission of what on any showing was an important episode. 'These things were not done in a corner.'

This instance has been quoted in order to show how real is the strain of the tension at this point. We are trying to take the measure of the difficulty which besets the student of the Bible. At the central point of all the tension becomes unendurable; because this is the point at which God impinges on man's life with His Gospel, which involves for man the inevitable issue of Salvation or Judgement.

What then should the historian in this instance have done? Many, no doubt, would defend the expedient here adopted, on the ground that this book was concerned with the political rather than the religious history of Israel. Yet, as we have said, these were important events even from the political point of view; and in any case, the volume in question alludes to the religious outlook of such men as Haggai and Zechariah, and of Ezra, as these affect the history. It was assuredly within the historian's province, and part of his duty, to narrate the external facts, together with the interpretation of them which the apostles of Jesus gave when they proclaimed His resurrection. But that inevitably raises questions about the ultimate meaning of all history, questions to which Christians, Jews, and atheists give radically different answers; and these are questions which the historian, as such, is not competent to solve. That which is ultimately in question at this point is the validity of the whole 'undenominational' view of truth which is involved in the existence of the modern secular of secularized university. The point at which it is raised is the history of those Events in which it is claimed that God was reconciling the world to Himself. In the last analysis, the issue lies between a theocentric and an anthropocentric view of the world and of human existence.

This is the real and the fundamental issue. It has for a long time past been a concealed issue; had it not been so, it is impossible that two Christian scholars would have taken the line that they did. It has been concealed by the fact that the choice has seemed to lie between a church dogmatism based on 'faith', and the scientific historian's duty to truth; and further, it has seemed that the choice of the latter way still allowed full scope for religion and religious experience. It has seemed, in the parallel study of the metaphysical questions involved in Christian faith, that it is possible to describe that study as the 'philosophy of religion': as if it were a discussion of certain philosophical questions which concern those people who have had a certain religious experience, but can be neglected by others. But that is to conceal the real issue; for the questions debated under the name of the 'philosophy of religion' deal with things which the Christian must believe to be true not only for religiously-minded men, but for all men. The true name of this study is 'natural theology', and the name 'philosophy of religion' ought to go on the scrap-heap. The true antithesis is not between 'faith' and 'reason', but between two different beliefs, of which the one uses reason on a secularistic basis, leaving God out of account, and the other uses reason on a theological basis, acknowledging God as the ultimate reality.

Of course it is true that the ordinary study of botany, geology, astronomy, or even history, need not begin by an explicit acknowledgement of the existence of God, even though the Christian believes that in studying these things he is studying the works of God. These are abstract studies, in the sense that they isolate some one sphere of knowledge for special investigation; they are departmental studies, strictly limited in their scope. But when it is a matter of co-ordinating all knowledge, as is done by philosophy on the human side and by theology from the side of revelation, then the existence of God becomes the primary issue; and this issue enters into history at the point where, according to the Christian claim, Eternity has impinged upon Time in the 'eschatological' events of redemption.

Thus the final analysis of the problem shows that Liddon was right in scenting in the Old Testament scholarship of his day presuppositions contrary to those of Christian faith, even though these scholars were right, against him, in demanding an exact exegesis which should make use of modern knowledge, and could accuse him of a dogmatism based on ignorance. What he rightly discerned was that somehow, behind the issue of Faith and Criticism there lay concealed the deeper issue of Faith and Secularism.

3. The Crucial Question of the Resurrection

We have seen how St. Paul acknowledges the Christian appeal to history at the central point of all: if Christ be not raised, our faith is vain, and we apostles are found false witnesses of God. But it has seemed difficult to many among us to allow that faith in the truth of our religion can be dependent on a truth of historical fact on which the historian has the last word. Père Congar has misgivings about the Anglican appeal to history, since it seems 'in the last resort to submit the faith to the judgement of the professors, and not to the apostolic succession of the *magisterium* as such'.[1] The Catholic Modernists took the other course, and accepting the judgement of the professors, proposed to cut the connection between history and faith. Many others have taken a similar line. The best statement of this position is probably that of Dr. Emil Brunner, who urges that the spiritual fact of the Lord's resurrection must be treated as distinct from the material facts of history; the historian cannot prove the Resurrection, and if ever he seems to do so, it is not the Resurrection that he proves: similarly he is not able to disprove it. Can our present discussion throw light on this problem?

Dr. Brunner states the point thus: 'Easter, the Resurrection of the Lord, is not an "historical" event which can be reported. If it were, could it be Easter? Easter is not an occult process for whose reliable description by eye-witnesses we would need as ideal a group of eye-witnesses as possible, under strict supervision. What use are "eye-witnesses" for the event of Easter? What sort of an occult process do people imagine it to have been, that it could be described in semi-scientific terms? Easter, the Resurrection communication of the Christ, is itself revelation, the divine self-testimony which, as such, allows of no objectivity because it is addressed wholly to faith.' The Apostles are the original witnesses, 'but their testimony is not that of eye-wit-

[1] M. J. Congar, *Chrétiens désunis*, p. 229.

nesses but of witnesses of faith. Their witness is based upon the fact that they have received this revelation, which can then become the basis for our faith'.[1] The explanation has been given a little earlier: 'It is not the historical credibility of the Resurrection narratives which bears witness to Christ, but the self-testimony of Christ conveys to the believer the historical credibility of the narratives. Hence to all who read these narratives only with the interest of students of secular history they will always remain incredible, whereas faith will be undisturbed by all historical criticism.'[2]

Something of great importance is being said here. The purely secular student will misunderstand the story, much as Caiaphas did. But something is wrong in the statement, when no historical vindication is permitted of the testimony to the Resurrection; the consequence is, that we are refused any opportunity to prove that the historical testimony is not mere propaganda and the story pure fiction. We need to be able to do this; but that means that we must submit the records to investigation by Christian and non-Christian students alike. Another point is that it is not true that it is simply the self-testimony of Christ which vindicates the truth of the narratives. Brunner goes back on this error a few pages later, where he says: 'No psychologist or historian has yet been able to represent as in any way or to any extent probable how a group of disciples which had been broken up by a terrible catastrophe could have come from purely inner reasons to such a faith which was finally condensed into visions.' In order to give a natural and psychological explanation of such a process, as the liberal Christians do, 'one has to make everything which the witness of the New Testament puts down as the *effect* of the Resurrection into its *cause*: faith in the fact of the Divine Sonship of Jesus'.[3]

Does not the root of this inconsistency lie in the dilemma: *Either* the narratives must be read from a secular point of view—*Or* there must be a faith undisturbed by all historical criticism? Either an 'unprejudiced', 'scientific' study of history, or a dogma

[1] E. Brunner, *The Mediator*, E.T., 1934, p. 575. 'Occult process' is plainly a periphrasis for 'miracle'.

[2] Ibid., p. 575.   [3] Ibid., p. 579.

which ignores history? Either a Liberalism which surrenders to secularism, or a doctrine of Inerrancy? It is the old dilemma which has been with us from the start: either we must surrender to the scientific outlook, or we must shut our eyes to history, clench our fists, and 'believe'.

But is not this precisely an instance of the subtle falsehood of the materialistic outlook? There is a truth of physical fact (which of course is really *true*, because it can be proved); on a different level, unrelated to it, there is religious belief, but only accessible to people with a special religious sensitiveness (and no one can show that it is more than mere wishful thinking). The falsehood of this is that it tears apart the two which by the Incarnation have been made one. The method of the Divine work through the Incarnation, as in the whole Sacred History, is that God speaks His word through men, and Spirit reveals itself through Flesh: till at last the Son of God is made man, and dies and rises again. The whole work of divine Revelation takes place through verifiable historical events. The fact is confessed in the creed that He died and rose again when Pontius Pilate was Governor of Judaea; and it is by historical methods that we prove that the Resurrection story is not a mere cult-legend, nor a myth like those of paganism.

But while it was open to rationalism to disprove the Resurrection, if it could, it was not possible for it to prove that the Resurrection is true; on this latter point Brunner is right. It is a point that appears to stand firm, beyond all doubt, that when the Apostles proclaimed that they were witnesses of the Resurrection, they were challenging the Sadducees to refute their testimony, if they could. To the Jew, resurrection involved the re-animation of the body; if then it could have been shown that the body of Jesus had not been re-animated, the testimony to His Resurrection would have collapsed. There is evidence, as we have seen, that the Jews never attempted to deny the fact of the empty tomb. But to acknowledge the empty tomb was not and is not the same thing as to confess that the Lord is risen, for a rationalistic explanation was always possible. Indeed, everyone who rejects the Christian Gospel must either deny the evidence for the empty tomb or give some rationalistic explanation of it:

he can say with the Jews that the disciples stole the body, with Kirsopp Lake that perhaps the women came by mistake to the wrong grave, or with a recent Scandinavian professor that perhaps there was an earthquake, and the body disappeared in a crack in the rock. That is to say, as Lake fully admits in his book on the Resurrection, it is impossible to settle this question on purely historical grounds.[1] The historian comes at last to a point where he can do no more, and we are left in the position of the crowd listening to St. Peter on the day of Pentecost; having heard his testimony to the Divine work in history, and being unable to refute it, they have next to face up to his exhortation to repent, believe, and be baptized.

If the Sadducees had been able to prove that the body of Jesus had not been raised from the dead, the gathering would have broken up in confusion, and there would have been no baptisms that day. It is the same in principle to-day. If, when it is critically examined, the Biblical narrative begins to gape and crack, and shows that the essential features of the story have been interpolated into it by later editors, and that an earlier form of it can be discerned which treats it as a tale of purely natural events, then the testimony has been discredited and can no longer claim serious attention. The case has collapsed in the effort to state it. If, however, this does not happen, there remains the further question to be faced, much in the same terms as those in which St. Peter posed it at Pentecost.

We have dealt with the Resurrection as the crucial issue which has been put in the forefront of the Christian preaching by the Apostles and by the Church ever since. The virginal conception of our Lord, which stands correspondingly at the beginning of His earthly life, has never been put in the same place in Christian apologetics: doubtless for this reason among others, that of it there could in the nature of the case be only one witness, and she could only tell her story without being able to call any evidence. In this instance, a jury of scientifically-trained observers would be the reverse of impartial, in proportion as they shared the assumption that all particular events are to be ac-

---

[1] See Ramsay, *The Resurrection of Christ*, pp. 51–2 (1945): Kirsopp Lake *The Historical Evidence for the Resurrection of Jesus Christ* (1907), p. 253.

counted for by natural causes; they could not believe that this alleged event had happened without calling in question the finality of that assumption. It is only in the light of the Christian conception of the *Einmaligkeit* or uniqueness of the Divine work of salvation that the virginal conception begins to be credible. To say this is not to prove that it is true. There must still be a careful historical inquiry, to prove whether the accounts consist of legends in which the traces of an earlier non-miraculous belief are readily discernible, or if, on the other hand, the evidence is found on examination to be unexpectedly tough: if, when it is studied in the light of the belief of the apostolic Church about the person of our Lord, it begins to appear that even if some element of legend be acknowledged in the narratives, the virginal conception itself remains as an obstinate fact lying at the base of the tradition.[1]

With this may be contrasted the belief in the Assumption of our Lord's Mother, when this is understood to mean, not the pious belief in her glory and blessedness in her Son's Kingdom, which all Christians might be expected to hold, but that her body disappeared from this earthly scene shortly after her death. For this there is no positive evidence; and the assertion of it should therefore be regarded as a dangerous symptom of 'modernism' in very orthodox circles. The essence of Modernism is the notion that the Christian Faith consists of doctrines believed by 'faith' without support from historical investigation. Further, when her bodily Assumption is accepted in this way, the suspicion at once arises that our Lord's Resurrection is assumed to rest on similar grounds.[2]

---

[1] This paragraph is intended as a criticism of the weak conclusion of the Report of the Doctrinal Commission (*Doctrine in the Church of England*, 1938, p. 82) that 'the subject is one on which the historical evidence by itself cannot be other than inconclusive'.

[2] This question is associated in my mind with a discussion at a conference between some of us Anglicans, and Fr. Boulgakov and some other Russian Orthodox. We asserted the necessity of critical investigation of the historical facts; their reply made it clear that to them 'criticism' meant 'Harnack'; they, not unnaturally, preferred to put their trust in Orthodox tradition. It was interesting to notice that a Roman Catholic who was present supported the bodily Assumption, on the ground that no relics of our Lady are known to exist; and this, for what it is worth, is a piece of historical evidence.

4. The Crucial Question of our Lord's Messianic Claim

The Resurrection of our Lord is a point where the Christian Faith stands or falls. According to the Markan narrative, He Himself posed the question whether He was or was not the Promised One by claiming authority in the Temple, and forced the chief priests to answer Yes or No. The reply of Caiaphas was to get Him condemned to the accursed death of crucifixion. If God did not vindicate Him by the resurrection on the third day, Caiaphas had, and still has, the last word.

The Resurrection is therefore not an isolated portent, but stands in the context of His whole messianic mission, and of the fulfilment in Him of the messianic prophecies. But here we come to a second crucial question, equally crucial with that of the Resurrection; this is the central problem with which the study of the gospels is occupied to-day. It is acknowledged on all hands that the evangelists and the other New Testament writers understand the mission of Jesus as messianic and as the fulfilment of prophecy. But since the whole of the evidence comes to us from within the believing and worshipping Church, and the evangelists are not merely compiling historical memoirs but are at the same time meditating on Him on whom all their faith and hope are fixed, is it possible with any certainty to go behind them and assert that He Himself so understood His mission? How can it be proved that this messianic interpretation of the work of Jesus is not a later interpretation superimposed on a life-story which was originally that of a prophet, perhaps, or a reformer? Of each and every text in which His mission is interpreted in terms of Old Testament prophecy, whether in the evangelists' own words, or in words attributed to Him, it can be and is asked, How can it be proved that this interpretation or this saying is original and authentic?

Such are the questions raised by the leaders of the form-critical school; and we ought to be grateful to them for stating the questions, because they compel us to face up to the Christian appeal to history, and indeed to the whole problem of the authority of the Old Testament and of the Bible generally.

If it were to be demonstrated beyond reasonable doubt that we cannot make any positive affirmation about what our Lord believed and taught, and cannot assert that He believed Himself to be the promised Messiah, the Servant of the Lord, and the Son of Man, then we can no longer acknowledge the Gospel of the divine Kingdom to be true; for it would be fantastic to assert that He was the Christ without knowing it, and that He redeemed the world without thinking that He was doing anything of the kind. The strange corollary is also involved, that everything that is important and creative in the New Testament was first perceived and stated by His admiring followers, having been hidden from Him. If He did not believe Himself to be the Promised One, the answer would have to be that He was not. If that were so, we should still have to say that the New Testament gives us the true interpretation of the Old Testament;[1] but as Charles Williams wrote somewhere, in that case the Messiah to whom the Old Testament writers looked forward, and whose advent in history the New Testament writers believed themselves to be describing, has not yet come. The answer to the question, 'Art thou He that should come, or look we for another?' would in that case be that we are still waiting for His coming.

To such a question there can be no summary answer; it needs a whole treatise or series of treatises. Our duty here, is simply to insist that this is the question, and to state what it is. We have had lately an extremely valuable work by Prof. W. Manson of Edinburgh[2] dealing with it, and showing that in answering it there are two methods which must be followed. The first is, to take a broad view of the evidence as a whole, and see whether any explanation of the rise of the Christian movement is possible, if the whole messianic claim of Jesus was an afterthought; and the second, to examine the text in detail, and see whether one or another citation of the Old Testament or allusion to it in our Lord's sayings bears the marks of having been originally made by Him.

On the former point, Prof. Manson writes thus: 'There are

[1] This point is worked out later on in this book; see pp. 199 ff. 237 f.
[2] W. Manson, *Jesus the Messiah*, 1943.

facts which antedate the rise of the Christian tradition as we have it, and which as such stand above the tides and the ever-shifting currents of opinion on the gospels. The first of these—and it is as reasonably certain as any fact of history—is that before any of the acts or words of Jesus were proclaimed to the world as the sign of proof of a divine redemption offered to the world in him, Jesus was already acknowledged as the Messiah of Israel, the coming Son of Man. This confession stands so near the beginning of Christian history that beside it no other starting-point is perceptible. Dating as public proclamation from the Easter days of the primitive community, it is the absolute presupposition of the Church's tradition, and the substratum of Christian theology in all later forms of its development. A second fact—not perhaps so generally admitted but upon analysis just as incontestable—is that the confession in question, by the very circumstance of its being made with reference to a Jewish teacher who had died a death of shame upon a cross, cannot have originated except upon grounds already given in the life and mind of the Crucified himself. At these points historical analysis takes us to positions lying well behind the literary criticism of the gospels, and the latter cannot, save at its peril, omit them from its reckoning.'[1]

The argument is thus brought back to the point which stands as central in the whole New Testament preaching: the fact that He died upon a cross, and was believed in nevertheless as Lord and Messiah, not in spite of the fact of His crucifixion, as though this were a terrible negative argument, the force of which it was necessary somehow to minimize, but because of it: 'God forbid that I should glory, save in the cross.' The argument is that this is impossible, had He not Himself seen it so, and accepted the way of the cross beforehand as the way of the divine Kingdom, as the gospels say He did.

The second question demands the detailed examination of the texts as given by the evangelists, with a view to determining whether at certain points the messianic allusions in them can be

[1] W. Manson, op. cit., p. 2. He adds that Isa. liii would not have sufficed of itself, when applied afterwards to Jesus, to prove that He had been the Redeemer; for the Servant is not said to have died under a curse such as that attached to crucifixion (p. 6 f.).

shown to go back to our Lord Himself. This argument is always likely to be less than conclusive, when each individual instance is taken separately; its force will rest partly on the first argument, and partly on the cumulative force of a number of instances. Thus, for instance, the quotation attributed to our Lord at the Last Supper of the text from Zech. xiii, 7 ('I will smite the Shepherd, and the sheep shall be scattered', Mark xiv, 27) cannot have been first quoted in Greek by whoever first quoted it, since the *LXX* reads 'shepherds'; Mark therefore, who usually quotes from the *LXX*, deserts it here. Again, on Luke xi, 20, 'If I by the finger of God cast out devils, then verily the Kingdom of God has arrived among you', Prof. T. W. Manson comments that there is here a subtle allusion to Exod. viii, 19, where Moses and the magicians are standing before Pharaoh; the magicians have reproduced two of his miracles, but now can do no more, and are constrained to recognize the finger of God in the production of lice by Moses. 'The argument by which Jesus refutes the charge of being in league with Beelzebub to cast out the demons, runs the same course. He first shows that the thing which he is doing is something which demons cannot reasonably be expected to do. That is the obvious sense of the parables of the Divided Kingdom and the Divided House. Dog does not eat dog. If then the demons are out of the question, his opponents will be constrained to say, as the Egyptian magicians said, "This is the finger of God". . . . The passage is also interesting as showing that our Lord's acquaintance with the Hebrew Bible was not only wide . . . but also very intimate and detailed.'[1] The inference that this Old Testament allusion goes back to our Lord rests on its appositeness to the original context; and it is to be noticed that Matthew deletes the word 'finger' and writes instead 'Spirit' (Matt. xii, 28).

Or again, in the saying about turning the other cheek and surrendering coat and cloak, as given in Matt. v, 39–40, no less than five words—the Greek words for 'resist', 'smite', 'cheek', 'turn', 'go to law'—correspond to those of the *LXX* version of the third of the Servant-poems, Isa. l, 6–8.[2] We ought

---

[1] T. W. Manson, *The Teaching of Jesus*, p. 83
[2] W. Manson, *Jesus the Messiah*, pp. 31–2.

to infer that the hearers are not being given merely precepts of the spiritual life, clothed in picturesque oriental language, but are being told that they must reproduce in their lives the pattern of the Servant of the Lord. The point of the sayings consists not in an abstract ethical ideal, but in a piece of concrete imagery. If so, it becomes in the last degree unlikely that the imagery should have found its way into the saying in the course of transmission; it comes from the mind which originally conceived the saying. If then it is admitted that the Sermon as a whole is from our Lord, He is here found to be thinking in Old Testament terms, and further to be using a part of the Old Testament that is highly relevant to His messianic claim.

These instances are given merely as samples of a method of proof, whereby it is possible to go back behind the written word of the evangelists to the tradition which they received, and with more or less probability to trace that tradition, in these instances, to the Lord Himself. They certainly indicate that the testimony of the New Testament writers that He Himself interpreted His mission in the light of the Old Testament is exceedingly hard to refute.

We asserted at the beginning of this section that this question of the historicity of our Lord's messianic claim is as crucial to the Christian Faith as is the Resurrection itself. That becomes apparent when it is seen that the central point in this problem is the action of our Lord at the Last Supper, when according to the testimony of the Apostles He interpreted His death as the Sacrifice of the Messiah, by which the New Covenant prophesied by Jeremiah was to come into effect. All Catholic Christians and all orthodox Protestants would feel that if this be not history, the heart of their religion would be knocked away. It means everything to us that He did this, with this intention, and commanded us to do it, for His *anamnesis*. For this very reason the appeal to history and to historical verification becomes necessary, that we may know whether our faith rests at this point on the truth.

In these matters each generation has its own battle to fight. In the last few pages we have been concerned with the quite recent phase of the study of the gospels; and no doubt in forty years' time some fresh questions will have been asked and new problems raised. If we who in our generation are entrusted with the proclamation of the Faith can feel confident about the appeal to history, that does not mean that we can settle in advance the special problems which those who follow us will pose, in ways strange to us. The Faith will remain, and the Form of the Church will remain, while the intellectual atmosphere and the topics of discussion alter.

5. The Task of the Christian Student

It has not been irrelevant, in a book on the authority of the Old Testament, to deal as we have done with two questions which belong to the study of the New Testament; for when we think of the Bible as the Book of the divine Kingdom it becomes impossible to treat the Old Testament separately from the New. The Bible is the Book of the Faith; and it is one Faith throughout, in two stages. It would indeed be hard to believe the Faith of the Old Testament to be true, if for twenty-five centuries after they were uttered no fulfilment of the messianic prophecies had appeared; we shall meet this question later, when we come to speak of Christianity and modern Judaism. The Church regards its Bible as one whole, and the advent of the Messiah and His resurrection from death as the central points in the fulfilment. Certainly, apart from belief in the Resurrection there could have been no New Testament, for there would have been no Gospel to proclaim. The Old Testament books similarly are all written in the light of the Faith of Israel, regarded as something altogether unique.

It is impossible in the last resort for there to be right understanding either of the Old Testament or of the New, unless the books are read in the light of this Faith; for there can be no complete sympathy with the books on the part of the reader, unless he believes that Faith to be true. This point becomes fully clear in the New Testament. In St. John's gospel, chapter vi, the multitudes are confronted with Jesus, who feeds them in the wilderness; and in the subsequent discourse on the Bread of Life a mystical interpretation of that Meal is given, in the light of the Christian Eucharist, with the Manna as its type. But the teaching on the Bread of Life is presented as leading of necessity to a process of Judgement, to which those who hear the teaching are subject. The multitudes see and believe not (v. 36); the Jews 'murmur' (v. 41, like the Israelites in the wilderness), and they 'fight' (52); some who are disciples of Jesus 'murmur' (61), are 'caused to stumble' or 'scandalized' (61), do not believe (64), cannot come to Jesus (65), and go back and walk no more with Him (66); last of all the Twelve themselves are sharply tested (67-9); one of them is a devil (70), and is going to betray Him (71). All who hear, without exception, become subject to the Judgement, and so, it is implied, is every reader of the gospel. No man can read it as an interested outsider; everyone is compelled to take sides, to react, to be judged. We, too, who speak of the crucial issues of the Resurrection of our Lord and His messianic claim, are thereby expressing our judgement on the truth of the Christian Gospel; and we cannot escape from so judging, for the responsibility is laid upon us. Yet while we pronounce our judgement, we ourselves are being judged; in the act of judging we are pronouncing judgement on ourselves.

So it is with the Old Testament also. We can enter into the meaning of the Old Testament as we use its words as the vehicles of our approach to God in adoration, penitence, thanksgiving and supplication, and as we ourselves tremble at the prophetic warnings of divine judgement. Hence the liturgy of the Church is the true school for the right interpretation of the Bible.

Yet this statement needs to be heavily qualified. There is such a thing as the literal and original meaning of the text, which can only be learnt by patient research; and the outlook of the modern reader is of necessity so different from that of the Semitic writer of 3,000 years ago that he will make every sort of mistake in the interpretation of the text, unless his understanding of it is disciplined by critical study. This double point is well illustrated by some words recently written with reference to another study, that of the history of the Ministry in the early Christian centuries:

'The historical problem . . . has been posed in a radically new form in quite modern times—within the last three generations. . . . The first concern of the Christian historian must be the establishing of the Christian historical facts. Yet his safeguard does not lie in any easy determination to exclude theology altogether from his handling of the historical material available. If this were possible to achieve, it would amount scientifically only to the worst possible distortion of the facts. The truly historical interpretation of Church history can never be untheological. Just because what is under investigation is a complex of facts in the specifically religious history and psychology of a period in the Christian past, the then contemporary theological interpretation of those facts is capitally relevant, from the most coldly scientific point of view. The historian's real difficulty is not the importation of theology into our understanding of Church history, but the fact that none of us, without long study and the most discriminating care, can fully share the then contemporary theological interpretation. We have all of us inherited ideas of different kinds from other, later periods of Church history, ideas of which pre-Nicene Christians had no clear consciousness.'[1]

All this applies, *mutatis mutandis*, to the study of the Old Testament. The study of it from a purely secular point of view or from that of the comparative study of religions will be bound to miss everything in the Old Testament that ultimately matters; yet it is nevertheless true that a vast amount of valuable light has been shed upon it by scholars who fall under such designations. Everything that throws light on the secular history is of importance for the right understanding of the spiritual history; and from this point of view Dr. Oesterley has given an instructive list of the qualifications of the ideal exegete: knowledge of the original languages, Hebrew and Aramaic, and also of the allied languages and dialects; of Semitic comparative religion; of archaeology; of folk-lore; of the historical background of each book; of the geography; of the literature of other peoples; of literary style.[2] Yet all this, however important, is no more than prolegomena to the real task, which is to reach a right understanding of the things which the Biblical authors actually wrote,

---

[1] Dom Gregory Dix, essay on 'The Ministry in the Early Church', in *The Apostolic Ministry*, ed. Kirk, 1946, p. 185 f.

[2] W. O. E. Oesterley, in *Record and Revelation*, pp. 417–26.

why it seemed to them important that just these things should be said, and what were the insights of faith that filled their imagination and impelled them to speak and write. It is the union of the insight of a personal faith with adequate knowledge and critical discrimination that alone can lead to good exegetical work.

The study of the prolegomena is assuredly not complete—when will it be?—but at least the ground has been thoroughly covered, and the whole main outline of the history determined. Everyone is saying that the theological interpretation of the Biblical history has lagged behind the study of the outward facts; and it is to be expected that the immediate future will see important constructive work done, on the spiritual history as seen from the inside. Some words written fifteen years ago about New Testament criticism are no less relevant to that of the Old Testament:

'It is a very strange and almost unaccountable fact that the older critics, having accomplished the literary analysis, and having with extraordinary skill achieved the solution of the main problems presented by the literary analysis, seem to have exhausted their critical faculties. For either, ignoring the further critical problems raised by it, they hastened at once to reconstruct the Jesus of History, or else, stopping short at this point, they doubted the ability of the critical method to achieve any historical reconstruction whatsoever. Thus the critical method was suspended as it were in mid-air. But their own critical work demanded that an even more critical procedure should follow. The critic is not free, having accomplished the literary analysis, to select this or that element in the tradition, and to pronounce it true to the original history; nor, conversely, to discard this or that element as due to the imposition upon the original history of Christian faith, or of primitive Christian superstition. Still less can literary criticism be indulged in as though it had no historical implications. Unless historical reconstruction be undertaken, the older critical method is rendered completely sterile. Nevertheless, the transition from literary analysis to historical reconstruction demands an increasingly critical procedure.'[1]

[1] Hoskyns and Davey, *The Riddle of the New Testament*, 1931, pp. 107–8.

The Task of the Christian Student

It is possible that Phythian-Adams had this passage in mind when he wrote, with reference to the true relation of the documents preserved in Exodus and Numbers to the older oral tradition of the Wilderness-period:[1]

'The general attitude of modern Biblical Scholarship seems rather to be that of an exhausted conqueror who is unable or unwilling to exploit his victory to the full . . . It has halted at the very moment when it should have advanced with ruthless ardour . . . It had been hoped that when critical analysis had separated out from the medley of documents those sources which might be treated as the oldest and therefore the most reliable, the task of the historian of Israel must become comparatively straightforward. But this is a fond delusion. Whatever exactly happened *when Israel came out of Egypt*, it will not be discovered by treating these heterogeneous fragments as the component parts of a puzzle-picture which can be 'reconstructed' provided the right pieces are used. Nor, again, is the truth to be extracted by more and more complex surgical operations upon J. and E., or upon any of their now rapidly increasing progeny. In *that* sense, we can never hope to hold it in our hands at all.'

Allusion has already been made to this book, as a good example of right critical procedure. The explanations given there may or may not be right in detail. But assuredly the method is right; for it is bsaed on an endeavour to solve the literary problem by trying to see it in the light of the faith by which Israel lived, made by a scholar who himself shares that faith. If it is necessary to cite an example of bad critical procedure one might point to an essay published some ten years earlier, on the Religion of Israel from Moses to Saul, in which it is not even noticed that the loss of the Ark to the Philistines must have been an exceedingly serious blow to the faith of the Israel of the day.[2]

The constructive work which waits to be done on the Old Testament will start as from within the faith of Israel; and that

---

[1] Pythian-Adams, *The Call of Israel*, 1934, pp. 57–8. Some literary dependence of the one document on the other is suggested by the use of the words 'exhaust' and 'reconstruct'.

[2] W. F. Lofthouse in *The People and the Book*, 1924, pp. 221–53.

indeed is the natural place where a Christian should start. Such work will use the utmost critical discrimination, and employ all available resources; but it will never lose sight of its main objective, namely to enter into and understand the faith which inspired the ancient Israelite writers, and the authority which the tradition of their faith exercised over them. Thereby it will throw light also on the authority which belongs to the Bible permanently, and in general on the manner in which the divine element in the Bible is mediated through the human. It will be treating the Bible as the Book of the Divine Kingdom.

It will start, therefore, with the endeavour to determine the literal meaning which the text originally bore, using so far as possible all the helps which modern knowledge gives; ignorance must not be preferred to knowledge, even when it has patristic or other ecclesiastical authority. It will not stop there; even within the Old Testament the question often arises, what meaning an earlier narrative bore in the eyes of a later editor, as shown by his own additions to it, and this is often a 'typical' interpretation.

Our duty is plainly to do something to implement what has been said, by giving some indication of the lines which a right criticism must follow; and our next task is, as was said at the end of the last chapter, to inquire into the process of the formation of the Old Testament canon, see what needs of the faith of Israel were met by the provision of such a canon, and learn thereby what the word 'bible' means.

CHAPTER V

THE CANON OF THE LAW

'The Old Testament, as we know it, is the corpus of religious literature of post-exilic Judaism. The Jewish
legend that Ezra miraculously restored the ancient
writings after their destruction (2 Esdras xiv, 9 ff., 40-48), is
not all untrue. Not only was a very large proportion of the
canonical scriptures actually written in this period—far larger
than we commonly realize—but whatever of earlier literature
has survived has done so because the scribes of the sixth and
following centuries judged it worthy to survive; and all has come
down to us with their mark upon it.'[1]

This is of capital importance. The Christian reader usually
thinks of the continuous record of Israelite history as ending
with the exile, and of the following centuries as 'a mere epilogue,
or a barren waiting-time till the rise of Christianity'; he has for
this period only a few historical fragments, separated from one
another by centuries of which there is no history; besides, as
most of the literature dating from this period is anonymous, it
seems to be as barren of personalities as it is of events. But really
'it is our perspective that is at fault. If the age of the prophets
saw the rise of creative ideas, it was in the post-exilic period that
they first became effective in the life of a community'.[2]

The false perspective that comes easily to the ordinary reader
of the Bible is shared often by the theological student, who in
gaining his first vivid impression of the great prophets, and
eagerly identifying their genuine prophecies, is apt to deal
somewhat impatiently with these which, as he now learns, were

[1] Dodd, *The Authority of the Bible*, pp. 154-5.
[2] *Ibidem.*

133

added at a later time, labelling them 'non-authentic'. Similarly, the later editings of the historical books are not as a rule of great importance for determining the true history of the events; but there can be no right understanding of the Old Testament as a whole if they are neglected.

While, however, it was in the time of Ezra that the Pentateuch was formally accepted as canonical, the idea of an authoritative sacred book did not then appear for the first time. Deuteronomy had held that position throughout the exilic period. Deuteronomy is thus 'the fundamental document of Judaism'; and 'when the community was reconstituted under the inspiration of Ezekiel and the Second Isaiah, it was a revised Deuteronomy that provided what we may call its "constitution". The Jews became the people of a book, and that book Deuteronomy'.[1] The decisive step which made possible the whole later development was taken at the reformation under king Josiah; and 'in the authority and sanctity assigned, at this conjuncture, to a book, we recognize the beginnings of the Hebrew Canon'.[2]

1. Deuteronomy

'And Hilkiah the high priest said unto Shaphan the scribe I have found the book of the law in the house of the Lord. And Hilkiah delivered the book to Shaphan, and he read it. . . . And Shaphan read it before the king. And it came to pass, when the king had heard the words of the book of the law, that he rent his clothes' (2 Kings xxii, 8, 10, 11), and proceeded to appoint what we should call a commission of five persons to take neces-

---

[1] Dodd, op. cit., p. 146. I assume in the following treatment that Deuteronomy can still be confidently regarded as embodying the law-book of Josiah's reformation; though (as I myself think) the core of it already existed in Hezekiah's reign, and it also received additions up to the early years of the exile.

[2] Ryle, *The Canon of the Old Testament*, 1893, p. 61. This is still a standard book on the history of the Canon, and a better book than Sanday, *Inspiration*, 1893; but it needs to be corrected at certain points by up-to-date books such as Oesterley and Robinson, *History of Israel*, vol. ii, or Lofthouse, *Israel after the Exile*. The best treatment of the subject in English seems to me to be Budde's article on the 'Canon' in the *Encyclopædia Biblica*.

sary action; the commission went to consult the prophetess Huldah, and reported to the king (v. 20).

How much of our present book of Deuteronomy was in the hands of Shaphan cannot be exactly determined; there is general agreement that the book received considerable additions afterwards.[1] Whatever were its exact contents, the king at once recognized it as authoritative, in spite of the fact that it certainly differed widely from the law which was then in force. It is possible that the words attributed to Hilkiah, that he had found *the* book of the law, mean that they all knew that a law-book existed somewhere, and that this was none other than the book used in the partial and abortive reformation carried out by king Hezekiah, according to 2 Kings xviii, 4.[2] In any case, Josiah accepted the book as authentic; and it must be remembered that the claim of the book to external authority, whatever precisely that was, would be powerfully reinforced in the king's eyes by the intrinsic authority of the prophetic teaching which it contained; almost every page of it bears the impress of the teaching of Amos, Hosea, Isaiah, Micah. Anyhow, he so accepted it, and it was soon put into operation.

The decisive act was the making of the Covenant, when 'the king stood by the pillar, and made a covenant before Yahweh to walk after Yahweh and to keep His commandments and His testimonies and His statutes, with all his heart and all his soul, to confirm the words of the covenant that were written in this book: and all the people stood to the covenant' (2 Kings xxiii,

---

[1] See the commentaries. An obvious instance is that the description of the horrors of the siege of Jerusalem in xxviii, 52–7 is more likely to have been written after the event; also that of the misery of exile in vs. 58–68.

[2] Sellin, *Introduction to the Old Testament*, E.T. 1923, pp. 74–7. The main difficulties urged against this suggestion are, first, that doubt has been cast on the actuality of Hezekiah's reformation: can it be proved that it is not a deduction of a Deuteronomic historian from the fact that Hezekiah was a godly king? Further, the memorable and resounding phrases of Deuteronomy, which can be recognized in almost every writer for the next two hundred years, do not begin to appear till Jeremiah. But for my part, I cannot escape from the impression that Sellin is right. There is no reason why the same faith should not have led to the same practical conclusions in Hezekiah's reign as in Josiah's; and the Hezekian reformation is further referred to in Rabshakeh's speech, 2 Kings xviii, 22, in a manner which puts the truth of it almost beyond doubt.

3); and 'they cut the calf in twain and passed between the parts thereof; the princes of Judah and the princes of Jerusalem, the eunuchs and the priests and all the people of the land . . . passed between the parts of the calf' (Jer. xxxiv, 18–19).

What was the precedent for this? What gave them the idea? We ought perhaps to think of the narrative in Joshua xxiv, which had certainly been written before this time:[1] Joshua there calls a national assembly at Shechem, and preaches a sort of sermon to the people about the national faith, reminding them of the call of Abraham, the Exodus, the deliverance from the Amorites, Balak and Balaam, and the conquest of Canaan, and calling them to choose whether they mean to serve Yahweh or go after other gods. When they repeatedly protest their intention to serve Yahweh, 'Joshua made a covenant with the people that day, and set them a statute and an ordinance in Shechem. And Joshua wrote these words in the book of the law of Yahweh' (Joshua xxiv, 25–6).[2] The whole scene bears a remarkable likeness to that of the covenant which Josiah made at Jerusalem, with the Book of Deuteronomy in his hand.

Deuteronomy itself seems to contain a direct allusion to Josiah's Covenant in its account of the Covenant in the plains of Moab in chapter xxix: 'These are the words of the Covenant which Yahweh commanded Moses to make with the children of Israel in Moab, besides the Covenant which He made with them in Horeb' (xxix, 1). The Covenant at Horeb is of course treated always as the primary and essential Covenant, by which Israel became the People of Yahweh;[3] any additional Covenant

---

[1] This chapter is 'attributed to E with practical unanimity among modern critics' (Carpenter and Harford-Battersby, *The Hexateuch*, 1900, vol. ii p. 357); Deuteronomy everywhere shows the influence of the J and E documents.

[2] These last words have caused difficulty in the minds of some scholars: it is said immediately after, that Joshua took a great stone to stand as a witness, and it is not clear why the Book and the Stone should both be necessary. Hence Dillmann and Nöldeke suggested that the words about the Book were added by the Deuteronomic editor of the Book of Joshua (Carpenter and Battersby-Harford, p. 358); this seems to be not unlikely.

[3] The Covenant at Horeb is referred to explicitly in Deut. xxix, 24–5, and in 8 other places where the word 'covenant' is connected directly with the Decalogue or with the Tables of Stone on which the Decalouge was inscribed,

would bear the same relation to it as a renewal of baptismal vows, such as is sometimes made in a Christian congregation on the occasion of a parochial mission, bears to the vows of the baptismal rite itself; it would be a deliberate ratification and confirmation of that to which the people were already bound. The twenty-ninth chapter as a whole is, of course, to be read as addressed directly to the people at Jerusalem. We get a clear indication of this in v. 14: 'Neither with you only do I make this covenant and this oath; but with him that standeth here with us this day before Yahweh our God, and also with him that is not here with us this day'. There need have been no absentees when Israel was assembled as a compact body, ready to invade Canaan; but there must have been many who had stayed at home to look after the farms when the Covenant was made at Jerusalem. After this the people are reminded of the Exodus, and how Yahweh had led His people since then, and they are warned of the danger of going after other gods, and threatened (as they had been threatened by Isaiah[1]) with the fate of Sodom and Gomorrah if they should turn away from Yahweh, and think that they could have peace, while they walked in the stubbornness of their heart, and forsook the Covenant which He made with them when He brought them forth out of the land of Egypt. A choice lay before them of life and good, or death and evil (xxx, 15 ff.).

It is impossible to affirm that the stories of the Covenants made under Moses in Moab and under Joshua at Shechem rest on genuine historical reminiscence. But the Covenant under Josiah at Jerusalem stands in the clear light of history, and it is one of the decisive moments in the story of the Israel of God. It marks the end of the long conflict of the Faith of Yahweh with the pagan religions of Canaan. It means that the decisive victory has now at last been won. The people, headed by their king, have solemnly and publicly pledged themselves to Yahweh as the true God. The Book is necessary to define the terms of the

---

besides 4 allusions to the Ark of the Covenant, and 9 places where the same Covenant is referred to in general terms. The subsidiary Covenant in Moab is referred to again in xxix, 9, 12, 14. The word is also used in vii, 2, in the prohibition of covenants with the Canaanites.

[1] Isa. i, 9, 10.

Covenant, and state the Faith which Israel now acknowledges as its own.

Some eight centuries before, the tribes had entered Canaan from the desert, united by a glowing faith in Yahweh as their national God.[1] But it was, humanly speaking, extremely unlikely that they would be able to retain this faith in anything like its authentic shape, when they settled down in the country, and learnt the arts of agriculture from their Canaanite neighbours; for they could not fail to learn at the same time the appropriate religious rites without which it was impossible to expect a harvest to ripen. It might seem inevitable that a syncretism should take place, and that Yahweh should take His place as one of the fertility-gods of the land; and this, of course, was the thing that was always tending to happen. In time of war, when the tribes or some of them, united for defence against some aggressor, the old faith in Yahweh would come back; in time of peace, the nature-religions would crowd in to take its place. The picture given us by the editors of the Book of Judges, of a sort of see-saw between Canaanite apostasy and periodical returns to faith in Yahweh in times of war, must have some foundation in fact.

But now at last the marvel had happened, thanks above all to the work of the prophets. The records of Samuel, Nathan, Elijah, Elisha, Isaiah, agree in showing them to have been men who held a position of strong moral ascendency and leadership. Though, like Elijah, they had often felt themselves to be standing almost alone, or, like Isaiah, to have only a small nucleus of disciples on whose loyalty they could count, they bore their witness, and stood before the nation as great men of God. Now their work had its reward, when at long last the nation solemnly professed its allegiance to Yahweh, and adopted a law-book in which the whole cycle of rites was transferred to Him, to be celebrated in His honour, with His flag hoisted over it. The peril of a syncretistic paganized religion had been overcome; the

---

[1] This is attested not only by the narratives but also by the early prophets, who look on the wilderness period as the time when Israel had been 'holiness to Yahweh', Jer. ii, 3; cf. Hos. ii, 14–15, Amos, v, 25.

agricultural rites were now subordinated to the faith of Israel in the God who had brought it out of Egypt.

But it had been a fearful conflict. Hosea had seen the national faith as all but submerged in the nature-religions; he could only hope that Yahweh would take Israel back into the desert, stripping her of the arts of civilization in order to purge her from the religious practices that went with them, and recall her to her first love. Amos, a little earlier, had seen no prospect but that Yahweh would cast His people off altogether. This terrible doom fulfilled itself, as regards the northern kingdom, with the fall of Samaria; and the continued existence of the southern kingdom hung on a thread. Under the awful terror of the 'war of nerves', a new revival of religion took place: not now of the worship of the country baals, but of darker religious rites drawn from a variety of pagan sources, offered to as many gods as possible, to Moloch, to the host of heaven, in the hope that if one set of offerings were ineffective, another might be of some avail. Against all this the great Isaiah had set his face and stood as firm as a rock; his faith had been triumphantly vindicated when Sennacherib failed to take Jerusalem. But under Manasseh pagan superstition had come back worse than ever, and Jerusalem had been filled with the blood of martyrs. A remnant only was left, and they watched and prayed and waited, till the pagan reaction had spent itself, and men began to be aware that Isaiah's faith had won the moral victory. At last it was possible for there to be a great national confession of faith and of adherence to the living God, while the sword of judgement was still suspended over their heads.

Therefore the authors of Deuteronomy go back over the national history. We did wrong, they say, ever to enter into relations with the Canaanites; we ought to have exterminated them utterly, made no marriages with them, and uprooted all the emblems of their religion. They do not explain how in that case the people would ever have learnt the arts of agriculture; it is an entirely fancy picture which they give of what might have been done in the past, even though the Deuteronomic editor of the Book of Joshua represented it as having been systematically carried out. That it was not so carried out is proved by the whole course of the history, and by the direct evidence of the first chapter of Judges.[1] Nor was it in any way possible for the programme of extermination to be carried out in the days of Josiah. The thing that was possible and that needed to be done was that there should be a purge of paganizing elements in the existing practice of the people. Not only must the new superstitions be cleared away, but also, what might seem in a sense to be regrettable, the country shrines must be destroyed; for henceforth there must be one altar only and one set of sacrifices, to proclaim the faith that 'Yahweh is our God, Yahweh is one' (vi, 4).

Such is the context in which we must read Deuteronomy. We must see it as a great and decisive confession of faith made by the People of God on the eve of its passion, and sealed by the solemn act of the Covenant.[2] Of that Covenant the Book was an essential part; for it set out in words the faith which the people now acknowledged to be their faith. The Book contained legal enactments, inspired by the prophetic teaching; it contained also splendid exhortations, in a glowing style of oratory that was a new thing in the language of religion. These conveyed the spirit in which the law was to be kept; and they remain to this day as classical expressions of the meaning of the spiritual service of God. Backslidings, of course, there were after this, as there had been before; Jeremiah saw much that brought him bitter disappointment. But an act had been performed, on which there could be no going back. The colours of Israel's faith had been nailed to the mast.

Such is the line of answer that must be given to the question which needs above all to be asked: *what did it mean* when the Book

---

[1] There appears to be at least one authentic instance to the contrary, in the case of Jericho, where the recent excavations have substantially corroborated the statement of the Book of Joshua that the city was dedicated to Yahweh as a sacrificial offering by Israel on its first entry into Canaan. See Garstang, *Joshua-Judges*, 1931, pp. 143–8.

[2] Ryle seeks to explain the significance of Deuteronomy as having been a 'people's book' (*The Canon of the Old Testament*, pp. 58–60); its object was to make the laws known to the people, whereas previously they had been known only to the priests who gave *torah* at the shrines. This interpretation seems to be based on a parallel with early Roman history; it has no doubt a certain truth, but it misses the really important points.

of Deuteronomy became 'scripture'? This book now held a place which no writings had held before. Elijah had waged a notable conflict against the imported worship of the Tyrian Baal, and had won. But the scene on Mount Carmel had been rather of the nature of a demonstration; there was no covenant and no book, and the pagan outbreak was actually 'liquidated' by Jehu in a style which has become familiar in modern times, and which aroused the disgust of Hosea.[1] Books had been written in the course of the long conflict with the pagan religions; there had been poems, songs, royal memoirs, narratives of the great events of the past. Without doubt many of these took shape in the 'schools of the prophets'; an interesting sign of this is the fact that in the J.-narrative of the Plagues of Egypt Moses has no rod, but speaks like a prophet, 'Thus saith Yahweh', and what he says comes to pass. We cannot tell to what extent, in these narratives as a whole, stories were deliberately re-told in order to exclude paganizing features which may have been creeping in. Certainly the prophetic books were read: Jeremiah had read Hosea, and elsewhere the influence of the narrative books can frequently be discerned. But they were read as edifying literature, or as words which Yahweh had spoken to an earlier generation; they were not 'canonical' in the sense in which that term could be applied to Deuteronomy after B.C.621. Deuteronomy was now the Book of the Covenant (2 Kings xxiii, 2).

2. The Pattern of the Messianic Hope

To them at the time it seemed that the great national confession of faith and of repentance had come too late. At the end of the description of Josiah's reformation and the great passover that followed, the prophetic writer says of him that 'like unto him there was no king before him, that turned to Yahweh with all his heart, and with all his soul, and with all his might, according to all the law of Moses; neither after him arose there any like him' (2 Kings xxiii, 25). He continues: 'Notwithstanding Yahweh turned not from the fierceness of His great wrath, wherewith His anger was kindled against Judah, because of all

[1] Hos. i, 4.

the provocations that Manasseh had provoked Him withal'
(v. 26), and then without a word of comment relates the un-
timely death of the king, in the prime of life, at the hands of
Pharaoh Necho. 'Lord, why hast Thou thus dealt with us?' is
his unspoken question; and his answer, 'because in the reign of
Manasseh we involved ourselves so deeply in apostasy from Thee
that even our repentance under Josiah could not avert our just
judgement'. But to us who have the history spread out before us
it is clear that the real work of Deuteronomy was to prepare the
People of God for a death and a resurrection: to enable it to go
into exile, and through the chastening discipline of suffering
learn a faith that was stronger than death. The presupposition
and the necessary starting-point of the spiritual process that was
now to begin, was that before the catastrophe happened the
nation had made its covenant with God and acknowledged as
authoritative the book of His law and His judgements.

Two hundred years later there was another Covenant; it is
described in Nehemiah viii–x, and its probable date is B.C. 397.
Once again, under very different circumstances, Israel bound
itself to the divine service, accepting a revision of the 'Law of
Moses', as set out in a collection of writings which included,
together with later compilations, the most ancient and authentic
records of the Deliverance on which Israel's existence was
based.[1] Our task is to make some kind of a survey of the spiritual

---

[1] The view which is taken here is that the Book promulgated by Ezra was
not the Priestly Code but the Pentateuch in the form in which it then existed,
and that this promulgation took place in the seventh year of Artaxerxes the
second (Ezra vii, 1, 8), i.e. about 397 B.C.; see Oesterley and Robinson,
History of Israel, vol. ii, pp. 135–7, and pp. 161 ff. below. I append for con-
venience a list of the most important dates, as given by Miss Hippisley and
printed in the appendix to the volumes of the Clarendon Bible series, pp.
6–9:

B.C.
596   First deportation to Babylon
586   Fall of Jerusalem
549–38 Isaiah xl–lv.
538   Capture of Babylon by Cyrus
537   Return of Zerubbabel and Joshua (Ezra i, ii)*
520–16 Building of Temple. Haggai and Zechariah
c.450   Isa. lvi–lxvi. Malachi.†
445   Return of Nehemiah (Neh. ii)

history of the time, and see what was happening to Israel's faith during these momentous years.

We must begin with the two processions of captives which went to exile in Babylonia: the first in 596, leaving the Judaean state still in being and the city standing; the second in 586, leaving the city in ruins, its walls broken down, its temple burnt with fire, and the whole structure of its corporate life destroyed:

'Thy breach is great like the sea; who can heal thee? . . .
All that pass by clap their hands at thee;
They hiss and wag their head at the daughter of Jerusalem, saying,
Is this the city that men called The perfection of beauty, The joy of the
whole earth?[1] *. . .*
O wall of the daughter of Zion, let tears run down like a river day and
night. . . .
The youth and the old man lie on the ground in the streets;
My virgins and my young men are fallen by the sword:
Thou hast slain them in the day of Thine anger; Thou hast slaughtered,
and hast not pitied.'

(Lam. ii, 13, 15, 18, 21.)

But it is something more than a physical calamity that is depicted in Ezekiel's vision of the Valley of the Dry Bones (Ezek. xxxvii, 1–14);[2] something more than the ruin of the social structure of a nation uprooted from its home and forcibly deported to a foreign land. Worse than these was the apparent absence of that spiritual sensitiveness which alone could make the survivors worthy of the name of Israel. 'It was dead, that body from which he had believed that life was to go forth to quicken the universe'; a further stage had come, the stage of

---

?397   Ezra's return
335   Samaritan schism

* On the return in 537 see Oesterley, pp. 71–81, where it is argued that in 537 the leader was Sheshbazzar (Ezra i, 8, 11).

† It would be safer to regard Isa. lvi–lxvi as belonging to various dates between 516 and 445.

[1] Quotation of Ps. xlviii, 2.

[2] I cannot believe that the recent theories which place Ezekiel's ministry chiefly in Palestine are either required to explain the evidence or helpful in interpreting it. I take it that ch. xxxvii refers primarily to the spiritual condition of the exiles, to whom he prophesied (v. 7).

utter dissolution, when each limb looked as if it had nothing to do with any other. Can these bones live? As he prophesies, his voice seems to him a mere sound in the air. 'But there is a noise and a shaking; then a frightful movement of the bones towards each other, each claiming its fellow to which it had once belonged. This strange union of dead things betokens a power which has not yet declared itself. And soon the sinews and the flesh come up upon them. They have acquired form, though they have no life. Then said He unto me; Prophesy unto the wind, Thus saith the Lord God, Come from the four winds, O breath, and breathe upon these slain, that they may live. So I prophesied as He commanded. And the breath came into them, and they lived, and stood up on their feet, an exceeding great army.'[1]

When the catastrophe happened, there remained to those Israelites—as to a certain small group of their descendants some 616 years later—only one ray of hope in the darkness: it had been predicted. Though many of the accredited prophets had encouraged a wishful optimism, Jeremiah at least had consistently told them to prepare for the worst. There was a remnant who had believed his teaching, and who were now saying from the bottom of their hearts, We have sinned. The marks of their punishment had gone so deep that they have never been effaced; and every aching sore was to them a reminder of the sin of the People of Yahweh in hardening their necks and turning away from Him after other gods. Yet it had all been prophesied in Yahweh's name; and the very fact that Israel's relation to Him consisted not in a quasi-natural kinship, as in the case of the ordinary tribal god, but in a Covenant, meant that He was in no way involved in Israel's fall. And the prophetic voice had also told them that His purpose with His people was not yet finished: even in exile 'ye shall call upon Me and ye shall go and pray unto Me, and I will hearken unto you. And ye shall seek Me, and find Me, when ye shall search for Me with all your heart' (Jer. xxix, 12–13). 'When thou art in tribulation, and all these things are come upon thee, in the latter days thou shalt return to Yahweh thy God, and hearken to His voice; for Yahweh

[1] F. D. Maurice, *Prophets and Kings of the Old Testament*, 1852, pp. 472–3.

thy God is a merciful God; He will not fail thee, neither destroy thee, nor forget the Covenant of thy fathers which He sware unto them' (Deut. iv, 30-1).

They prayed to their national God in a foreign land, and found that faith was still possible. The life of old Israel had died; their homes, traditions, worship, all were lost; Israel in their persons had died—and behold they lived. They had been chastened and not killed. They were sorrowful, yet there was a spring of hope in them which gave promise of a future joy. Because they had believed the prophetic announcement of Yahweh's just judgement on their sin, they were able to hear the promise of a future Salvation: 'I know the thoughts that I think towards you, saith Yahweh, thoughts of peace and not of evil, to give you hope in your latter end' (Jer. xxix, 11). These great words occur in the letter which Jeremiah wrote to the exiles of the first deportation, to tell them not to expect to be able to return in a few years and resume their old life at Jerusalem: 'After seventy years be accomplished for Babylon I will visit you, and perform My good work towards you, in causing you to return to this place' (v. 10).

With Jeremiah the classical pattern of Israel's messianic hope begins to appear. It can be summarized under the following headings:

(i) A Second Exodus, not this time from Egypt but from the north country and the other countries whither the Israelites had been driven (Jer. xvi, 14, 15, and xxiii, 7, 8).

(ii) A New Covenant, resting on personal knowledge of God and bringing forgiveness of sin (Jer. xxxi, 31-4), and an outpouring of the Spirit of Yahweh, causing the people to keep His commandments and do them (Ezek. xxxvi, 27), and bestowing prophetic insight (Joel ii, 28).

(iii) The Return of the Presence of Yahweh to dwell in the midst of Israel, that they might be truly His People and He their God (Ezek. xliii, 1-7; Isa. xl, 1-11).

(iv) The calling in of the Gentiles to share, incompletely or fully, in the blessings of the Covenant and the knowledge of the true God which Israel possessed (Isa. xlv, 22-4; xlix, 6; lvi, 6-8).

Right at the centre of this series of promises of spiritual renewal stand the poems which describe the Servant of Yahweh (Isa. xlii, 1–4; xlix, 1–6; l, 4–9; lii, 13–liii), in which the pattern of the ideal Israelite is set forth, and an interpretation given of the meaning of suffering in God's work of Salvation.

These passages are all very well known, and it is not necessary here to print them out at length, or comment on them in detail, except for the third heading, which has been much neglected and demands more detailed treatment.[1] The other passages will be mentioned at various points in our exposition.[2]

Jeremiah spoke of a new Exodus, not from the land of Egypt, but from Babylon and the other lands of the exile (xvi, 14 f.; xxiii, 7 f.). The importance of this promise is that it marks the beginning of the 'spiritual' or 'mystical' interpretation of the story of the first Exodus, as giving the pattern of a new and greater Deliverance. Henceforth, when the Israelites heard the story, they were to think of it as to be re-enacted in the future on a more imposing scale. Hence we find a clear allusion to the Exodus-narrative in Isa. lii, 11–12: 'Depart ye, depart ye, go out from thence, touch no unclean thing. . . . For ye shall not go out in haste, neither shall ye go out by flight: for Yahweh will go before you; and the God of Israel will be your rereward.' There would again be the Pillar of Cloud before and behind. But the Second Exodus would take place with quiet deliberation and in perfect safety.[3]

There would be a return. Yahweh, because He loved Israel with an everlasting love, would gather His scattered flock (xxxi, 3, 10). Rachel, weeping for her children, would see them

---

[1] Pp. 148–55 below.

[2] Most of the texts are printed out in my *Throne of David*, chs. ii (on the messianic hope) and iii (on Israel's universal mission). The treatment of these subjects in that book was worked out in the first place from a New Testament starting-point, in order to trace through the Old Testament the things which are there fulfilled. The defect of the treatment in that book is that too little attention is there given to the dates of the various prophecies, and consequently to the way in which the hope itself was moulded by the events of the history, and above all by the crisis of the exile, which we are now studying.

[3] Some other refs. to the Exodus in Isa. xl–lv: xl, 3; xlii, 15; xliii, 2, 16 ff.; xlvi, 9; xlviii, 20 f.

again, and her work would be rewarded (vv. 15–17). Yahweh had heard Ephraim too—the remnant of the northern tribes—accepting his chastisement and repenting (v. 18 f.). At last the weary and sorrowful soul of Judah would be at peace again (vv. 23–5). For the restoration would be no mere renewal of the old Covenant, with its *torah* given by a priest or written down in Deuteronomy; there would be a New Covenant, written in their hearts, resting on personal knowledge of Yahweh, and bringing forgiveness of their sins (xxxi, 31–4). Ezekiel had spoken in a similar strain, of the return to Palestine of an Israel sprinkled with water to cleanse away the old idolatrous spirit; a new heart, a heart of flesh, in place of the stony heart; and a new spirit, the Spirit of Yahweh Himself, causing them to keep His judgements and do them. So His Name, which had been profaned, should be hallowed; and His penitent people, seeing how they had profaned it, would loathe themselves in their own sight (xxxvi, 22–31). In place of the false shepherds who had misgoverned and misled His People, Yahweh Himself would be in their midst as their Shepherd, with a Davidic prince to act as ruler in His Name (xxxiv, 11 ff., 23 f.).

Thus amid the splendour of Babylon, where 'instead of the one modest temple and the recently dismantled local shrines, the newcomers saw huge seven-storied buildings dedicated to gods whose worship was conducted with a pomp and display undreamt of in Judah',[1] they came to feel no sense of inferiority. The Second Isaiah taught them to see the vanity of those splendid images, made by men, able to initiate nothing and needing to be carried because they could not go; and to fix their whole faith and hope on Yahweh, the one true God, compared with whom all the nations of men were like a drop dripping from a bucket, a just God and a Saviour, to whom at last every knee must bow, and the Lord of History, who was bringing Cyrus in to execute His purpose and let His exiles go free (xlv, 21, 23; l, 13).

Did His saving purpose include a restoration of the Davidic monarchy? Isaiah had spoken of a Shoot of the stock of Jesse who should reign in Jerusalem (xi, 1), and Jeremiah of the

[1] Lofthouse, *Israel after the Exile*, p. 4.

Righteous Branch whom Yahweh would raise up to David (xxiii, 5), and Ezekiel of His servant David who would be prince among them (xxxiv, 24); and the effort of Haggai and Zechariah was directed to the proclamation of Zerubbabel as Davidic king.[1] We do not know what was the end of this; but nothing more is heard of any such messianic claim to temporal power for four hundred years, and there is the possibility that the Syrian governor may have thought it advisable to look into the matter, and Zerubbabel have come to a violent end.[2]

But Haggai and Zechariah had a deeper motive and a higher hope than king-making. As Oesterley says, 'More effective than encouraging words is the prophecy that Haggai utters of the near approach of the Messianic time for which the Temple must be ready', and 'Zechariah (ii, 5, 10–12) contemplates the actual presence of Yahweh in the midst of his people'.[3] Here we reach the central point of the hope which formed itself in the minds of the Babylonian Jews. When once Yahweh had brought His people to true repentance for their sin, and they had paid the punishment acknowledging it to have been deserved, He would redeem them again by a second Exodus, consecrate them to Himself by a New Covenant, and bring them back in triumph to their own land, that He might set up His Kingdom over them and establish His Presence in their midst, that they might wholly be His people, and He their God.

3. The Promised Return of the Presence

The conception of the Tabernacling Presence had been a

---

[1] Haggai ii, 23, is explicit, and Zech. iv, 6 ff., indicates Zerubbabel as the leader; 1 Chron. iii, 19, mentions him as a descendant of David. See Oesterley, *History*, ii, 99–103. But in Zech. iii, 8, where 'the Branch' is being spoken of, Zerubbabel's name does not appear, while in vi, 11–13 Joshua the high priest is designated as the Branch. Oesterley thinks that this name has been substituted for that of Zerubbabel (p. 102); and these confusions in the text seem clearly to indicate that the prophet's hopes with regard to Zerubbabel were rudely disappointed by some event of which no record remains.

[2] This is mentioned as a possibility by Oesterley, p. 152 n., but he is careful not to commit himself to any definite assertion.

[3] Op. cit., pp. 83, 99.

living element in the religion of Israel from the beginning.[1]
Nathan in 2 Sam. vii, 5–6, is told by Yahweh to warn David not
to build Him a house to dwell in, because since the day that He
brought up the children of Israel out of Egypt He has walked in
a tent and a tabernacle. 'Yahweh hath said that He would dwell
in the thick darkness' seems to be an authentic utterance of
Solomon at the dedication of the Temple.[2] When 'the Ark of the
Covenant of Yahweh Zeba'oth which dwelleth between the
Cherubim' (1 Sam. iv, 4) was lost in battle, Phinehas' wife
named her child I-chabod, saying, The Glory is departed from
Israel, because the Ark of God was taken (vv. 21–2). When
Hezekiah in time of great need prays to 'Yahweh the God of
Israel that dwellest between the cherubim' (2 Kings xix, 15;
Isa. xxxvii, 16), and similar phrases are used in Ps. lxxx, 1 and
xcix, 1, the reference is the same.[3]

Amos thinks of Yahweh's Presence as localized in Jerusalem:
'Yahweh shall roar from Zion, and utter His voice from Jerusalem'. Deuteronomy regularly alludes to Jerusalem as 'the place
which Yahweh thy God shall choose to cause His Name to dwell
there', and the same phrase is used in Jer. vii, 12, of Shiloh as
the place where the Ark had once been, but which was now
desolate. When David goes in and sits before Yahweh (2 Sam.

[1] See Phythian-Adams, *The People and the Presence*, 1942, for a valuable exposition of it, besides his treatment of it in *The Call of Israel* and *The Fulness
of Israel*. Perhaps the general failure to do justice to this conception has
been the most conspicuous of all the failings of modern critical scholarship.
Marshall's statement at the beginning of an otherwise valuable article on the
Shekinah, in *H.D.B.*, vol. iv, that not only the word but the conception
originated after the close of the Hebrew Canon is an extreme statement of a
widespread misconception.

[2] 1 Kings viii, 12. See Phythian-Adams, *The People and the Presence*, p. 11,
and the references given there.

[3] See the unusually full commentary on the word *cherub* in the *Oxford Hebrew Lexicon*, pp. 500–1. This word is used in Ps. xviii, 10 = 2 Sam. xxii, 11 of
'the living chariot of the theophanic God', and in Gen. iii, 24 (J) of the guards
of the Garden of Eden. Otherwise it occurs only (but for the passages already
named) in P's description of the Tabernacle; in Kings and Chronicles of the
Cherubim of the Temple, in the accounts of its dedication; and in Ezek. i,
ix, 3, x and xi, 22 of the cherub-chariot, in xli, 18–25 in the decorations of his
ideal Temple, and in xxviii, 14, 16, where 'the king of Tyre is scornfully
compared with one of the Cherubim'. Further, 'it is probable that the
Seraphim of Isa. vi, 2–6 are another form of the cherubim'.

vii, 18), or when Deuteronomy orders that three times in the year all Israelite males are to appear before Yahweh (Deut. xvi, 16), the meaning is that they go to the place where the Tabernacling Presence is.

When finally Jerusalem is destroyed in B.C. 586 and the Ark is again taken, Ezekiel gives a 'mystical' description of the departure of the Presence, symbolized by the Cherub-chariot, from the doomed city. First It rests above the threshold of the House (ix, 3 and x, 4–5), then at the door of the east gate of the temple enclosure (x, 18–19), and then, finally departing, on the Mount of Olives (xi, 22–3), after the last sentence of judgement has been pronounced on the idolatrous city, and the promise has been made that to the exiles He will be a Sanctuary for a little while in the countries where they are gone, and that He will take the stony heart out of their flesh, and give them an heart of flesh, that they may keep His ordinances and do them (xi, 14–21).

But Ezekiel also told them that when His purpose of judgement had been accomplished, and when the Temple at Jerusalem had been rebuilt, to be the place of His dwelling, He was coming back:

'And behold, the Glory of the God of Israel came from the way of the east;

And His voice was like the sound of many waters;

And the earth shined with His glory.

And the Glory of Yahweh come into the house by the way of the gate whose prospect is toward the east. And the spirit took me up, and brought me into the inner court; and behold, the Glory of Yahweh filled the house. And I heard One speaking unto me out of the house; and a Man stood by me. And He said unto me,

Son of man, this is the place of My throne,

And the place of the soles of My feet,

Where I will dwell in the midst of the children of Israel for ever.

And the house of Israel shall no more defile My holy Name.'

(xliii, 2, 4–7.)

But all was contingent on Israel's repentance; only when the people showed signs of being 'ashamed of all that they have done' (v. 11) was he permitted to show them the form of the house and the ordinances thereof, and let them measure the pattern.

The message of the Second Isaiah begins with the announcement that Yahweh's hour has come. The exiles are to bring a message of comfort to desolated Jerusalem (Isa. xl, 1), bidding His way to be prepared in the desert; let them announce the Glad Tidings[1] of victory, that Yahweh, like a victorious King, is assuming His throne. 'The Glory of Yahweh shall be revealed, and all flesh shall see it together: for the mouth of Yahweh hath spoken it' (v. 5). Let the heralds of the Glad Tidings lift up their voice with strength, and 'say unto the cities of Judah, Behold your God' (v. 9). He is coming as a mighty one, to feed His flock like a shepherd (vv. 10–11). 'How beautiful upon the mountains are the feet of him that bringeth Good Tidings, that publisheth peace, that bringeth Good Tidings of good, that publisheth salvation; that saith unto Zion, Thy God reigneth' (lii, 7).

We see now what brought Sheshbazzar to Jerusalem in 537, and Haggai and Zechariah in 520, and what Haggai meant when he said that 'the desirable things (i.e. the offerings) of all nations shall come, and I will fill this house with Glory, saith the Lord of Hosts' (ii, 7), so that the glory (splendour) of the Temple, filled with the Presence, will surpass that of Solomon's Temple (v. 9). Similarly Zechariah sees a man with a measuring-line, come to measure Jerusalem, in view of the promised Advent:

'For I, saith Yahweh, will be unto her a wall of fire round about,
And I will be the Glory in the midst of her.'

(ii, 5.)

'Sing and rejoice, O daughter of Zion,
For lo, I come, and I will dwell in the midst of thee,
            Saith Yahweh;
And Yahweh shall inherit Judah as His portion in the holy land,
    And shall yet choose Jerusalem.

[1] For this word, besorah, see Lowther Clarke, The Divine Humanity, pp. 87–101.

Be silent, all flesh, before Yahweh:
For He is waked up out of His holy habitation.'

(ii, 10, 12, 13.)

Malachi, two generations later, had this same hope of the
advent as the motive-power of his appeal for the purging of the
temple worship from the slovenliness into which it had fallen:

'Behold, I send My messenger,
And he shall prepare the way before Me;

And Yahweh, whom ye seek, shall suddenly come to His
temple' (iii, 1); but the messenger will have to sit as a refiner
and purifier of silver, to purify the sons of Levi, if they are to
offer to Yahweh offerings in righteousness, and the Sun of
Righteousness is to arise on them with healing in His wings
(iii, 3; iv, 2).

This hope of the Advent occurs in many psalms; we shall see
in the next section that it is perhaps right to think that it is presupposed in the Priestly Code. There can be little doubt that it
fills the mind of the Chronicler, in whom what is commonly
described as his ecclesiastical interest is in part a projection of
the messianic order of things on to the history which he narrates. So, he might say to himself, it will be when the Day
dawns; so it was in the good old days, when the Presence dwelt
in the sanctuary, at least under the good kings such as Jehoshaphat, Hezekiah and above all David himself, the type of the
King that shall be. When therefore he describes the dedication
of Solomon's Temple and the coming of the Presence to take up
Its abode in the sanctuary, his mind is fixed less on the history of
seven hundred years before than on the wonderful Event in the
hope of which he lives:

'And it came to pass, when the priests were come out of the
holy place (for all the priests that were present had sanctified
themselves, and did not keep their courses; also the Levites
which were the singers, all of them . . . arrayed in fine linen,
with cymbals and psalteries and harps, stood at the east end of
the altar, and with them an hundred and twenty priests sounding with trumpets:) it came to pass, when the trumpeters and

singers were as one, to make one sound to be heard in praising and thanking the Lord; and when they lifted up their voice with the trumpets and cymbals and instruments of music, and praised the Lord, saying:

> *For He is good;*
> *For His mercy endureth for ever:*

that then the house was filled with a cloud, even the house of the Lord, so that the priests could not stand to minister by reason of the cloud; for the Glory of the Lord filled the house of the Lord' (2 Chron. v, 11–14).

It can come as something of a shock to realize that none of these men saw anything that could be called a fulfilment of their expectations. What needs to be said is said in the Epistle to the Hebrews: 'These all died in faith, not having received the promises, but having seen them and greeted them from afar, and having confessed that they were strangers and pilgrims on the earth' (Heb. xi, 13). The hope whose fulfilment was believed to be imminent by Second Isaiah, and in succeeding generations by Sheshbazzar, by Haggai and Zechariah, and later by Malachi, was disappointed, and for four centuries after Ezra there was no belief that it had been fulfilled; no one ever asserted that the Presence had returned to dwell in the Most Holy Place in the Second Temple.[1] Indeed, the rubric of the Day of Atonement that the blood of the sin-offering was to be sprinkled 'upon the mercy-seat, and before the mercy-seat', to 'make atonement for the holy place, because of the uncleannesses of the children of Israel' (Lev. xvi, 15–16), could only be intended as a purification of the Sanctuary against the time of His Coming; for it would be utterly inconceivable that after He had come, there should be a purification of the very seat of His sanctifying Presence.

But at long last men were seen in Israel, their faces radiant with joy, proclaiming that the Presence had returned. The Book of the Glad Tidings according to Mark opens with the prophecies of the Return of the Tabernacling Presence in Malachi and

---

[1] Cf. p. 234 below.

Second Isaiah,[1] and the whole New Testament rings with the announcement that He has come; and the point is formally stated in John i, 14, 'The Word was made flesh and tabernacled[2] among us, and we beheld the Glory.'

The delay of the Advent was the supreme trial of the faith of post-exilic Judaism. There is indeed a partial parallel to it in the delay of the Christian hope of the Second Advent; generation after generation through all the Christian centuries has looked for the Lord's Return. But there is a difference; for the Christian Church has had for its central article of faith that the Promise has been fulfilled; thus, while looking forward to the consummation of the divine purpose in the End of history, it has the record in the gospels of the fulfilment in history, and it has the sacrament of the Tabernacling Presence of the Lord at the altar, as the outward and visible sign and means of His indwelling in His spiritual Temple of His Body the Church.[3] But post-exilic Judaism could only look forward in hope to an Event which had not yet happened, but which when it happened would completely transform Israel's whole life. Those men died without having seen the fulfilment for which they had hoped. Many prophets and kings had desired to see those things which our Lord's disciples saw, and had not seen them; and to hear those things which they heard, and had not heard them (Luke x, 23–4). But He also spoke of 'Abraham, Isaac and Jacob and all the prophets' as 'in the Kingdom of God' (Luke xiii, 28).

4. The Priestly Document and the Pentateuch

About the time when Malachi was prophesying in Jerusalem, the Priestly Document must have been taking shape, or have

---

[1] Mark i, 2, 3. These prophecies are quoted also in Matt. xi, 10=Luke vii, 27 (cf. Luke i, 17, 76) and Matt. iii, 3=Luke iii, 4–6.

[2] ἐσκήνωσεν. 'There can be no reasonable doubt that the Greek word σκηνή (=tabernacle) was from its resemblance in sound and meaning used by bilingual Jews for the Hebrew *Shekinah*. . . . The *conception* of the Shekinah appears in Greek dress under the word δόξα' (glory)—Marshall, *H.D.B.*, iv, p. 489. This page contains an interesting but not exhaustive list of places where the conception occurs in the New Testament, and Jesus is identified with the Shekinah.

[3] John ii, 21; 1 Cor. iii, 16–17; Eph. ii, 19–22; 1 Pet. ii, 4–10.

been lately written, in Babylonia. There is no doubt of the pre-occupation of these writers with the conception of the Tabernacling Presence. We have seen earlier how in their narratives of the Wilderness-period the simple Tent of Meeting outside the camp became the splendid Tabernacle or Dwelling in the midst of the camp (Num. ii); and how in this whole description the aim of these writers is not to write what we call history, but rather to say something about the worship of the restored Temple which could be said in no other way.[1] Hosea had said that a penitent Israel would go back into the Wilderness, and there return to her first love (Hos. ii, 14–15). Now Israel was penitent, and was rebuilding its faith on the old foundations; it was longing to be able to apply to itself the words that it read in the 'Law of Holiness'; it believed that Yahweh had brought Israel out of Egypt, had set His Tabernacle among them, and His soul had not abhorred them; He had walked among them, and He had been their God, and they His People; for He was Yahweh their God, who had brought them up out of the land of Egypt, that they should not be their bondmen, and had broken the bars of their yoke, and made them go upright (Lev. xxvi, 11–13). They were longing for the return of the Tabernacling Presence as of old; and in a sense they were again in the Wilderness, looking forward to their re-possession of the Promised Land.

It is possible that this hope of the Return of the Presence can alone explain certain aspects of the Priestly Code.[2] It is hard otherwise to make sense of the terrible strictness of the order that there can be no sacrificial atonement for 'high-handed' or 'presumptuous' sins, but that if such occur the guilty soul must be cut off from Israel (Num. xv, 22–31); only sins done unwittingly are provided for. It was certainly not that these writers were

[1] P. 60 above.

[2] See Phythian-Adams, *The People and the Presence*, pp. 100–110, *The Way of At-one-ment*, pp. 27–34. I do not wish to lay any great stress on this idea, because it seems to need a more thorough demonstration, before it can be maintained that no other explanation of the facts is tenable. I mention it because it seems to throw much-needed light on this chapter (Num. xv), and to cohere with the general picture that we must form of the faith which animated the Priestly writers.

ignorant of the pertinacity and resourcefulness shown by wayward human nature in being ignorant of the rules laid down for it to keep, or wilfully transgressing them. They relate the awful example of the man who gathered sticks on the Sabbath (Num. xv, 33–6). When the Manna was given, and orders were posted about it, of course there were some who tried to keep the manna till next day, and others who went out to get some on the Sabbath, when they had plainly been told that there would be none (Exod. xvi, 19, 27). If there were no atonement for guilty faults, the camp would have become a shambles. The answer must surely be that the Priestly Code presupposes the act of God promised by Ezekiel, that when Yahweh took Israel from among the nations and brought them to their own land, He would take away the stony heart out of their flesh, and would give them a heart of flesh, and put His Spirit within them; the result would be an entire and humble readiness to walk in His ways and delight in doing His will. If *after that* any were found wilfully disobeying, it would be proof positive that such persons were no true members of the redeemed Israel, and must be cut off.[1]

It is possible to test this point by the Christian fulfilment. The new heart and the new spirit find their most perfect expression in our Lord's words, 'I thank Thee, O Father, Lord of heaven and earth that Thou hast hid these things from the wise and prudent and hast revealed them unto babes' (Matt. xi, 25= Luke x, 21); and when the Promise had been fulfilled, and the outpouring of the Spirit had taken place, this fact made necessary the awful judgement on Ananias and Sapphira in Acts v for a sin which, measured by ordinary standards, would not be counted very grave, but which, for those people living in that state of grace, was altogether deadly.

For the Jews in Babylon, the story of the Conquest of Canaan in the Book of Joshua (which, as originally edited, formed one whole with the five Books of Moses) was no mere chronicle out of the dusty past, but a living symbol or type of the task which lay before them in the immediate future. As they looked for a new Exodus and a new Covenant, so they were preparing for a new entry into the Promised Land. Once again, they stood out-

---

[1] *The People and the Presence*, p. 106.

side Palestine, and they looked forward to the day when they might cross the Jordan and their feet stand within the gates of Jerusalem. But this was to be more than a merely physical return; it was to be a re-possession not merely of the sacred sites but of Israel's ancient traditions. They had therefore to look beyond the literal meaning of the story of Joshua; a military conquest was for them out of the question. Theirs was to be a spiritual warfare, to make good Israel's spiritual inheritance; its true symbols were therefore not the shield and spear, but the sanctuary, the altar and the priesthood, prayer and sacred chant and psalm.[1]

But no less in this warfare they need to be 'strong and very courageous, to observe to do according to all the Law which Moses My servant commanded' (Joshua i, 7), and never be affrighted nor dismayed, because Yahweh is with them (i, 10). The Ark of His Covenant passes over Jordan before them (chap. iii), and the Captain of Yahweh's host, with His sword drawn in His hand, leads on to Jericho, and the signal for the fall of the city is the solemn sounding of the Trumpets (vi, 5).[2]

Such was the hope which inspired the Babylonian editors of the Hexateuch. They were not annalists, carefully collating historical traditions, but churchmen, with their faith rooted in the

[1] Here assuredly we have the key to the descriptions of military operations in the Book of Chronicles, written in the next century, which to our literal minds appear strangely unconvincing. When in 2 Chron. xiii Jeroboam is defeated by Abijah in a quite extraordinary campaign, he has first been treated to a homily in which he has been reproached for having an invalid priesthood ministering to the golden calves, whereas at Jerusalem the liturgy is correctly performed. It is not rash to assume that the true context of this is the situation in the late fourth century, when the Samaritan Temple at Gerizim had lately been built. Another similar passage is ch. xx, where Jehoshaphat goes to war, and his soldiers do not fight, but sing psalms and praise God. The writer is really thinking of another sort of warfare, which alone he understands; he knows the strength of faith and the power of prayer, but the military problems of supply and tactics do not interest him.

[2] These chapters of Joshua appear to have been put into their present shape mainly by a Deuteronomic editor, to whom, for instance, the words quoted above from i, 7 are usually assigned. But in that case they will still have been edited most probably in Babylonia. For this general interpretation of the Book of Joshua, I owe much to W. Vischer, *Das Christuszeugnis des Alten Testaments*, Bd. ii, Zürich, 1942; but some of his exegesis seems to be fanciful.

great works of God in the past, and looking with fervent hope to His action in the future.

Yet we do an injustice to the men of that age if we attribute to them no sense of history at all. To us, indeed, the treatment of the history by the authors of the Priestly Document and still more by the Chronicler seems so utterly at variance with all our notions of historical probity, that it requires very little reading between the lines of almost any modern commentary to see that the commentator feels quite out of sympathy with writers who view the history through so deeply tinted clerical spectacles. Yet the editors of the Hexateuch, in an age and country where scientific history, as we know it, did not exist, nevertheless show the sincerity of their appeal to history by the fact that they preserve in their Hexateuch old and authentic documents dating from pre-exilic times. It could scarcely have been difficult for them to have suppressed the narratives and laws in J., E. and Deuteronomy, and to have retained only the revised and up-to-date 'Priestly' versions of them. Indeed, by doing so they would have avoided a number of rather flagrant inconsistencies, as, for instance, when the old records tell of altars being erected and sacrifices offered in many other places in Palestine besides that which Yahweh chose to cause His Name to dwell there; and in the patriarchal period, though the Priestly writer himself makes no mention of any sacrifice being offered by anyone, not even Abraham, till the Law has been given to Moses and the Tabernacle set up, they incorporate into their narrative the old stories of sacrifices being offered, from Cain and Abel onwards. The reason for the preservation of the older documents can only be found in the fact that these Babylonian Jews believed that there had been a series of Events in which God had bared His arm and redeemed Israel, and therefore had a real historical conscience; it was the tradition of the Events that was authoritative, not their own notions about them. Such an act of loyalty to history was the proper corollary of their faith in a God who had revealed Himself in history.

We must further notice how they prefix to the collected traditions of Israel a preface relating the story of the chosen nation to the general history of mankind. A process of 'narrowing-down' is depicted; it is explicit in the Priestly narrative, but is implied no less in the structure of the earlier sources. Noah has three sons; but leaving Ham and Japheth on one side, we follow the story of Shem (Gen. x). 'Shem . . . begat Arpachshad two years after the flood; and Shem lived after he begat Arpachshad five hundred years, and begat sons and daughters. And Arpachshad lived five and thirty years, and begat Shelah' (xi, 10–12), and after him other sons and daughters; but we follow on with the line of Shelah, Eber, Peleg, Reu, Serug, Nahor, Terah, Abram. At this point Lot is left on one side; and then Ishmael, and then Esau. This principle is none other than what St. Paul calls the *eklogē*, the Election or Selection (Rom. ix, 7 ff.) whose ultimate purpose is that in Abraham's Seed all the nations shall be blessed and the Gentiles justified through faith (Gal. iii, 8).

In beginning thus with Adam and not with Abraham, the Priestly writers seem to show the influence of Second Isaiah's theme, that as Yahweh is the one true God, so the knowledge of Him must at last become available for all mankind. We ought not, then, to be surprised that the creation-epic in Gen. i shows affinities with Babylonian myths; we should rather have been surprised if it had not, since its primary purpose was to equip the Israelite living in surroundings where they were on everyone's lips, with a treatment of the subject which made the pagan myths look very trivial. Prominent in those myths was *Tiamat* or *Tehom*, the primaeval monster whom Marduk cut in two to make the heaven and the earth; the English versions translate it 'the Deep'. 'This Deep was of old time reckoned a thing of vast importance in the constitution of the world, and was associated with the crudest notions of mythological cosmogony. Any name for the material which goes to the making of the world would have been deficient had the *Deep* not been included. . . . So the Deep is given a place, an indifferent one, between the earth and the waters. No further mention is made of it. Let anyone read through the wearisome articles in dictionaries and commentaries about the cosmological speculations and uncouth traditions that were clamouring by prescriptive right for a place in such a story as this, and he will be impressed with the relief and spiritual enlargement bestowed by its wonderful silence which cuts off once and for all the burdensome entail.'[1] Darkness was upon the face of *Tehom*. No more need be said. The Babylonian myths, like their gods, are vanity. 'I am the Lord, and there is none else.'

The Israelites for whose benefit the creation-story was written were exiles in a strange land, surrounded by pagan influences, and needing to be armed and equipped to resist them. St. Paul's exhortation, 'Watch ye, stand fast in the faith, quit you like men, be strong' (1 Cor. xvi, 13), could have been given in Babylon five hundred years before. It was necessary that every Jew should know for himself what the faith and the vocation of Israel really were, and so take the measure of the Babylonian gods as 'the work of men's hands, wood and stone, which neither see nor hear nor eat nor smell' (Deut. iv, 28), and see that his own faith was something different in kind. 'Did ever people hear the voice of God speaking out of the midst of the fire, as thou hast heard, and live? Or hath God assayed to go and take Him a nation out of the midst of another nation, by temptations, by signs, and by wonders, and by war, and by a mighty hand, and by a stretched-out arm, according to all that Yahweh your God did for you in Egypt before your eyes? Unto thee it was showed, that thou mightest know that Yahweh He is God; there is none else beside Him' (Deut. iv, 33-5).

While then they must know how Yahweh had created the world, and know the stories of the faithful Abraham and the other patriarchs, the story of the redemption from Egypt and the Covenant was altogether central; with it went the expectation that the living God, who had so acted in the past, would in the future, perhaps very soon, provide a new Exodus, a new Covenant, and a re-possession of Canaan. They must also know the law by which their own lives was to be regulated. All that part of it which related directly to the sanctuary and its sacrifices was for the present inoperative. But they must keep the Sabbath: 'for it is a sign between Me and you throughout your generations; that ye may know that I am Yahweh which sanctify

---

[1] Coggin, *The First Story of Genesis as Literature* (Heffer, Cambridge, 1932) pp. 4-5.

you' (Exod. xxxi, 13,); and the laws of ritual purity, especially
in restricting intercourse with Gentiles: 'neither shalt thou make
marriages with them; thy daughter shalt thou not give unto his
son, nor his daughter shalt thou take unto thy son; for he will
turn away thy son from following Me, that he may serve other
gods' (Deut. vii, 3, 4).

In the last two paragraphs we have summarized the contents
of the Hexateuch. But it was necessary not merely that the books
should be written, but that they should be read and learnt; for
this purpose the Synagogue arose. No details of its origins are
known; but the meeting of the Elders of Israel in Ezekiel's house
can confidently be regarded as its prototype. It was a new thing
in the history of the world that there should be buildings in
which people assembled for religious exercises. Everywhere in
the ancient world there were sanctuaries, but the people were
never allowed inside them; they were built to house the image
or other symbol of the deity, and provide a strong room for the
offerings. The people assembled round the altar, in the open
air. When Christians go to church, the building to which they
go is still a synagogue with a pulpit and a lectern and seats;
the other essential articles of furniture are the table of the Last
Supper and something to represent the River Jordan. A syna-
gogue-building is permanently necessary where there is a
rational belief in which the people need to be instructed, and a
liturgy of the Word in which they join. The synagogue came
into existence in order that the people might hear the Scriptures
read till they knew them, in large measure, by heart. The
Scriptures needed to be collected and put in a fixed shape that
they might be thus read.

5. The Canonization of the Pentateuch

In the seventh year of Artaxerxes (the second), Ezra, who was
'a ready scribe in the Law of Moses' (Ezra vii, 6), went up from
Babylon, and 'on the first day of the fifth month came he to
Jerusalem, according to the good hand of his God upon him.
For Ezra had set his heart to seek the law of Yahweh and to do
it, and to teach in Israel statutes and judgements' (vv. 9, 10).

The Canon of the Law

The work that lay before him there was first to carry out a purge of the heathen marriages which many at Jerusalem had contracted (chaps. ix, x), and then to promulgate the Law. This is described in Neh. vii, 73–x. 'And they spake unto Ezra the scribe to bring the book of the Law of Moses, which Yahweh had commanded to Israel' (viii, 1).

It is first to be observed that the scene is modelled on a synagogue meeting. There is the raised pulpit, or tower, of wood; the reading out of the law-book, at the request of the people (v. 1); the people meanwhile stand (v. 5); there is the blessing of God and the Amen (v. 6), and afterwards the exposition of the Law, which is the origin of the Targum (v. 8).[1] The law-book was the Pentateuch, as Dr. Oesterley shows: 'When it is said in Neh. viii, 3: "And he read therein from early morning until midday", and again in v. 8: "And they read in the book, in the law of God . . ." there is nothing to show that any book *as a whole* was read. We are therefore led to the conclusion that what was read consisted of extracts from the Pentateuch, in the form which it had assumed by this time, and that those extracts were portions which were generally applicable to all the people, and that these portions were among those which had been added during the Exile. . . . If this theory of the reading of the Law is in any degree correct, it will be seen how important the work of Ezra was; for he was the first to bring the fulness of the Judaism of Babylonian Jewry to Palestine.'[2]

Some three weeks later, according to Neh. ix, 1, they were ready to make the Covenant. In it they undertook to 'walk in God's Law, which was given by Moses the servant of God, and to observe and do all the commandments of Yahweh our God, and His judgements and His statutes'; to guard their racial purity; and to keep the Sabbath, refusing to trade even with non-Jews on that day, and the Sabbatical Year, by remission of

---

[1] Oesterley, *History of Israel*, ii, p. 137 f. See the whole passage, pp. 128–39, on Ezra and his work.

[2] Ibid., pp. 136–7. The decisive proof that it was the Pentateuch and not the Priestly Code that was then accepted, seems to be that this alone will explain how the Book of Joshua came to be detached from the other five. It was on the Books of Moses that the Covenant needed to be based (Neh. viii, 1; x, 29).

debts (x, 29–31). Other arrangements follow, for the carrying on of the temple service. The whole is preceded by the magnificent eucharistic prayer, which according to the *LXX* is chanted by Ezra *solo*, but in the Hebrew text by eight Levites in unison. It is a classical statement of the mighty acts of God: possibly the noblest liturgical formula to be found in the Old Testament. First God is praised for His own great glory, and for the creation of heaven and earth.[1] Then commemoration is made of the call of Abraham; of the deliverance from bondage in Egypt with mighty signs and wonders, and the giving of the Law on Mount Sinai, the Sabbath being specially mentioned; of the gift of the manna, and the command to enter into the promised land (ix, vv. 7–15). Then they recall the disobedience of Israel in the wilderness, and in spite of this the divine mercy, forgiving their sin, and giving them the pillar of cloud and fire, and the Spirit, and the manna, and the water for their thirst, and victory over Sihon and Og, and multiplying them, and bringing them into Canaan and subduing the land before them (vv. 16–25). Yet again in Canaan they were disobedient, and forsook the law and slew the prophets; many times they sinned, but when they called upon their God, He sent them saviours to deliver them; they sinned again, but in His mercy He did not make a full end with them, nor forsake them, 'for Thou art a gracious and merciful God' (vv. 26–31). So at last we come to the petition which is made on the ground of these His continued acts of mercy; 'Let not all the travail seem little before Thee, that hath come on us . . . since the times of the kings of Assyria unto this day'; for the punishment was all most justly deserved, and in consequence they are subject to foreign rulers to whom they pay tribute. 'And yet for all this we make a sure covenant, and write it; and our princes, our Levites, and our priests, seal unto it' (vv. 32–8).

So another Covenant was made; like the Covenant of Deuteronomy, a great reaffirmation of the Faith of Israel, and like it, involving the acceptance of a Book containing history and ex-

---

[1] Here, at the end of v. 6, the *Sanctus* could have followed, as in the Christian eucharistic prayers which follow this model. Dom Gregory Dix in *The Parish Communion* (ed. Hebert, 1937), p. 120.

hortation as well as law. The Israel which confesses its faith is now a penitent Israel, chastened by suffering, but nevertheless looking forward in hope to God's future action, when He shall come to establish His Kingdom and make Israel to be wholly His people, and He be their God. From this time onwards the Book of the Law is fully canonical. But whereas Deuteronomy had been imposed by a believing king and the prophetic party on a nation which was only half prepared to receive it, the Pentateuch was accepted whole-heartedly by a far larger body of the faithful, without any coercion from the civil power. In far larger measure now we see the shape of 'the Church' beginning to emerge: that is, a spiritual society constituted as such by faith in the unseen God.

CHAPTER VI

THE COMPLETION OF THE CANON

1. The Law and the Prophets

The work of Ezra marked an epoch in the history both to the Israelite nation and of the Canon of Scripture. It was not without reason that later tradition assigned to him a central place in the formation of the canon, and that legends gathered round his name. From his day onwards Israel was in the full sense the people of the Law, and possessed a fully authoritative Sacred Book.

The Church, in accepting the Old Testament as inspired and authoritative, thereby accepts and endorses the work, first of the Priestly editors of the Pentateuch, and then of Ezra who saw it acknowledged as Scripture. Yet at this point many Christians have not unnatural misgivings. The high ideal and the ultimate failure of the reformed Judaism are well stated in the following quotation:[1]

'Thus the walls, both material and disciplinary, are rebuilt higher and stronger, in order to keep the heathen out and the holy people in. It was hoped that so, at last, the people of whom God had said, "Out of Egypt have I called My son", would be realized in history—actualized—and found worthy to inherit the blessing promised to Abraham's seed; and it was just this highly orthodox reformed community which crucified God's Son when He came.'

The problem is this. The promulgation of the Pentateuch and the reform associated with it bound Israel to a certain exclusiveness with regard to its heathen neighbours. Nehemiah waged his conflict with Sanballat, Tobiah and Geshem, and both he and

[1] From a set of lecture notes in use at Kelham.

The Completion of the Canon

Ezra carried out 'purges', to stop the intermarriage of Jews with pagans. The first of the series may have been that which is described in Neh. xiii, 23, of marriages with women of Ashdod, Ammon and Moab. A big purge was carried out by Ezra, and is described in Ezra ix–x; it may be this that is summarized in Neh. xiii, 1–3, and it seems to be alluded to in the narrative of the Reform itself, Neh. ix, 2, and mentioned in the actual text of the Covenant, x, 30. In these passages appeal is made to Deut. vii, 3, where intermarriage with the Canaanites is forbidden, to Deut xxiii, 3–6, where it is said that the Ammonite and the Moabite are not to enter into the Assembly of Yahweh to the tenth generation, and also to the evil example of Solomon, 1 Kings xi, 1 ff. On the other hand, in Second Isaiah, Zechariah, Ruth, Jonah, several of the Psalms, and elsewhere, we find a very generous attitude towards the people of other nations, as for instance where the Servant of Yahweh is to be a light of the Gentiles (Isa. xlii, 6; xlix, 6), or where the House of Yahweh is to be a house of prayer for all people, and the 'stranger' will be joyful in it, praying and offering sacrifice (Isa. lvi, 6–8).

The modern Christian sympathizes naturally with the latter of these two attitudes, with what is called the 'universalism' of the prophetic writers as contrasted with the 'particularism' or 'nationalism' of the priestly reformers. It is easy for him to see in Ezra and his party the line which led to the unattractive rigorism of the Pharisees, and in the other attitude the generous spirit of our Lord and His apostles. Consequently in one writer after another it is suggested or openly stated that the Reform of Ezra was really a false step, the deliberate acceptance of a lower ideal and the rejection of a higher. But here we come to the central point of difficulty: it is that with Ezra's reform is associated the acceptance of the Pentateuch, which was the first and chief instalment of the Old Testament. To regret or to disparage Ezra's reform is to cast doubt on the rightness of the acceptance of the Pentateuch as canonical.

Here is a tangle to unravel. There are three points which need to be considered before we attack it directly. First, there is the degree of authority which the Church attaches to the Old Testament and to the Pentateuch in particular, when it accepts

The Law and the Prophets

it as canonical; for there is a sense in which the Old Testament is superseded by the New, and the Law by Grace. In the gospels our Lord is stated to have explicitly criticized the Old Testament at certain points; and in the New Testament as a whole, Justification is proclaimed to be through faith and not by the works of the law, the permission for divorce is withdrawn, the Jewish Sabbath and ritual uncleanness and animal sacrifice all pass away, and the Israel of God opens its doors to converts from all nations.[1] But in each case the law and the prophets are not destroyed but fulfilled; in each case the positive principle which the New Testament proclaims has been fully stated in the Old Testament. Nor is it that our Lord rejects the ceremonial law and reaffirms the moral law, nor that He rejects the law and acknowledges the prophets. On the contrary, He finds the moral law also to be incomplete, and therefore reinterprets the Decalogue as well as providing a new rite to take the place of the animal sacrifices; and He is explicit in affirming that it is both Law and Prophets that He has come to fulfil.

In such a question as this all Christians regard the authority of our Lord and the Apostles as primary; and the guidance that we are given on such a question as the judgement to be pronounced on the work of Ezra seems to be this. We are not expected, indeed we are not allowed, to treat the Jewish Law as the final answer to the problem, since it is not the final word of God; we must expect to find a certain imperfection and incompleteness in it. But we must expect to be able to see that the answer then given was relatively right, a step in the right direction and not a false step. Salvation was from the Jews: Jerusalem and not Gerizim lay in the line of the true Tradition of the Faith, pointing on to a fulfilment of sacrificial worship in which both Jew and Samaritan should at last come to worship the Father in spirit and in truth (John iv, 22–4).

Second: this question is specially difficult for us because our own controversies are tangled up in it. It is necessary for the Biblical student not only to criticize the Scriptures, but to be

---

[1] These six points form the basis of the study of the relation between the Old Testament and its fulfilment which I have given in *The Throne of David* (1941). See also pp. 200 f. below.

critical also of his own habitual ways of speaking and thinking; and this applies all round. Thus, on the one side, it is very easy for the pastor and preacher, and not least the Catholic, convinced of the importance of institutional religion, to work with all his might to build the walls higher and stronger to keep 'secular' influences out and keep the holy people in; to concentrate on 'the righteous remnant' and those whom the Bible calls 'the poor', and forget the warnings of the Bible about the danger of a self-centred religiousness, and the prophetic insistence on the universality of the Gospel. On the other side, it is no less easy to interpret the Old Testament prophet and priest in the light partly of the Reformation controversies, and partly of that modern Protestantism which equates 'spiritual' with 'non-sacramental'; or again, the prophets can be understood too simply in the light of some modern ideal.[1] In the present instance 'particularism' can readily suggest in our minds the fierce nationalism which has been characteristic of most European nations in recent years, and 'universalism' the international concord for which we all long. But the truly critical mind is that which is active in self-criticism. It is not, indeed, that we should seek a true and objective understanding of the Bible by eliminating all consideration of the modern questions on which it throws light; to do so is to cut off the living sympathy without which there can be no right understanding of it, while not escaping, even so, from the influence of unconscious prejudices and presuppositions. The better way is to be as fully aware as possible of the modern parallels, and at the same time to cultivate a spirit of self-criticism with regard to them and so to be able to seek guidance from the Bible in dealing with them.

Third: part of the difficulty of the particular problem of which we are thinking arises from the defectiveness of the historical evidence. It is highly important, for a right understanding of the prophets, to know at least approximately the situation in which they wrote; the Book of Jonah is completely misunder-

[1] There is a bad instance of this in a modern missionary hymn (*English Hymnal*, 548), where the text 'the earth shall be filled with the knowledge of the Lord,' Isa. xi, 10 (or 'with the knowledge of the glory of the Lord', Hab. ii, 14), is first misquoted and then applied to modern world-wide missions to the exclusion of any other reference.

stood by those who think it to be the life-story of the son of Amittai who lived about 770 B.C.

But all the prophecies of the period are anonymous, except those of Haggai and Zechariah, and the only historical books, those of Ezra and Nehemiah, have been left in confusion by the Chronicler's editing. It would make a great difference if we only knew the contexts and occasions of the last eleven chapters of Isaiah, or the exact situation that called out the Book of Jonah; above all, if we knew more about the antagonism between Jerusalem and Samaria which led in the end to the schism. But here it seems to be impossible to determine with any certainty how far the Chronicler, for whom antagonism towards northern Israel is a chief preoccupation, has projected into the events of 537 and 520–16 the situation of 200 years later. When the Samaritans went into schism, perhaps 335 B.C., they took with them the completed Pentateuch, and therefore cannot have wholly rejected Ezra's reform; on the other hand, the fact that they went into schism means presumably that it was over them that the issue of Jewish exclusiveness was fought out. It seems inevitable, in the nature of the case, that there should have been suspicion and bad feeling between Jerusalem and Samaria ever since the Babylonian Jews had begun to return to Palestine. But it is impossible, owing to the defectiveness of the evidence, that such a suggestion as that of L. E. Browne in *Early Judaism* (1920) that Isa. lxiii, 7–lxiv, is the work of a Samaritan prophet, should be more than a conjecture. We have, then, as our authorities, a series of texts at whose context we cannot do more than make guesses on the basis of the internal evidence.

Yet in its broad lines the situation is plain enough. In the texts we have set out before us the two tendencies, commonly labelled, or mis-labelled, particularist and universalist. Our first question should be, whether Second Isaiah really belongs to the second of these, or should be regarded as the father of them both. The former position is taken by Prof. T. W. Manson, when he says that 'from the time when the Servant Songs were composed, there were two ideals of the Remnant. The one ideal, that of a Remnant that saves by self-sacrifice and suffering, is embodied in the Servant of Jehovah and in the figure of the Son

The Completion of the Canon

of Man in the teaching of Jesus. The other ideal, that of a saved Remnant, is embodied in Ezekiel's vision of the restored Israel and finds its issue in Pharisaism.'[1] Here Second Isaiah and Ezekiel are assigned to opposite sides; and certainly Ezekiel has nothing to say of any hope of salvation for the Gentiles. But if we apply another test we get a different result. Both prophets agree on certain other points of cardinal importance, notably the hope of the Return of the Presence of Yahweh, and that the Babylonian Jews are to go to Jerusalem for it; and this demands the re-building of the Temple and the re-constituting of the worship there. Second Isaiah therefore, when he puts into the forefront the Return to Jerusalem, is the inspirer not only of Zechariah, who indeed shows plain traces of his influence, not least in his 'universalism',[2] but also mediately of Nehemiah and Ezra.

Further, the ground on which his 'universalism' rests is his deep realization of the uniqueness of Yahweh. Bel, Nebo and the rest are unreal, less than nothing, vanity, powerless to do anything good or evil, having no existence outside the minds of the men who created them. Yahweh is the true God, the only God, the maker of the ends of the earth; and He who in the beginning made all men must at the last be known by all men:

> '*Look unto Me and be ye saved, all the ends of the earth,*
> *For I am God, and there is none else.*
> *By myself have I sworn,*
> *The word is gone forth from My mouth in righteousness,*
> *And shall not return,*
> *That unto Me every knee shall bow,*
> *Every tongue shall swear.*'

(xlv, 22–3.)

But He of whom these things are said is the God of Israel; hence the prophet says, two verses later:

> '*In Yahweh shall all the seed of Israel be justified,*
> *And shall glory*' (v. 25).

Faith in Yahweh as the national God of Israel rings through the

---

[1] *The Teaching of Jesus*, 1935, pp. 230–1.
[2] Zech. i, 17; ii, 11; viii, 20–3.

whole prophecy from beginning to end; the paradox is, that this particularist faith in Yahweh as the national God leads on of necessity, through the demonstration that He is the real and the true God, and so stands in an utterly different class from all other objects of worship, to the certainty that at last He must be known to all men.

We can then say quite confidently by what road the prophet has reached his 'universalism': not through any calculation of the possibilities of an evangelistic campaign, but from the other end, by meditation, adoration, intercession. Second Isaiah is a seer on a mountain-top, pondering on the counsels of God, and taking long views of His purpose. The same applies to the Servant-poems, whether they were written by him or by another, and whether he meant them to apply to some particular Israelite, or to the ideal Israelite, or to Israel as a whole, or to the ideal Israel, or to One who should come;[1] for the essence of these poems consists in that which they say, in the picture which they draw. A pattern is there set forth of faithful love and service to Israel and to Gentiles, and of suffering which turns out to be redemptive and sacrificial. How, or in whom, it should find its historical fulfilment, may have mattered to the prophet relatively little; it was, in any case, not his concern. The thing that did matter was that this was the true pattern. If it was true and according to the mind of God, God would fulfil it in His own time.

Much the same applies to other classical statements of the hope of the salvation of the Gentiles. Ps. cii dates itself as exilic, for Jerusalem is in ruins: 'Thy servants think upon her stones' (v. 14). But the very fact that they are grieved that she is in the dust indicates that it is Yahweh's will to build up Zion and appear in His glory; if these thoughts are in their minds, it is He who has put them there. Then the nations shall fear His Name; then a People shall be created which shall praise Him, the prisoner shall be released, those going down to death shall find mercy; men will declare the Name of Yahweh in Zion and His worship at Jerusalem, when the nations and the kingdoms

[1] Cf. Dr. Oesterley in Oesterley and Robinson, *Hebrew Religion* (1930), pp. 265–70.

are gathered to serve Him (vv. 16–22). Here, then, we have fundamentally the same scheme of things as in Second Isaiah: the restoration of desolate Jerusalem, the Return of the Presence, the glorifying of Yahweh's Name, and the coming of the nations to join in His worship. Some prophets and psalmists think that when the Day of Yahweh comes, and His sentence of judgement on Jerusalem is finally reversed, it will be the privilege of the Gentiles to convey the exiles back thither, to build the walls for them, and to bring costly presents; others, more sensitive, are not content that the Gentiles should merely behold, as from a respectful distance, the Glory of Yahweh, but should themselves come to seek *torah* at Jerusalem, and to pray and offer sacrifice.[1]

But these are visions of the future, and acts of supplication to God for the coming of His Kingdom. We had best then ask what possible course of action there was for a prophet seeking to give effect to his message. The first duty before him would be to bring the Israelite people themselves to a better understanding of their glorious faith and their high vocation. In Second Isaiah's day the pastoral work of the Scribes was only at its beginning. Ezra, 150 years later, could rely on the support of a strong and compact community; Second Isaiah reproached them for the faintness of their faith:

> '*Hear, ye deaf:*
> *And look, ye blind, that ye may see.*
> *Who is blind, but My servant?*
>   *Or deaf, as My messenger that I send?*
> *Who is blind as he that is at peace with Me,*
>   *And blind, as Yahweh's servant?*
> *Thou seest many things, but thou observest not;*
> *His ears are open, but he heareth not.*
> *It pleased Yahweh, for His righteousness' sake,*
> *To make the teaching great and glorious.*
> *But this is a people robbed and spoiled. . . .*'
>   (Isa. xlii, 18–22, R.V., mg.)[2]

[1] See e.g. for the first, Isa. lx; Ps. lxxii; and for the second, Isa. ii, 3–4; xlii, 1–4; lxvi, 21–3.

[2] Other similar passages are xl, 27; xliii, 8, 22 ff.; xlvi, 12; xlviii, 1–8; xlix, 14; l, 1; li, 12.

It would be the pastor's duty not only to teach them at the synagogue-meeting the vanity of the heathen gods, but to bring back those who showed signs of lapsing from their religion and of marrying Babylonian girls. Here he could appeal to the authoritative Book of Deuteronomy, which prohibited such intermarriage. Only so could the exiles be built together into a strong and compact community. Yet in spite of Second Isaiah's dissatisfaction with them, it is plain that there was sufficient faith among them to make it possible for him to call on them to pack up and undertake the journey to Jerusalem.

But if the prophet was certain that somehow and at some time the Faith must go to the Gentiles, it was less easy to see what could immediately be done. Should one speak about the God of Israel to the Babylonian family living next door, and if so, what should one say? It might be possible to break down their polytheistic belief; but might not the conclusion of the argument seem to them to be that Bel was the only God? It would be hard to make them see that the God of another nation, and a conquered and subject nation at that, could mean anything to them. If they did—if the immense difficulties of this catechetical process were overcome, and the result were that the convert was not exchanging one superstition for another, but was really learning the amazing truth that the Father of all the gods had adopted small and despised Israel as His chosen people, and then had allowed His own city to be destroyed and His people enslaved that they might learn to know Him truly—if the Babylonian family had begun to see what all this meant, what then was the next step? They must be adopted into Yahweh's nation, be circumcised, become proselytes. That was possible, even in those early days in Babylonia; and there is evidence that proselytes were being actually received at Jerusalem within a century after this, in Isa. lvi, 6–8, a prophecy which presupposes the restoration of the Temple, and presumably falls between 520 B.C. and 444. There the 'strangers, that join themselves to Yahweh, to minister unto Him, and to love the Name of Yahweh', and who keep the Sabbath and observe the Covenant, are promised that they shall have access to the Temple, and offer there acceptable burnt-offerings and sacrifices, so that the Temple will become a house of prayer for all nations, and the centre of unity for the gathering-together not only of the exiled Israelites, but of other nations also.

But the gathering in of proselytes could scarcely happen on any but the most minute scale while the Jewish Church was outwardly so insignificant as it was in Babylonia, and when the Temple was not yet restored. In any case, the difficulty of bringing the converts to a right understanding of the Faith was in fact so immense, that it would seem almost inevitable that the hope of their conversion should be postponed to the day when the Glory of Yahweh should be revealed, when all sorts of things would become possible that now were impossible; and to that day we know that Second Isaiah looked forward. Zechariah, his disciple makes the connection explicit:

> *'Sing and rejoice, O daughter of Zion:*
> *For lo, I come, and I will dwell in the midst of thee,*
> > *Saith Yahweh.*
> *And many nations shall join themselves unto Yahweh in that day,*
> > *And shall be My people;*
> *And I will dwell in the midst of thee.'*

(ii, 10–11.)

The immediate duty of the exiles was to return to Jerusalem in readiness for Yahweh's Return; for there could be no doubt that Jerusalem was the appointed place for His future action. One band after another of Babylonian Jews returned thither; and increasingly as Babylonian Jewry grew in strength and compactness, the returned exiles must have contrasted with the 'people of the land' much as Caesar's trained and disciplined soldiers contrasted with the unruly tribesmen of Gaul and Britain. The 'people of the land', the remains of the pre-exilic population, were carrying on in the old casual way, serving Yahweh and pouring out drink-offerings also to the Queen of Heaven, and seeing no harm in marrying women of the neighbouring tribes and going with them to their ancestral religious rites. We know from the Elephantine papyri what degree of polytheism, and how purely pagan an outlook, were possible to Jews who still regarded themselves as worshippers of Yahweh.

It is not suggested that the Jews of Jerusalem had sunk to that level; but they were far below the standard of the Babylonian Jews who now came among them: men whose deepest conviction it was that for *this* sin above all, the sin of forsaking Yahweh and going after strange gods, Israel had suffered its appalling punishment, and that all possible hope for the future was conditional on renouncing idolatrous worships and cleaving steadfastly to Yahweh alone. They were men who took their faith seriously, knew by heart their laws and sacred narratives, their prophecies and psalms, and already perhaps observed the rule of prayer to God three times a day.[1]

It is easy to see what attitude these men would feel compelled to take towards marriages with women of Ashdod or Moab, and how sincere might be the penitence of returned exiles who had lapsed from the higher standard which they had previously known, when Ezra's return recalled them to it; for in the account of Ezra's purge it becomes plain that it was 'they of the captivity' (x, 6), including priests and Levites, and princes and rulers (ix, 1, 2), who had been 'chief in this trespass'.

It is easy to see also, how suspicious the Samaritans would naturally be when Nehemiah repaired the walls of Jerusalem, thus giving the city a certain municipal independence, and enabling him to shut the gates against them (Neh. xiii, 19), in order that he might have the Sabbath observed properly. 'The Jews must be socially and municipally secure (they could not of course be politically independent) if they were to be religiously untainted. Nehemiah therefore began work at once upon the city walls. The Samaritans understood him from the first. They were as resolved as their grandfathers to have no Deuteronomic Jerusalem on their borders.'[2]

We ought then to expect that our disciples of Second Isaiah would be found insisting that the walls, both material and disci-

[1] Ps. lv, 17; Dan. vi, 10. The acrostic psalms, such as xxv, in which the couplets or strophes begin with the letters of the alphabet in order, were, of course, so written in order to assist the memory.

[2] Lofthouse, *Israel after the Exile*, 1928, p. 235. For further comments on the further course of Samaria's relations with Jerusalem, and how they accepted in the end the Deuteronomic law of the single sanctuary, but regarded Gerizim and not Zion as the place which Yahweh had chosen, see p. 237.

plinary, be made higher and stronger, not indeed to keep the heathen out, but to keep the holy people themselves in such a spiritual condition that their light might shine before men. At all costs Israel must be saved from falling back into a syncretistic religion that was pagan at heart. It must guard its faith in Yahweh as the one true God and as the God of Israel. The choice had to be made between a strictness which guarded the purity of Israel's faith by keeping Gentiles at arm's length, and a laxity which would have surrendered the whole essence of that faith and the lessons painfully learnt in the Exile. The time was indeed to come when Jew and Gentile should become 'one Man in Christ Jesus', without any loss of the integrity of the Faith. But only His coming would make that possible; and meanwhile it is impossible seriously to question the relative rightness of the choice which Nehemiah and Ezra made, in spite of the spiritual dangers to which they and their followers were thereby exposed.

To us it is an extremely familiar truth that no building up of an institutional system can protect the heart of man from the tempter who attacks from within; we at least have no excuse for thinking that the provision of these external safeguards is all that is necessary. But in post-exilic Judaism these things were being done for the first time. They had yet to find out by experience how possible it is for human pride to make capital out of spiritual privilege, to delight in exercizing discipline over one's own life in order to seek praise for it, and over others in order to have the satisfaction of exerting power, and to make the ecclesiastical system an end in itself and not a means for its true end which is the glory of God.

It was one thing, however, to try to guard the Israelite people from the bad influence of paganism, and another to adopt towards all pagans an attitude of aloofness and contempt. Something like this must have been the attitude at which the author of the Book of Jonah aimed his biting sarcasm; and it is most important to notice that in this book Jonah is represented as fully aware all the time that Yahweh is full of mercy and compassion, however distasteful that fact is to him, and fully aware also of his own duty towards the pagans, even when he is actively engaged in running away from it. Similarly the Book of

Ruth, with its sympathetic delineation of the love and loyalty of the Moabite girl, and the unexpected sting at the end, that this foreign woman was the ancestress of the great David himself, must have been written (or re-written) in order to criticize those who were fond of quoting the anti-Moabite law of Deut. xxiii.

These two instances, both later than Nehemiah, of the 'universalist' attitude of mind, stand in the national literature side by side with those which expressed the need for the unique vocation of Israel to be guarded by a certain exclusiveness. It was further possible to appeal to the canonical writings in support of the 'universalist' view. Second Isaiah's prophecy and the other prophecies and psalms which spoke of Israel's universal mission, can hardly yet have become 'scripture'. Yet there was in the Book of Genesis the Promise to Abraham, that in his seed all the nations should be blessed. These texts could be understood in two ways: either that in Abraham's seed all the nations would receive divine blessing, or that they would 'bless themselves by Abraham', desiring for themselves that they might be as happy as he.[1] The latter is likely to have been the meaning of the original eighth-century writer. But we are concerned now with the meaning as understood in post-exilic times; and here we have the fact that the Septuagint translators give the rendering familiar to us. It was, then, in the post-exilic period at least, possible for the text to be understood as declaring 'that the blessings of which Israel is to become the organ and channel are to be communicated ultimately to the world'; while even the second rendering meant that these same blessings 'would attract the regard of all peoples, and awaken in them the longing to participate in them'.[2]

Here then we have two truths, that Israel was called to a

---

[1] The first rendering, which is that of the English versions, follows the natural meaning of the *niphal* form which occurs in three of the five statements of the promise—in Gen. xii, 3; xviii, 18; and xxviii, 14; but the *hithpael* form which comes in the other two, xxii, 18 and xxvi, 4, must be construed in the second sense. 'Most modern scholars consider that the two passages of which the sense is clear should determine the sense of the three in which the sense is ambiguous'; for the *niphal* 'may have either a reflexive or a passive sense' (Driver, *Genesis*, p. 145).

[2] Driver, Ibid.

position of special privilege and was bound to guard its integrity by maintaining its exclusiveness, and that the blessing thus given to Israel was held by it in trust for all nations; and we have the further fact that Judaism was not in a position to reconcile them. It had a mission to all nations, but was prevented from carrying out that mission by the fact that it was itself one of the nations, and could only evangelize the Gentiles by detaching them from their own traditions and incorporating them into its own; it could not bring Gentile and Jew into unity, because it could only require the Greek to cease to be a Greek and become a Jew. Further, its law was a Jewish law; and while the Gentile could be, and was, attracted by the godliness of the faithful Jews by their faith in one God, by their intelligent worship, by much that he could read in the Books of Moses, and most of all, possibly, by the figure of the Servant of Yahweh, the Law was the framework round which the Jewish national life was built; the Servant, too, was an ideal figure, not to be found anywhere in concrete reality. Only when the Servant had actually appeared in the flesh, and the righteousness of God had been manifested not in the precepts of the Law but in His Person, could the dilemma be resolved and the door be opened for all nations to enter within Israel. 'He is our Peace, who hath made both one'; the Person of the Messiah was to be the centre round which Jew and Gentile could be gathered together in unity. So and only so could the two truths be reconciled, and the Israel of the New Covenant at once maintain its integrity and in a sense even its exclusiveness, and fulfil its mission to all mankind.

Thus the reform of Ezra failed and was bound to fail in carrying out the fulness of Israel's mission; it could not carry out the duty laid on it by Second Isaiah. The time for that was not yet come. Yet we cannot rightly say that it took a false turning, or rejected a higher way; we are bound to acknowledge it to have been relatively right in guarding the uniqueness of Israel's vocation, and saving the spiritual life of Israel from pagan contamination. It was further right in imposing on Israel the discipline of Law. It was necessary for Israel to be drilled and disciplined in that daily waiting on God, of which the perfect fruit is the 119th psalm. Law and rule were necessary to the Jew,

The Law and the Prophets

because they are permanently necessary. The demand made on a man by such a rule continually reminds him of his duty of obedience to the will of Another, and stirs him up to learn in daily life what that will is. There is always the danger of scrupulosity; yet even so, discipline is better than indiscipline, and conscientiousness than laxity.

But a further discipline was necessary; the discipline of failure. Man had to learn that the most thorough obedience to a legal code could not finally bring him justification and peace with God,[1] because it could not save him from self-righteousness. Through the Law came the knowledge of sin, not only because it is humanly impossible to keep all the precepts of a Law without tripping up somewhere, but for the deeper reason that it cannot save man from the sin of pride; he who has kept the whole law cannot escape in the last resort from taking credit for the fact, and comparing his own virtue with the failure of the unfortunates who do not reach that level of attainment. Only when the Righteousness of God has been embodied in a Person and when Justification is offered, not through personal merit but through His Mercy, can saint and sinner alike come to peace with God. God hath concluded all under sin, that He might have mercy upon all.

Ezra's reform had to end in failure; and one sign of its failure is that it caused the Book of Ecclesiastes to be written.[2] It is also possible, from this point, to see why the sanguine hopes of the fifth century that the Reform might be crowned with the Return of the Presence of Yahweh to dwell among His people, had for the time being to be disappointed. There had to be the Law, and there had to be the experience of the failure of the Law, before Salvation could come.

[1] One of the two chief words translated 'perfect' is the word *shālem*, 'at peace with' God, as in 1 Kings xv, 14: 'the heart of Asa was perfect with Yahweh all his days.'

[2] Cf. p.105 above. The Book of Job is commonly assigned to the period before Ezra; but is it not possible that its true date is the fourth or even the third century, since the point at which we have now arrived appears to give us its true context in the spiritual history?

The Completion of the Canon

2. The Canonization of the Prophets

At some time subsequent to Ezra the books of Joshua, Judges,
Samuel and Kings, and those of Isaiah, Jeremiah, Ezekiel and
the Twelve Prophets were added to the Law, not indeed as
standing precisely on a level with it, but yet so that it became
possible to speak of 'the Law and the Prophets' as the description of Holy Scripture. This phrase is used several times in the
New Testament,[1] where indeed it denotes the whole Old Testament, and not only its first two parts; but it occurs first in the
preface to the Greek *Ecclesiasticus*, written by Ben-Sira's grandson about 131 B.C., and proves that he regarded the Prophets as
Scripture. The same is made probable for the writer of Daniel,
one generation earlier, by his statement that he 'understood by
the books the number of the years whereof the word of Yahweh
came to Jeremiah the prophet' (ix, 2); clearly the Book of
Jeremiah is part of a collection. There can be no doubt that the
same is true of Ben-Sira himself, who in his panegyric on the
saints of Israel in Ecclus. xliv–l follows the narrative in the books
of the 'earlier prophets' from Judges to Kings (his mention of
Elijah and Elisha showing that he is using Kings, not Chronicles), and then names in order Isaiah (where the words
'he comfort ed them that mourn in Zion' show that Second
Isaiah form ed part of the book), Jeremiah, Ezekiel and the
Twelve.

The earlier limit for the canonization of the prophetical books
must be placed after the time when the latest of the prophecies
were written, early in the Greek period, and after the time when
the Samaritans went into schism, taking with them only the
Pentateuch, probably about 335 B.C.; the lower limit is the date
of Ben-Sira, about 200. As there is no tradition of any public
act by which the Prophets were accepted as canonical, it seems
safe to say that the process of their acceptance was gradual; and
that is almost as much as to say that the liturgical tradition of the

---

[1] Matt. v, 17; vii, 12; Luke xvi, 16, 29, 31; Acts xiii, 15; cf. the Law, the
Prophets and the Psalms. Luke xxiv, 44.

Synagogue had much to do with the canonization, and that it was through being read as lessons that these books won general recognition as Scripture. That in New Testament times a prophetic lesson was read is clear from Luke iv, 17 ff., and from the allusion in Acts xiii, 15, to the two lessons from the Law and the Prophets, and in v. 27 to 'the voices of the prophets that are read every Sabbath day', besides the lesson from the Law, Acts xv, 21.

But our chief concern at present is to see whether the canonization of the Prophets introduced any change in the conception of the meaning of Scripture; notably whether it was now that idea of inspiration first came to be understood as involving inerrancy. The prophets spoke words in God's Name; when their writings came to be regarded as Scripture, side by side with the Law, was it now for the first time that men came to think of the words of Scripture, not merely as authoritative in a general sense, but as the exact expression of truth as from God's own mouth? We shall best approach this question by considering the most important instances of the use of the prophets' writings by later generations, and the predisposing conditions which existed towards the ultimate recognition of the Prophets as canonical Scripture.

The Pentateuch, as we have seen, consisted essentially of the story of the Redemption and the Covenant on which Israel's existence was based, and the Law which Israel was pledged to observe. It therefore held a primacy which it has always retained in Jewish tradition. No subsequent additions to the canon could be on the same level; the Israelite could not be pledged to prophecies or to psalms, as he was pledged to the fundamental rule of Israel's belief and practice. But the Pentateuch also contained a long introduction, consisting of the pre-history of the Patriarchs, with the story of the creation of the world and of mankind as a preface to that; and this might seem to invite and almost to demand the continuation of the history after Moses. Not only had the Book of Joshua originally formed one whole with the Pentateuch so that it might retail a quasi-canonical character; but also the continuation of the story led on to David, and his name connected itself with the Messianic hopes of the future.[1] It might then seem inevitable that the Scriptures which told the story of the beginnings of the Divine purpose for the world and for Israel should include also the prophecies which told of the completion of that purpose.

Further, those prophecies had been 'inspired'; the prophets had always spoken in Yahweh's name. The prophetic formula, 'Thus saith Yahweh', invited comparison with the formula of the law-books, 'And Yahweh said unto Moses'. There was always a sense of the immense and incalculable debt which Israel owed to the unique series of prophets who had taught her what her faith really was, and had brought her through the crisis of the Exile. There was also the indisputable fact that their prophecies had in an astonishing way been fulfilled. Amos and Hosea had foretold the captivity of the northern kingdom: it had happened. Isaiah had said that Jerusalem would pass through a fearful ordeal and would be delivered: it had come to pass. Jeremiah had foretold the captivity of Jerusalem: it had happened. Ezekiel laboured to convince the exiles of the first deportation that the fall of the city was certain: 'and when this cometh to pass (behold, it cometh) then shall they know that a prophet hath been among them' (Ezek. xxxiii, 33). Zechariah, seventy years later, is quite clear: 'Your fathers, where are they? and the prophets, do they live for ever? But My words and My statutes, which I commanded My servants the prophets, did they not overtake your fathers? and they turned and said, Like as the Lord of Hosts thought to do unto us, according to our ways and according to our doings, so hath He dealt with us' (i, 5, 6). The same appeal to the word of Yahweh by the former prophets comes in Zech. vii, 7–14, in a prophecy whose purpose is to recall and re-enforce the moral and social teaching of his predecessors. It was because the prophets themselves had believed in the future fulfilment of their prophecies that they had put them in writing: 'Now go, write it before them on a tablet, and inscribe it in a book, that it may be for the time to come for ever and ever' (Isa. xxx, 8). Many allusions show that the

---

[1] Cf. the 'Branch', Jer. xxiii, 5; Zech. iii, 8; vi, 12; 'My servant David', Ezek. xxxiv, 23–4; xxxvii, 24–5; and the constant preoccupation of many of the Psalms and of Chronicles, with this messianic theme.

books were read. Jeremiah in his early prophecies reproduces the teaching of Hosea. Ezekiel (xxxviii, 17) wonders whether his own prophecy about Gog and Magog is not to be the fulfilment of Zeph. i, 13-14; iii, 8: predictions which are commonly taken to have originally referred to the danger from the Scythian invasion which in fact did not materialize. The later prophets abound with turns of phrase reminiscent of the earlier.

But however much the use which was made of the prophetical books prepared the way for their collection into a canon, all the quotations which we have mentioned take the prophets to have been simply inspired messengers who had *in their day* spoken the words of Yahweh. There is no suggestion that the prophecies were canonical in the allusion to them in the eucharistic prayer in Neh. ix: 'Thou testifiedst against them by Thy Spirit through Thy prophets, yet would they not give ear' (v.30). It is not till Ecclus. xlvi-xlix that we get clear signs that the prophetic books stood together in a collection.

When, however, the recognition of the prophetic books as Scripture had definitely happened, a change had come over the conception of Scripture by the bringing together of the two ideas of canonicity and prophetic 'inspiration'. Of course, the Pentateuch was thought of as possessing divine authority. But the formula 'The Lord said unto Moses' had not prevented such important additions as the ritual of the Day of Atonement being (according to the usual opinion) added to the Law after its first promulgation; not even the express prohibition in Deut. iv, 2 and xii, 32, against adding anything to the law-book or diminishing from it prevented either this or the large additions which are held to have been made to the original Deuteronomy—perhaps, indeed, the prohibitions themselves were added because of copious alterations known to have been made in some copies of the Book. We cannot therefore argue that, at any rate in that earlier period, the recognition of a book as Scripture would immediately result in the fixing of the text. That is to read back into an earlier age the developed idea of 'inspired scripture', which we find in Philo, Josephus and the Talmuds.

Clearly we have reached an important point in our discussion, with this thesis that the recognition of the Prophetical books as

Scripture marks the beginning of the 'traditional' view of Inspiration. Two things need to be said first. (*a*) It must be remembered that during the period when the Holy Ghost was actually speaking by the prophets, there was no purely external test, such as according to the traditional doctrine is constituted by the presence of the words in the text of Holy Scripture, to assure the hearer that some particular words which he heard were words of God. The inspiration of a prophet could always be challenged. We have two notable stories in which 'true' prophets (Micaiah and Jeremiah) are confronted with 'false' prophets giving a completely opposite message (1 Kings xxii, Jer. xxviii). But while no doubt it would be highly convenient if prophets, journalists, statesmen, and writers of books went through life with labels attached to them, that is not how things happen; and in those days the hearer had before him two men, both claiming to speak the word of Yahweh, but saying diametrically opposite things. The appeal was of course to the verification of the predictions by the event. But that lay in the future; and the decision which had to be made was made, then as now, according to the choice which the hearer made between the two conceptions of God represented by the two sides.

(*b*) Then again, there is a world of difference between a view of Inspiration which denies and one which affirms the continuing presence of the Holy Ghost. The denial is typically represented by the Mohammedan phrase, 'Allah is one, and Mohammed is His prophet'. God has spoken, once for all, and there is nothing more to come; we have got it all in black and white in the Koran, and there it is for us to explain according to our ability and our liking, possibly even to explain away. There is no Holy Ghost to say new and inconvenient things. There need be no anxiety on that score. The opposite view of the matter finds expression in the words of Moses in Deut. xviii, 15: 'Yahweh thy God will raise up unto thee a prophet from the midst of thee, of thy brethren, like unto me: unto him shall ye hearken.' You do not know beforehand what he will say; beware therefore lest you harden your hearts, as in the day of the provocation, for you must listen for the new things which you have yet to learn, beyond what I have been able to teach you hitherto, or you to understand. We hear the same note in the gospel: 'I have yet many things to say unto you, but ye cannot bear them now. Howbeit, when He, the Spirit of the Truth, is come, He will guide you into all the truth' (John xvi, 12–13). Here is something which is at all times quite vital to the religion of the Israel of God.

Therefore the disappearance of prophecy from Israel in the last three centuries before Christ is a phenomenon that raises serious questions. Tradition fixed the date of Ezra as the time when prophecy ceased, and no book was admitted to the canon of Scripture which was not believed to date from his time or earlier. Actually, at least Jonah and Joel among the prophetic books, as well as various prophecies embedded in or attached to other books, are now held to be later than Ezra. But none of these can be much later than 300 B.C.; and by the time of 1 Maccabees it was a fixed belief that for the time being at least, prophecy was finished.[1] It is not that during this period the Holy Ghost was inoperative; those who at an earlier time might have been prophets now taught in synagogues or wrote in other literary forms. But the fact remains that the living word of God addressed to the contemporary situation was no longer expected to come in the old way. Prophecy had come to an end.

Budde attributes to the authors of the Priestly Code the belief that prophecy had no further function:[2] 'Ezra gave to the community in the canon of the Law all that it required. It was not new when he gave it; he only gave over again what God had once already given through Moses to the people as his one and all. If the people had remained true to this Law, not only would they have escaped all the disasters of the past, but also they would never have needed new revelations from God through his prophets. These prophets contributed nothing new; they were sent only to admonish the unfaithful people to observe the Law, and to announce the merited punishment of the impenitent. The Law thus had permanent validity, while the work of the

---

[1] See 1 Macc. iv, 44–6, where they cannot decide, for lack of a prophet, what to do with the desecrated altar of burnt offering; also ix, 27; xiv, 41; and the Song of the Three Children, v. 15.

[2] K. Budde, in *Encyc. Biblica*, s.v. 'Canon', col. 661, §31–2. Cf. Sanday, *Inspiration*, p. 169.

prophets was transitory; the Law addressed itself to all generations, the prophets each only to his own, which had now passed
away. The generations that had sworn obedience anew to the
Law under Ezra, therefore, had no need for the prophets.
Should similar circumstances recur, it might be expected that
God would send prophets anew; but the prevailing feeling was,
no doubt, that the time of unfaithfulness, and consequently of
the prophetic ministry, was gone for ever.'

Whether Budde is right or wrong about the Priestly Code, he
has, at any rate, correctly interpreted one strain in Judaism.
The prophets who speak throughout the Book of Chronicles
mostly denounce unfaithfulness to the Law; though there is also
an interesting passage in which the Sons of Asaph 'prophesy'
with harps, psalteries and cymbals, after the order of David,
in giving thanks and praising the Lord (1 Chron. xxv, 1–3).
The pattern of the Righteousness of God and of man's service
of Him, according to this writer, is that which is given in the
Law and the liturgical worship in the Temple; all is systematized
according to the rules of the right moral and ceremonial practice, and therefore the prophetic message also is understood as
having fitted into this scheme. Yet it had been one of the key-
points of the prophets' actual message that the true service of
the transcendent God can never be simply equated with any
such set of rules.

On the whole, then, we may accept Budde's statement as
describing, at any rate, a tendency which was involved in the
work of Ezra and his colleagues. But at the same time we must
remember that the Priestly editors of the Pentateuch preserved
in it the traditional descriptions of Moses acting as a prophet,
and above all that of the outpouring of the Spirit of Yahweh in
Numbers xi on the seventy Elders and also on Eldad and Me-
dad, and Moses' recognition of these unofficial charismatics.
Further, if we were right in affirming the messianic outlook of
the Priestly Code, its rigour presupposed the expected Return
of the Presence and the Gift of the Spirit. The prophet Joel,
whose date may perhaps be soon after Ezra, vividly delineated
the coming Day when the Spirit would be poured out on young
and old, and all Israelites would become prophets. So long as

this eschatological element was present, it would seem that the due balance of the Faith was preserved; it was lost only when the eschatological hope faded, and the legal element took all the emphasis.

It was also true that several circumstances had discouraged prophecy, from the exile onwards. In the old days it was in places of public concourse that the prophet was accustomed to appear, above all at the religious festivals. But in Babylonia it was difficult for the Jews to have a place of assembly, except it were in some wholly Jewish village—till they began to have synagogues. Ezekiel's prophecies were given often to gatherings of the elders of Israel in his house. No doubt it was possible for prophets to speak in synagogues; where there were prophets, one would expect from the New Testament parallels that they regularly did so. Yet the typical figure in the synagogue pulpit would be the pastor, the instructor, the scribe; and it was his work that was then supremely needed, to train up the people in the habits of true religion and in the knowledge of the books which now are Scripture. The great prophets of Israel (as distinguished from the dancing-dervish type of *nabi* out of which they developed) had the high vocation of guiding Israel through a long period of severe crisis, from the beginning of the Assyrian menace to the national existence, through two centuries of acute tension, till the final disaster, and then of bringing her through death to resurrection. In Second Isaiah this work is complete. After him the prophets who appear do not rise to the former stature; but that which makes their greatness is the eschatological hope of the Advent which they announce. Apart from this, it belonged to the nature of the case that the pastor was the prominent figure. When another great crisis appeared, in the attempt of Antiochus Epiphanes to introduce a universal Hellenic culture, this crisis called forth the book of Daniel, which, though technically not one of the Prophets, is of prophetic quality. In that crisis the work of two centuries of synagogue training in Palestine was fully vindicated by the manner in which the people stood the test.

It is not surprising, then, that prophecy should die down; and in what is possibly the latest of all the prophetic utterances, the prophetic order is denounced as utterly corrupt and associated with 'the unclean spirit' (Zech. xiii, 2–6). As we have said, the end of prophecy did not mean that the Holy Ghost had ceased to speak; but it did mean that the theological balance, as between the Spirit and the Letter, had become upset. It was a serious thing that the inspiration of men by the Spirit of Yahweh to speak His word was believed not to have occurred since the time of Ezra, so that in the Talmuds 'until then' and 'from that time onwards' become the standing expressions used to denote the end of the prophetic period. A date before Ezra became the regular test for the admission of books to the third division of the canon; 'books like Ben-Sira and similar books written "from that time onwards" may be read as one reads a letter' (*San.* 28a), and do not 'defile the hands'.[1]

Thus we must conclude that the canonization of the prophetic books did in fact introduce a considerable change in the conception of Scripture, partly by the interpretation of inspiration as inerrancy, but chiefly because of the rise of the belief that there were to be no more prophets, and the loss of the belief in the present operation of the Spirit, which alone could keep the idea of Law in its right proportion.

4. The Writings

The Hebrew Canon was complete by the first century A.D. The last discussion about it was at Jamnia, *c.* A.D. 100, when it was decided rather that Ecclesiastes and Canticles had been rightly admitted to the canon, than that they ought to be admitted. In the New Testament, we find the Old Testament described as 'The Law of Moses, the Prophets, and the Psalms' (Luke xxiv, 44); in Matt. xxiii, 35, perhaps, and in the parallel Luke xi, 51, certainly, the allusion to 'the blood of Zachariah' who was murdered 'between the altar and the house' is a reference to 2 Chron. xxiv, 20–21, and means that 'the blood of all the righteous, from the first murder in the Bible to the last, shall

---

[1] Budde, op. cit., col. 667, §44. Cf. also the quotation on p. 191 f. below. Books that 'defiled the hands' would be 'holy books', such that contact with them might seem to need a ceremonial washing afterwards.

be required of this generation'. It is to be noted that the Hebrew Bible, not the Greek, is in this case referred to, since in it Chronicles occurs last. It is possible that in 1 Macc. vii, 16 f., the psalm 'their blood have they shed like water on every side of Jerusalem' (Ps. lxxix, 2–3) is quoted as Scripture, as the formula is 'according to the word which he wrote'; the date of this book is *c.* 100 B.C. Thirty years earlier, *c.* 131, Ben-Sira's grandson in his preface to Ecclesiasticus shows that he regards 'the law and the prophets' as scripture; he mentions them three times, and each time goes on to mention certain other books, which he calls 'the others that have followed in their steps', 'the other books of our fathers', 'the rest of the books'. From the fact that he varies the designation, it is inferred that these other books are not, like Law and Prophets, fixed and acknowledged collections of books; from the fact that he mentions them with the Law and the Prophets, that this uncertain number of books has nevertheless a certain scriptural character. Finally, Ben-Sira himself, in his panegyric on the saints of Israel, immediately after mentioning the Twelve Prophets goes on from Zerubbabel and Jesus son of Josedek to Nehemiah, thereby showing that he knows the Books of Ezra and Nehemiah, and therefore presumably also Chronicles (Ecclus. xlix, 11–14). From all this we may infer that the recognition of the third division of the Canon was gradual, as that of the second seems to have been, and that it is to be dated in the first century B.C.

The books thus acknowledged fall into groups. First, the Psalms; this, as the first and most important item in the collection, is found in Luke xxiv, 44, standing as the title of the whole. There are three Wisdom-books, Job, Proverbs and Ecclesiastes; three books of history, which originally were one, Chronicles, Ezra and Nehemiah. The fact that Chronicles stands last, in the *Baba Bathra* as in the Massoretic text, indicates its late acceptance; Ben-Sira (Ecclus. xlix, 11–13) seems to know Ezra-Nehemiah as a separate book, perhaps already detached from Chronicles in order to provide a continuation for the Book of Kings. There is the Book of Daniel, which stands by itself; and 'the five (festal) rolls, printed in modern impressions in the order of the feasts at which they are read in the synagogue:

Canticles (Passover), Ruth (Pentecost), Lamentations (9th Ab., Destruction of Jerusalem), Ecclesiastes (Tabernacles), Esther (Purim)'.[1] It would be tempting to conclude that the modern liturgical use gives a key to the original acknowledgement of these books as canonical; but this cannot seemingly be supported from the order of the books in the oldest sources, since the *Baba Bathra* puts Ruth first of all, before the Psalms, and Daniel before Esther, so that by A.D. 200 they had not been constituted as a distinct group, while the grouping according to the order of the feasts appears only in the later French and Spanish MSS.[2]

The principle on which the books were accepted seems to be that of including all the books of a religious character, and written of course in Hebrew, of which the date was believed to go back to the prophetic period, that is, the period that ended with Ezra. But even so, a certain discrimination was used; Baruch and Enoch were not admitted. Plainly this principle excluded the Hebrew original of our *Ecclesiasticus*; while 'Job was received as, according to general belief, a book of venerable antiquity; Ruth as a narrative relating to the period of the judges, and therefore (as was invariably assumed as matter of course in the case of historical narratives) as dating from the same time; the Psalms as broadly covered by the idea that they were "David's Psalms"; Proverbs, Canticles, and Ecclesiastes as resting on Solomon's name; Lamentations as resting on that of Jeremiah; Daniel as a prophet of the Persian period (which in its whole extent was supposed to fall within the prophetic age) overlooked in the earlier collection. The same consideration held good for Ezra, regarded as a history book. At the close comes the Book of Ezra—separated from the general work of the Chronicler—which, in its account of the Great Assembly, contained the original document on the close of the prophetic period, and so, as it were, puts the colophon to the completed canon.'[3]

This brings us a long way towards understanding why these

[1] Budde, op. cit., col. 649–50, §6.

[2] Budde, op. cit., col. 650–1, §9. The *Baraitha*, or unauthorized gloss, on the Talmudic tractate *Baba Bathra*, is printed out in full, in a translation, in Ryle, *Canon of the Old Testament*, Excursus B, p. 283 ff.

[3] Budde, op. cit., col. 667, §45.

books of the third division of the canon were acknowledged to be Scripture. The canonization of the Prophets had fixed the principle that Scripture was now to include prophecies inspired by God. There was no reason in principle why other books, dating from the period when God had inspired the prophets, and similar to them in general character, should not be canonized. Many of the psalms, in particular, breathed the very spirit of the prophets (many of them, no doubt, having actually been written by prophets); and most of the books had that educative value which made the Prophets valuable from the pastoral point of view.

When, therefore, we compare the second and third canons with the first, we see that the Pentateuch had a binding character which the other two had not; it laid down the things that the Israelite must believe and do to his soul's health. The Prophets had spoken of the messianic future; apart from this their value was mainly educative. The value of the Psalms and the other Writings was wholly educative. We must then think of the Pentateuch as the core of the Old Testament, remembering that the Samaritans, and the Sadducees in our Lord's day, regarded it alone as canonical; and we may regard the other two divisions of the canon as concentric circles round that core. The fact that there could be dispute as late as A.D. 100 whether two books were rightly accounted canonical, and that this dispute was not one that shook the Jewish polity to its foundations, shows that it is not inconsistent with the idea of Scripture that it should have a fringe. It was possible for there to be dispute about Ecclesiastes and Canticles. A dispute about Exodus or Isaiah would be inconceivable.

It is otherwise, of course, when it is believed that Scripture is inspired in such a way as to be free from all possible error in every part. Then, the notion of a fringe becomes altogether inadmissible. But there had been from the beginning a distinction made between the authority of the Law and that of all subsequent additions to the canon; and 'we know with certainty that . . . the idea of a property common to all holy books, that of "defiling the hands", was an invention of Pharisaic scholasticism, withstood by the Sadducees even after the destruction of

Jerusalem (*Yad.*, 4–6). Until this bridge had been securely constructed there could be no idea of a canonicity that included all three portions equally. This is proved by a fact to which we have already referred—the Sadducean recognition of nothing but the Law'.[1]

We do, in fact, find that by the first century the influence of the Scribes had produced a full-fledged doctrine of 'verbal inspiration'. In Philo of Alexandria the text is regarded as to such an extent inerrant that the exegete might find in it allegorical meanings dependent on the turn of phrase and even the punctuation, while totally ignoring the meaning which the writer was intending to express by them. He even attributes this inerrancy to the Greek translation.

Josephus thinks of the inspiration of the Old Testament records primarily as ensuring an unsurpassed degree of historical accuracy; he supports this by showing how the greatest care had always been taken to keep the priestly race pure and untainted; the records are thus completely accurate, 'nor is there any discrepancy in the facts recorded. The composition of the records is due to the prophets alone, who by the inspiration of God narrated the earliest and most ancient events, and compiled an exact history of their own time. . . . From the time of Artaxerxes to our own day there has been a continuation of the record of events; but these later records have not attained the same level of authority as the first, because there has not been an exact succession of prophets since that time'—and so the Book of Maccabees, for instance, does not share the infallibility of the Book of Kings. 'Our conduct', he continues, 'vouches for our implicit faith in our own writings; for during all the ages that have already gone by, no one has ventured either to add to them, or to take anything from them, or to make any alteration in them. It is an instinctive belief of all Jews from their earliest childhood to regard the records as decrees of God, to abide by them, and (if need be) gladly to die in their defence.'[2]

---

[1] Budde, op. cit., col. 665, §41.

[2] Josephus, *Contra Apionem*, i, §§6–8. Translation from Barry, *The Inspiration and Authority of Holy Scripture*, 1919, p. 22. The Greek for 'decrees of God' is Θεοῦ δόγματα.

The Writings

We shall see in the next chapter that the New Testament writers assume a very different conception of the 'truth' of Scripture from Josephus's narrow idea of a merely factual accuracy.

We are now at the end of our study of the Hebrew Canon. But the Greek Bible contained also a number of other books, approximately those which are now commonly called the Apocrypha. These circulated in the Jewish Diaspora; but they have never received any regular canonization other than that of the Christian Church. The eighth day of Tebet, when according to the 'Letter of Aristeas' the translators arrived in Egypt in the time of Ptolemy Philadelphus (reigned 285–47 B.C.), seems to have been kept in Philo's day as a festival; but 'Rabbinical Jews called that day the fast of darkness, for they regarded this translation as a national disaster, "like the day on which the golden calf was made".'[1]

The history of the Septuagint raises many difficult problems, not least that of its text, with which we are not here concerned; for while the use of the Greek Bible in Judaism and in the Church shows some mutual influence, its history is mainly that of the Church's Bible. It has remained the Bible of the Greek-speaking churches and of Eastern Orthodoxy generally, and through the old Latin translations the basis of that of the Western Church. Some of the Fathers, notably Origen and Jerome, insisted on the prior claim of the original Hebrew Canon; but the books of the Apocrypha have through the centuries been regularly treated in the Church as Scripture, and were acknowledged as fully on a level with the rest by the Council of Trent. The Reformed Churches, on the other hand, have always refused to acknowledge them; Luther, however, recognized in them a relative importance. We of the Church of England accept them as deutero-canonical; 'the other books (as *Hierome* saith) the Church doth read for example of life and instruction of manners, but yet it doth not apply them to establish any doctrine' (Art. VII). Yet a certain prejudice against the Apocrypha caused most Anglican exegesis in the nineteenth century to be unduly

---

[1] Nestle in *H.D.B.*, art. 'Septuagint', vol. iv, p. 439.

unwilling to recognize the clear traces of it which are discernible in the New Testament.[1]

The Apocrypha stands in much the same relation to the Hebrew Bible as the third canon of that Bible to the first and second. The classical tradition of the Faith of Israel is given in the Pentateuch, which tells of the Redemption and the giving of the Law, and in the Prophets who proclaim Israel's belief about God and interpret the story of His dealings with Israel, above all as regards the crisis of the exile and the messianic future. While the Psalms also belong for the most part to this classical tradition, the third canon consists mainly of commentary upon it, showing how it works out in the life of the community. The Apocrypha continues this commentary, from a point of view which is in general a little further removed from the classical tradition; the new Greek apologetic in the book of Wisdom lays the emphasis less on the events of the Redemption than on the revelation of God in the created world.

There appears further in it a certain rhetorical character, notably in the Book of Wisdom, but also to some extent in Ben-Sira. The Hebrew Bible, and particularly that central part of it which sets forth the classical tradition of the faith, shows a concentration and directness of style which arises from the fact that the writers are grappling with the decisive facts of God's action in history and the duty which this action lays upon men; there is in the writers a sense of constraint that impels them to say with outspoken directness the things that must at all costs be said. We have noticed how clearly this comes out in Deuteronomy; but it is apparent very widely, even in so relatively late a work as the first eight chapters of Proverbs, where the writer is as far as possible from uttering ethical commonplaces, but is setting himself with great earnestness to provide the young Jew, living among corrupting pagan influences, with sorely needed help in keeping himself unspotted from the world. The same note is heard in the earlier part of Ecclesiasticus; but the panegyric on the saints of Israel at the end of the book becomes somewhat

[1] Cf. Westcott's important study, *The Bible in the Church* (1864), which has for one of its main aims the vindication of the Hebrew Canon as alone authoritative.

rhetorical. To a greater degree the author of Wisdom seems to speak rather in a style which will be interesting and attractive to those brought up under the Greek culture. The history of the Maccabees stands nearer to the hellenized Josephus than to the prophetical Book of Kings. In other words, these books are markedly less 'biblical' than those of the classical tradition and the Hebrew Bible generally.

The Wisdom-literature as a whole does not belong to the classical tradition of the Old Testament; but it is an authentic development of Biblical thought. The 'wise man' appears indeed in pre-exilic times; the tradition of the 'wisdom of Solomon' is likely to have some historical foundation; in Jer. xviii, 18, the wise man is grouped with the priest and the prophet among the teachers of Israel; and some of the gnomic sayings in Proverbs may be pre-exilic, copied out by 'the men of Hezekiah King of Judah' (Prov. xxv, 1). But the Wisdom-literature proper (apart from the Book of Job, in which the great chapter on Wisdom, chap. xxviii, is held to be a later insertion) belongs to the Greek period. It was a new development of Hebrew thought, called forth by the need, above all, of defending the ethical tradition of Israel against the moral laxity which contact with Hellenism made easy; yet it was itself much influenced by the Hellenism to which it was the antidote. This is true above all of the conception of Wisdom itself, which is depicted in Prov. viii and elsewhere as existing almost side by side with God; Ben-Sira went further, and took the momentous step of identifying Wisdom with the Law of Moses, while in the Wisdom of Solomon the idea is again expanded much further, under Greek influence.[1]

The splendid conception of the divine Wisdom called forth a noble panegyric from Sir Edwyn Hoskyns: 'In the twenty-fourth chapter of the Book of Ecclesiasticus, Jesus the son of Sirach bursts into the song of the glory of Wisdom. Created from the

[1] In the 'Introduction to the Wisdom-literature', by E. J. Bicknell, in the *New Commentary*, pp. 307–11, the Wisdom-literature is defined as including, within the Hebrew Canon, Job, Proverbs, Ecclesiastes, and certain Psalms, esp. i, xxxvii, xlix, l, lxxiii, cxii, and parts of other Psalms, such as xviii, 20–6; and in the Apocrypha, Ecclesiasticus, Wisdom, and other passages such as Baruch iii, 9–37.

beginning, she was the mist of the story of the Creation (Gen. ii, 6). She inhabited the Abyss, and was honoured by the host of Heaven. In every people and nation She had sought a resting-place, but in Israel and in Jerusalem, the beloved city, She tabernacled, took root, and rested. The glorified people whom She honoured with Her presence came to Her; they ate and drank from Her as from a vine; and those who submit to Her guidance and serve Her are removed from the degradation of sin. To live under the book of the covenant of the Most High God and to obey the Law of Moses is to live in the tabernacle of the Wisdom of God. This is no isolated passage, for the author of the Book of Baruch (iii, 9–iv, 4) in similar fashion sings the praise of the Wisdom of God revealed in the Law. There is none that knoweth Her way, nor any that comprehendeth Her path. The nations have not known the way of knowledge, and have perished because they did not possess Wisdom. But God, who knoweth all things, knoweth Her, and gave Wisdom to Jacob. He presented Her to Israel, His beloved. Then it was that Wisdom appeared on earth, and was conversant with men. All they who hold Her fast are appointed to life, therefore, *Turn thee, O Jacob, and take hold of her: walk towards Her shining in the presence of the Light thereof.* The Wisdom of God, hidden from the eyes of all living (Job xxviii, cf. 4 Ezra v, 10), the clear effluence of the glory of the Almighty—but who nevertheless, pervadeth and penetrateth all things, and against whom evil doth not prevail (Wisd. vii, 24–viii, 1)—had taken form and shape in the Law of Moses, which is the Word of God (Deut. xxx, 11–14). Brought forth from the Beginning or ever the earth was, Wisdom was with God, His first creation, the artificer and master-workman of the universe. She stretched out Her hand and came to Her own, but because of the wickedness of men She was regarded by none and found no resting-place on earth; only in Israel had She been received, and there She tabernacled with men (Prov. viii, 22–30, cf. iii, 19; Wisd. vii, 13, 22; viii, 3, 4; ix, 1–11; 2 Enoch xxx, 8, cf. xxxiii, 3, 4; Prov. i, 20–30; 1 Enoch xlii). Renewed by Her, the faithful Israelites became the friends of God and His prophets and, since he alone loves God who lives with Wisdom, the Jews, living under the Law, became the children of Wisdom (Wisd. vii, 14, 27, 28; Ecclus. iv, 11, cf. Luke vii, 35; xi, 49).'[1]

4. The Meaning of the Word 'Bible'

We started at the beginning of the last chapter to answer the question, what meaning of the word 'Bible' emerges from the history of the formation of the Old Testament canon. The answer is to be found by considering that history in the light of the Faith of Israel, which gave the whole motive for the writing of the books, their preservation and their continued use. The books were not written as 'scripture'; they became scripture because an authoritative sacred book was essential to the existence of Israel as the People of Yahweh. The spiritual needs which called the Bible into existence can be summed up under three heads.

First, we have seen how the Bible is connected with Israel's confession of its faith. The earliest-written parts of the Bible, narratives, songs, psalms, prophecies, were in existence and were being read for centuries before they became Scripture. The canonization of Deuteronomy came with a great national confession of faith, when at the end of the long conflict of the Faith of Yahweh with the nature-religions the people bound themselves to serve Him alone; and this act could only be clinched by the acknowledgement of a document containing not only laws but exhortations expressing the spirit in which the laws were to be kept and appealing to the divine work of redemption which was the basis of Israel's existence as the People of Yahweh.

Under Ezra a second and similar confession of faith was made, involving this time the acceptance of the Pentateuch. Israel had sinned, and had been punished; penitent exiles, returned from Babylon, reaffirmed the old faith and professed their steadfast purpose to serve their God truly, according to His holy Law. This was clinched by the act of binding themselves to the Pentateuch, which contained not only the revision of the Law, but also the literary treasures which contained their most ancient traditions.

[1] E. C. Hoskyns, *The Fourth Gospel*, pp. 152-3.

The Completion of the Canon

Second: the Old Testament, no less than the New, springs out of the mystery of redemption through suffering. Deuteronomy was promulgated on the eve of Israel's passion; and it was in the actual process of its passage through death to resurrection and newness of life that the prophecies were given which reveal the central secret of Israel's faith, and brought that faith to birth. These prophecies spoke of a Second Exodus, a New Covenant, an outpouring of the Spirit of Yahweh, and the Return of His Presence to dwell amidst His people; and they made a full and clear proclamation of Yahweh as the one true God, who in the beginning created the heaven and the earth, and of the mission of Israel to bring the knowledge of the true God to all the nations of mankind, and they set forth the Suffering Servant of Yahweh as the pattern of Israel's spiritual service. Therefore, while the central core of the Bible consisted of the Pentateuch, which firmly based Israel's faith on the events of the Exodus, it was necessary that it should come to include also the writings of the Prophets which expressed its belief about God and contained the promises of His future saving action.

Third: the Bible was connected in the most intimate way with Israel's worship. The first book to be canonized had affirmed the principle that the worship of the one God demanded one altar and one set of sacrifices; and it led to the institution of the Synagogue, a building in each place in which the faithful should meet to hear the Book read and to be instructed and exercized in His spiritual service. To serve Baal had meant the mere performance of a ritual. The service of Yahweh included this, but demanded also a reasonable obedience, and an understanding with the mind of His will for man. Therefore there had to be the Synagogue as well as the Temple, and the Book of the Divine Kingdom, declaring the history of its establishment and the terms of the service which it demanded, set forth in narrative, law, ballad, exhortation, prophecy, teaching, and psalm.

CHAPTER VII

THE OLD TESTAMENT IN THE NEW

1. The Fulfilment

The Gospel is the announcement of the divine answer to that whole side of the Old Testament which consisted of unfulfilled hopes. The high expectations of the exilic prophets had not materialized in any degree that could be taken as a fulfilment of the promises made in Yahweh's Name. Jeremiah had predicted a Second Exodus, and several bands of courageous men had returned to Palestine; but there had been no Deliverance with a mighty hand and an outstretched arm. A Covenant had been made under Ezra; but it had not been the New Covenant bringing forgiveness of sins. The Temple had been restored, but there had been no glorious Return of the Presence of Yahweh. The Law had been promulgated, but there had been no outpouring of the Spirit of Yahweh upon all flesh; instead, there had been a general sense that the day of the Spirit was over, and there had been a long uphill fight to guard Israel's integrity and maintain the observance of the Law. There had been rewards and encouragements, and those who had sought the Lord had not sought Him in vain. But His promised Day had not dawned.

At long last, in the fulness of time, there appeared in Israel men whose faces were radiant with joy, proclaiming that all that the Prophets foretold had come to pass. The Lord God of Israel had visited and redeemed His People. Jesus, of the seed of David, was the promised Messiah. In His advent, His ministry, death, resurrection and ascension, all had been fulfilled. The Spirit had been outpoured. The Glad Tidings consisted in a correlation of these recent historical events with the

Old Testament prophecies, which gave the meaning of the events. Indeed, there was no possibility of explaining who Jesus was, and what was the significance of His preaching and above all of His death and resurrection, and what was the true status of the Christian community, apart from the Old Testament Scriptures. It is scarcely an exaggeration to say that whenever a New Testament writer quotes or alludes to the Old Testament, it is in order to exhibit some aspect or other of the Divine Purpose that had been fulfilled in Jesus.

Yet there is a certain antinomy running through the Christian acceptance of the Old Testament. St. Paul, writing to the Galatians, solemnly warns them that they must on no account undergo the circumcision which the Law commands; to the Romans, he says that there is no peace with God to be attained by the observance of the Law; in Ephesians, that the exclusion of the Gentiles from the privileges of Israel, symbolized by the Wall of Partition in the Temple, has been broken down. The readers of Hebrews are told that the day of the Temple sacrifices is over. St. John makes it clear that the Jews who reject Jesus are no true sons of Abraham. Behind all this lie the actions attributed to Jesus Himself in the synoptic gospels: He had broken the rules of Sabbath observance; He had called the Pharisees hypocrites; He had declared the laws of ritual uncleanness to be no longer binding, annulled the Mosaic permission for divorce, and had performed, as the last act of His ministry, a rite, independent of the levitical sacrifices, in which He had declared the New Covenant to be inaugurated through His blood.

Yet, though the Jewish system is thus declared to be superseded, appeal is invariably made, for the justification of this, to the Old Testament itself. It is never said that the Mosaic Law is now seen not to have been the Law of God at all; on the contrary, it is God's Law, and it is holy and righteous and good. It is never said that the Prophets were right and the Law wrong, nor is the moral law endorsed and the ceremonial law repudiated; on the contrary, Jesus has come not to destroy but to fulfil both the Law and the Prophets. When St. Paul will justify the thesis that peace with God is found through faith and not by the works of the Law, he goes to Abraham for his proof. When Jesus Himself enjoins indissoluble marriage, He appeals to the Divine institution as given in the Book of Genesis. Thus the Gospel-message is not that a higher stage of spiritual development has now been reached, in which certain universal principles are proclaimed which the Prophets might have seen and put into effect if they had had fuller insight; it is that the very principles which the Prophets had seen and proclaimed, but had been impotent to put into effect, now come into full operation. The messianic days had arrived, and things which had before been impossible had now become possible.

They had become possible through the advent of a Person, who had made all things new. There was little that was new in His ethical teaching; most of His precepts were to be found scattered about the Old Testament. The command 'Thou shalt love thy neighbour as thyself' came from Lev. xix, 18; and if He could say, 'A new commandment I give unto you, that ye love one another' (John xiii, 34), the newness lay less in the commandment itself than in the added words 'as I have loved you', and in the new fact that 'the divine love has been poured out in our hearts through the Holy Spirit who was given to us' (Rom. v, 5). A Christianity which consisted in a demand for the observance of the spiritual and moral teaching of the Sermon on the Mount would have been no Gospel, but a new legalism more impossible than the old. The Gospel consists in the fulfilment of the Divine Purpose, in the perfecting of the Divine Kingdom, in the actuality of the Reign of Jesus as its King, in the Return of the Tabernacling Presence, making the New Israel to be truly the People of God and a living Temple where He dwells no longer merely among but also in them. 'For we are a Temple of the living God; even as God said, I will dwell in them and walk in them; and I will be their God and they shall be My People.'[1]

Thus the attitude of the New Testament to the Old is a highly critical attitude, and yet shows the most humble deference to its authority. It is God's Book, the record of His ordering of history in preparation for His own coming to accomplish His purpose

[1] 2 Cor. vi, 16; quoting Lev. xxvi, 16 (cf. p. 155 above), Jer. xxxi, 33.

of salvation; therefore it gives the indispensable key to the understanding of the Divine Advent which has now taken place. The Day of the Lord has come, as a day of salvation and of judgement: of judgement, because the utterly terrible thing has happened, that when He came to His own place, His own people received Him not, but because they knew Him not, nor the voices of the prophets which were read every sabbath day, fulfilled them by condemning Him; and of salvation, because no power on earth could prevent the Stone which the builders rejected from going into its place as the head of the corner. All this, both the hardening of men's hearts against God and the victorious fulfilment of the Divine Purpose, was there in the Old Testament Scriptures.

2. Prolegomena

The main question before us is, What do the New Testament writers understand by the word 'scripture'? What sort of authority has it for them? How do they show their sense of its authority by the manner in which they use it?[1] It is necessary to begin with a brief survey of certain necessary 'prolegomena': what is said explicitly about the Inspiration of the Old Testament, and what is implied in the manner in which they quote and use it.

There are two formal statements about the Inspiration of the Old Testament, both occurring among the later-written books.

2 Pet. i, 19–21: 'We have as more sure the prophetic word, to which ye do well to take heed, as to a light shining in a desert place, till the day dawn and the day-star rise in your hearts; knowing this first, that every prophecy of Scripture is im-

---

[1] There is no systematic treatment available of the use of the Old Testament in the New; all recent work of the New Testament pays thorough attention to the writers' use of O.T., but no one has systematized the results. There is a somewhat uncritical essay by A. H. McNeile in *Cambridge Biblical Essays* (ed. Swete, 1909) on 'Our Lord's use of the Old Testament'; a valuable but brief study by G. H. Box in *The People and the Book* of 'The value and significance of the Old Testament in relation to the New'. Prof. Tasker's book, *The Old Testament in the New Testament* was not published till after this chapter was in type; in it the New Testament books are discussed separately, and it is shown in what ways each writer uses the Old Testament.

patient of private interpretation; for not by will of man was prophecy brought, but men being carried by the Holy Ghost spake from God.' The readers must not listen to Gnostic teachers who find in the Old Testament strange new meanings.

2. Tim. iii, 14–17: 'But do thou abide in what thou hast learnt and hast been made faithful, knowing from whom thou hast learnt, and that from infancy thou hast known holy Scriptures which are able to make thee wise unto salvation through faith that is in Christ Jesus. Every inspired Scripture is also profitable for instruction, for reproof, for correction, for discipline in righteousness: that the man of God may be fully equipped for every good work.' The emphasis is on the practical spiritual value of Scripture, consequent on its divine origin.

Less explicit but in general very similar is Rom. xv, 4: 'Whatsoever things were written before were written for our instruction, that through patience and encouragement from the Scriptures we might have hope.'

The divine authority of the Scriptures is apparent everywhere in the formulae of quotation; these vary greatly in detail, and it would serve no useful purpose to give a list of them all here The simplest is 'it is written', with such additions as 'through the prophet' or 'in the second psalm'; or 'it was said to them of old time'. Often the writer is mentioned: 'David (or Moses) said (concerning Him)'; 'David in the Spirit calls Him Lord, saying'; 'that it might be fulfilled which was spoken by the Lord through the prophet, saying'; 'spoken by the Holy Ghost through the mouth of David'. Sometimes it is simply 'God said'. In Gal. iii, 8, the Promise to Abraham is introduced with the phrase, 'The Scripture, foreseeing that God would justify the Gentiles through faith, proclaimed the Gospel beforehand to Abraham, saying'. In one place the formula 'the Scripture saith' introduces a text from the Law and a saying of our Lord (1 Tim. v, 18).

In 1 Pet. i, 10–11, the prophets are seen to have had a true but imperfect grasp of the mystery of redemption through suffering: 'Concerning this Salvation the prophets sought and searched diligently, who prophesied of the Grace that should come to you, searching to what or what sort of time the Spirit of the Messiah in them was pointing, when It testified beforehand of the passion of the Messiah and the glory that should follow.' The correlation of divine inspiration with imperfect human insight is made again in the opening words of Hebrews, which defy translation but can be paraphrased: 'God having given to the prophets a variety of partial revelations in a variety of styles, has revealed Himself finally and inclusively in His Son.' It is perhaps right to see sometimes in the freedom which the writers allow themselves in making quotations a sense that the texts required to have their meaning more fully drawn out; though no doubt is ever cast on the reality of their inspiration.

The quotations are in a different language from the original. The fir st generation of Christians used the Hebrew Bible, but the New Testament is in Greek. As a general rule, its quotations follow the *LXX* translation, but the Hebrew text is often followed by preference.[1] The variations of wording present a complicated problem, and it is usually held that collections of texts, such as we find in St. Cyprian's *Testimonia* two hundred years later, were already in existence in the apostolic age; sometimes quotations agree with one another in differing from both the Hebrew and the *LXX*.[2] But it must also be remembered that they had not our facilities for looking up references: the formula in Heb. ii, 6, is 'Someone testifies somewhere, saying'. Further, while it is likely that a writer would usually be able to refer to the *LXX*, it must often have been difficult, especially after the breach with the Synagogue, to get access to a Hebrew text. St. Paul's quotations are usually from the *LXX*; those from the Pentateuch are exact in twenty-two cases out of thirty-one in Romans, and in four out of nine in 1 Cor., but those from the historical and prophetical books only in three out of twenty-two and one out of nine respectively;[3] it can be inferred that he quoted largely from memory, and that the Law and the Psalms were better known to him.

The Hebrew and the *LXX* were evidently regarded as equally

---

[1] See F. H. Woods in *H.D.B.*, art. 'Quotations', vol. iii, p. 184 ff.

[2] Cf. Mark i, 2 and Matt. xi, 10=Luke vii, 27; Rom xii, 19 and Heb. x, 30; 1 Pet. iv, 8 and Jas. v, 20.

[3] Woods in *H.D.B.* III, p. 187.

authoritative. In St. Mark, all the quotations except four are from *LXX*; of the exceptions, one is the *Shema'* (xii, 30), another the translation of the cry *Eli* from the cross, which is first given in Hebrew; another the prophecy from Zechariah about the smiting of the Shepherd (xiv, 27), which if quoted from *LXX* would have lost all point, since it reads 'shepherds' for 'shepherd'. St. Matthew's are usually translations from Hebrew, made by the evangelist or taken from a collection of *testimonia*; the exceptions are cases in which the *LXX* is followed because the Hebrew is inappropriate: Matt. i, 23 ('a virgin shall conceive'); xxi, 16 ('out of the mouth of babes and sucklings') and xii, 21 ('in His Name shall the Gentiles hope'). This last instance is interesting because it comes at the end of a long quotation from the Hebrew, and is substituted for 'the isles shall wait for His law'. John xix, 37, follows the Hebrew ('they shall look on Him whom they pierced'): an indication that the evangelist knew his Bible first in Hebrew. On the other hand, the explanation given in Acts ii, 30–1 of 'Thou shalt not suffer Thy holy one to see corruption' appears to depend for its appropriateness on the *LXX*: it follows that St. Peter cannot have actually so used it at Pentecost.

The texts are sometimes adapted for Christian purposes. In Matt. ii, 6, a text from Micah is deliberately corrected: Bethlehem, now that the Christ had been born there, was by no means 'the least among the princes of Judah'. In 1 Cor. iii, 20, St. Paul adapts Ps. xciv, 11: 'The Lord knoweth the thoughts of *the wise* that they are vain.' In Rom. x, 6–8, he gives a creative interpretation of Deut. xxx, 12 (the commandment 'is not in heaven . . . nor 'beyond the sea' . . . 'but very nigh unto thee . . . that thou mayest do it'); he renders it as meaning that the word is not in heaven, as though Christ had never become incarnate, nor in the abyss, as though Christ were engulfed there and not risen from the dead, but is here and very nigh, as the Gospel of Salvation proclaimed by us.

The manner in which the New Testament writers use the Old Testament is frequently criticized by modern scholars. The general criticism is expressed in the following passage from Dr. Oesterley:

The Old Testament in the New

'The claim of the apostle Paul to be "of the stock of Israel, of the tribe of Benjamin, a Hebrew of Hebrews" (Phil. iii, 5) is convincingly confirmed by his use of the Old Testament, and the way in which he interprets it. While his application of Old Testament texts to the people in his own times, as e.g. in Rom. iii, 9–18; ix, 22–6, is fully comprehensible and justifiable, there are other cases in which the exegesis is reminiscent of the methods of Rabbinical Judaism. As instances of this, reference may be made to 1 Cor. ix, 9 (cp. Deut. xxv, 4); x, 1–6 (cp. Exod. xiii, 22; xiv. 22; xvi, 4, 35; xvii, 6; Num. xx, 11); 2 Cor. iii, 15, 16 (cp. Exod. xxxiv, 34); Gal. iii, 16 (cp. Gen. xiii, 15; xvii, 7; xxiv, 7); iv, 21–31 (cp. Gen. xvi, 5; xvii, 16–19; xviii, 10, 14; xxi, 1, 2). Other New Testament writers also offer some illustrations of a forced and unnatural exegesis, e.g. Heb. i, 5–13 (cp. Ps. ii, 7; 2 Sam. vii, 14; Ps. xcvii, 7; civ, 4; xlv, 6, 7; cii, 25–7; cx, 1); iii, 7 ff. (cp. Ps. xcv, 7 ff.); v, 4–10 (cp. Ps. cx, 4); xi, 13–15 (cp. Gen. xxiii, 4); 1 Pet. ii, 4–8 (cp. Isa. xxviii, 16; Ps. cxviii, 22; Isa. viii, 14), not to mention some others. We shall not for a moment deny that the arbitrary use of Scriptural passages, divorced from their context, is perfectly justifiable for specific purposes, as in the New Testament passages referred to; but it can hardly be denied that from the purely exegetical, or, shall we say, the hermeneutical point of view, they are beside tl e mark.'[1]

Dr. Oesterley has put into words the difficulty which is widely felt. We shall endeavour to deal with most of the texts which he refers to. Certainly it must be freely admitted that neither the New Testament writers nor the Fathers after them possessed the equipment which the modern scholar has at his disposal for determining the literal sense of the Old Testament. They were not setting themselves to reconstruct with scientific accuracy the situation in which an Old Testament writer was placed and the message that he gave to the men of his own time. That duty lies upon us; we are bound to seek out the literal meaning of each Old Testament book and text in the first place. The New Testament writers had not got our methods of scientific history, as they had not got our railways, steamships and wireless. They

[1] Dr. Oesterley in *Record and Revelation*, p. 412.

had not our knowledge; but we have every need to defer to their wisdom.

3. Theological and Illustrative Use of Scripture

It will be well to go straight to the central point, which is expressed in St. Paul's argument in Galatians. If his exegesis of the texts to which he appeals is unsound, to that extent the argument will be at fault. But it can often be that while the particular instance chosen is unsound, the argument itself is sound, since there are other instances which are valid, so that the argument is true to the general sense of Scripture.

So it may be with the text from which the great argument in Galatians starts; 'the Scripture, foreseeing that God would justify the Gentiles by faith, preached the Gospel beforehand unto Abraham, saying, In thee shall all the nations be blessed' (Gal. iii, 8). It seems probable that the words of Gen. xii, 3, as originally written by the J.-writer, meant something partly different;[1] but St. Paul had before him the *niphal* form in the Hebrew, and the passive in the *LXX*, and he knew further that the universal mission of Israel did not rest on this one phrase in Genesis, but on fifty other passages; it was an authentic element in Israel's messianic vocation. It is this that St. Paul is expounding. He is setting out his philosophy of history, as he has learnt to see it; and he is arguing seriously from his Old Testament data, not devising a theory first, and then finding 'allegorical' illustrations of it from Scripture. The argument runs thus:

There was a Purpose of God, existing from the beginning, and attested by the Promise to Abraham; its final term was the justification of the Gentiles through faith, that they might come to peace with God, and salvation, and blessing. But how could the Purpose of Blessing be accomplished when human sin stood in the way: above all the sin of disobedience to the known will of God, whereby man incurs the curse of Deut. xxvii, 26? (Here is an excellent quotation, selected from many possible texts.) St. Paul finds the answer in the reversal of that argument which had once made the messianic claim of Jesus seem to him intolerable blasphemy; death by crucifixion, according to Deut.

---

[1] See p. 177 above.

xxi, 23, bore the curse of God. Indeed, it was for this very purpose that Caiaphas had conceived and carried out the plan of having Him put to death in that particular way. But now St. Paul had learnt that He had voluntarily taken on Himself that curse, and had 'become a curse for us', that by thus giving Himself as a ransom for many and overcoming death and sin He might turn the curse into a blessing, and save the blessing of Abraham, not for the Jew only, but for the Gentile too (iii, 13, 14).

Christ, then, is the promised Seed of Abraham; and St. Paul notes that in Genesis the word 'seed' is in the singular (v. 16; Gen. xxii, 18, etc.). No doubt the plural could not be used; it would mean 'crops' or 'seeds of various sorts'.[1] Nevertheless the point which he makes is of great importance; it is that the Promise is fulfilled, not in a multiplicity of descendants separately, but in the One in whose body all the redeemed are gathered into unity: Jew and Gentile, slave and free, male and female 'are all one Man in Christ Jesus' (v. 28), and so become corporately 'Abraham's Seed, heirs according to promise' (v. 29).

This justification is of course through faith; for there is no other true justification, no other way to peace with God. There is no peace with God to be gained through scrupulous observance of the Law (v. 11), as Saul the Pharisee had learnt by bitter experience. The Law, then, was but a stage in the divine education of Israel; in the Pentateuch the enactment of the Law comes 430 years after the promise to the Man of Faith (v. 17). (Here we may question the chronology, but the exact number of years is immaterial; and we may further say that we now know that the imposition of the Law in its completeness did not take place till the Reform of Ezra, while the completeness of the Promise that the Gentiles should share in the Covenant came with Second Isaiah. Thus even so, St. Paul's order holds good: the Promise comes first, and the Law comes after. He here explains, in fact, where Ezra's reformed Judaism failed.) The Law was indeed God's law (v. 21); it was added 'because of transgressions', to train up the people in the way of obedience

[1] McNeile in *The Old Testament in the Christian Church*, p. 10.

to God (v. 19), and as he explains more fully in the parallel argument in Rom. iv, 15, to demonstrate man's inability to attain to peace with God by works of his own. But when at last the Righteousness of God had been manifested in the person of the Messiah, then the law-keeping Pharisee and the law-breaking publican and sinner and the law-less Gentile could know themselves to be alike sinners, and all together receive free pardon and forgiveness through Him: 'the scripture hath shut up all things under sin, that the promise by faith of Jesus Christ might be given to them that believe' (v. 22). The Law had been a servile discipline (vv. 23, 24), to prepare the way for the enjoyment of sonship, through the One Son, Jesus the Messiah (iii, 25–iv, 7). The Jews had not been wrong in accepting the Law as divine; they had been fatally wrong in forgetting the Promise and regarding the Mosaic system as final.

He continues: But you Galatians, you who had begun to live under the new order of things, with the messianic Gift of the Spirit, why are you now all crazy to turn your backs on this and go Jewish, taking up again the 'weak and beggarly rudiments' of the Tradition of the Elders, and observing the 'days and months and seasons and years' of the Old Law (iv, 9, 10)? You would outdo the Rabbis themselves in Rabbinism. Well then, if you will have rabbinic exposition, I will give you a sample, from the story of Hagar and Ishmael; listen to me while I refute your Rabbis who tell you that in keeping the whole Law you will be following Isaac and the patriarchs. For in reality the covenant of bondage is that of Hagar and her son Ishmael, connected as it is with Arabia and Sinai; whereas the Promise made to the man of faith comes down through Sarah and Isaac. On the one side, the Law and the earthly Jerusalem; on the other, the Promise and the Jerusalem which is above and is free (vv. 21–31).

Thus St. Paul's much-criticized 'rabbinic exegesis' in this passage turns out to be a piece of strictly *ad hominem* argument, addressed to people who were clamouring for rabbinic exegesis; but the main argument which it crowns is a sound theological argument, substantially firm at every point. In this argument the Old Testament is treated seriously as authoritative; the aim

The Old Testament in the New

is to show from the Scriptures themselves that the divine Purpose for Israel, which the Old Testament was written to set forth, finds its completion and fulfilment in Jesus the Messiah and in Him alone. The Old Testament quotations are therefore vital to the argument, and indeed its whole weight rests upon them; and we have seen that they are all good quotations, or if they are partly invalid they can be supported by others which are valid.[1]

This, then, we may call the *theological* use of Scripture in the New Testament. There is also an *illustrative* use of Scripture,[2] in which the argument does not really rest on the texts quoted, but on other considerations or other texts, and the quotations are simply illustrations of it, such that the argument could stand without them. Of this illustrative use the Hagar-Ishmael allegory in Gal. iv, is an obvious instance. Another is St. Paul's quotation in 1 Cor. ix, 8-10, of the commandment in Deut. xxv, 4, that an ox at work is not to be muzzled, in order to show that ministers of the Gospel may claim financial support. It has

---

[1] The extent to which St. Paul's exegesis may be criticized, and yet be found to justify itself on a higher level, may be illustrated from his argument in Rom. iv. There, in vv. 16-21, he exhibits Abraham as the man of faith who against all natural possibility believed God's promise that Sarah should bear him a child. This is the theme of the account in Gen. xviii, where however in vv. 11 ff. Sarah 'laughs' incredulously and is rebuked. St. Paul does not notice that at the age of 86, only 13 years earlier, Abraham had begotten Ishmael, according to xvi, 16; nor that in xvii, 17, Abraham also had 'laughed' at the promise of a child to Sarah; yet it is from ch. xvii, not xviii, that he quotes in Rom. iv, 17. No doubt there is a discrepancy in the narratives in Genesis, due to diversity of sources; but he does nothing to reconcile the discrepancy. The point, however, on which his argument rests is the theological conception underlying the account in Gen. xviii, of which the key-verse is v. 14, 'Is anything too hard for (*pala*') the Lord?' *Pala*', with its derivative *niphla'oth*, is the word regularly used in the O.T. for God's 'mighty works'; hence St. Paul is expounding with entire faithfulness the meaning which the writer of Gen. xviii intended to convey, in order to show how one principle runs through God's dealings with His people under two dispensations.

[2] Lightfoot (*Galatians*, p. 199 f.), having set side by side Philo's allegorical exegesis of the story of Hagar and Sarah and that of St. Paul, says: 'With Philo, the allegory is the whole substance of his teaching; with St. Paul it is but an accessory. He uses it rather as an illustration than as an argument, as a means of representing in a lively form the lessons being enforced on other grounds.'

been much criticized, especially because in vv. 9–10 he seems
to go out of his way to deny the relevance of the literal sense. It
can hardly be called a conclusive argument; texts used in this
way can usually be countered by others. Yet it can truly be said
to throw light on the principle for which he is contending,
namely that a certain respect and consideration is due, as for the
labouring ox in old Israel, so for the labourer in the work of the
Church.

Another instance is his use of Ps. lxviii, 18, in Eph. iv, 8–11,
to illustrate the gift by the ascended Christ of the apostolic
ministry to the Church. Here he gives the appearance of mis-
quoting the psalm, which spoke of some king, perhaps David,
going up to Jerusalem in triumph after some campaign, leading
his train of captives, and receiving gifts from those who had
been the enemy; St. Paul changes 'received' into 'gave'. In this,
however, he seems to be following a recognized Jewish interpretation, preserved in the Talmud, which reads: 'Thou ascendedst
up to the firmament, O prophet Moses, thou tookest captives
captive, thou didst teach the words of the law, thou gavest them
as gifts to the children of men';[1] that which he 'gave' he had
'received' from God. Again there is an appropriateness in St.
Paul's illustration; the ascended Christ is a victorious conqueror. But it is an illustration, not a demonstrative argument;
it does not give the actual ground on which St. Paul's assertion
rested.

The distinction of the 'theological' and the 'illustrative' use of
the Old Testament comes out with great clearness in the passages
from the Epistle to the Hebrews to which Dr. Oesterley refers us.
It is here most necessary to attend carefully to the actual course
of the argument, and to see exactly what is its true basis. The
author can scarcely have believed that his thesis about the Highpriesthood of the Christ in chap. vii really rested on the fact that
in Gen. xiv no mention is made of Melchizedek's parentage
and genealogy, of his birth and his death; he was not seriously
arguing that he had no father or mother, and therefore the
Christ must be taken to be, like him, an eternal Priest. That

---

[1] Armitage Robinson, *Ephesians*, pp. 179–80, quoting from S. R. Driver,
Sermons on the O.T., p. 197.

is not what he says; he says not that Christ is like Melchizedek, but that on the contrary, Melchizedek is 'made like unto the Son of God' (vii, 3). Nor did his thesis really rest on the reference in Ps. cx, to the Messiah as 'priest for ever after the order of Melchizedek', though that passage was clearly important to him.

His thesis that the Christ is Highpriest is part of the whole interpretation of the Redemption in terms of sacrifice; and this interpretation was part of the original Christian tradition, and depended finally on the Lord's own act in performing a sacrificial rite at the Last Supper, in which He interpreted His death as the Sacrifice of the New Covenant.[1] This sacrificial view of the Redemption runs through the New Testament; and it demanded that a place be found in it for the Highpriest of the messianic Sacrifice. It could not be doubtful for a moment who the Highpriest must be. Neither St. Paul nor St. John explicitly names Him as Priest. But it is several times said that 'He gave Himself', as in Eph. v, 2, 'He gave Himself up for us, an offering and a sacrifice to God, for an odour of a sweet smell'; 'My flesh (which I will give) for the life of the world', John vi, 51;[2] 'He offered Himself without spot to God', Heb. ix, 14. He is the Highpriest in John xvii, 19, 'For their sakes I consecrate Myself', and in Rev. i, 13, where He is seen clothed in the Highpriestly vestment.[3] Behind all this lies the fact that at the Rite in the Upper Room He was the officiant.

The argument of Hebrews about His Sacrifice is most truly 'theological', in the sense in which we are using the word. The Christian Covenant is the New Covenant of Jer. xxxi, 31 ff.; this promise is quoted at length in viii, 9–13, and is seen to be completely fulfilled in Christ (x, 16 ff.). The sacrifice of the Day

---

[1] Much work has been done on this point in recent years. It is sufficient to mention Vincent Taylor, *Jesus and His Sacrifice*, esp. pp. 114–42, 175–86, 201–17; W. Manson, *Jesus the Messiah*, pp. 142–6; and Dom Gregory Dix, *The Shape of the Liturgy*, ch. iv, with his quotation on p. 77 of the dictum of Dr. Rawlinson in *Mysterium Christi*, ed. Bell and Deissmann, 1930, p. 241: 'The doctrine of sacrifice (and of atonement) was not read . . . into the Last Supper: it was read out of it.'

[2] There are several variant readings of this text; the words 'which I will give' are probably not authentic. But the meaning is not seriously affected

[3] See p. 216 below.

of Atonement is said in ix, 7–11 to bear the marks of imperfection, by the fact that the levitical highpriest alone could enter the Sanctuary, once a year, and that the sacrifice was only for ceremonial faults. The prophets further had shown in their criticism of the sacrifices that what God really wanted was not the offering of an animal but the self-oblation of man himself in rational obedience; and here he quotes Ps. xl, 6–8, 'Lo, I come to do Thy will, O God'—no isolated text, for Ps. li, 17, and Isa. liii, 10, could be added to press the point home. Thus the Sacrifice of the Christ, being the offering of Himself without spot to God (ix, 14), is shown to be the fulfilment in history of that which the Old Testament writers had discerned to be the true inwardness of sacrifice; and all his quotations are good quotations, according to the literal sense of the original texts.

But the argument that the Christ is the Highpriest was not so straightforward: and this for two reasons. First, the Old Testament had relatively little to say about the inwardness of the priestly character. It is hard to find more than scattered hints, such as the phrase 'a faithful priest' in 1 Sam. ii, 35; a phrase or two from Malachi, such as 'the priest's lips should keep knowledge' (ii, 7), and the treatment of the symbolism of the highpriestly vestments in Exod. xxviii. But also, and still more, the Christian conception of priestliness depends on the historical person of Jesus Himself. To this point therefore, the writer of Hebrews addresses himself, speaking at length of the true humanity of the Saviour and His experience of human temptation and suffering, and connecting this directly with His Highpriestly office; for it was by this human experience that He gained, as man, that intimate fulness of sympathy with tempted and suffering men which qualifies Him to be their Highpriest before God. This is the theme of chap. ii, 5–18; iv, 14–16; v, 5–10.

He comes, then, to Ps. cx, 4, where he finds a priesthood after the order of Melchizedek to be predicated of the Messiah (v. 6). The Lord's own interpretation of His Messiahship had indeed been so full and comprehensive that Priesthood, in this wide and deep sense, could truly be said to be included in it. But in Hebrews the effort is being made to present a formal theological statement. Since He is the eternal Son, the Heir of all things,

through whom the worlds were made (i, 3), and His Sacrifice
one and unique, and He Himself ascended into heaven (ibid.),
His Highpriesthood must be thought of as one, eternal, universal.
But apposite Old Testament texts were hard to find; the Old
Testament had not worked out the idea of priestliness. Psalm
cx, 4, however, gave a suggestive phrase, pointing to Gen. xiv,
the only other place where Melchizedek is mentioned.

Thus our author makes the best he can of Gen. xiv, with the
help of some forced exegesis. He would say, perhaps, that the
Holy Ghost had seen to it that in Gen. xiv no mention should
be made of Melchizedek's parentage or birth or death, because
He intended Melchizedek to stand as a type of the Messiah.
But plainly the exegesis of Gen. xiv is not the basis of his argument, for by itself it is far too weak to bear the weight. The
weight of the argument rests on the other considerations that
we have mentioned—the general thesis that the Redemption is
sacrificial, and the priestly character of Jesus Himself ('such a
Highpriest became us, holy, guileless, undefiled, separated from
sinners, and made higher than the heavens', vii, 26), besides the
hint given in Ps. cx, 4. The Highpriesthood of the Christ rests
on other grounds, and the use of Gen. xiv is 'illustrative'.

There are other instances of 'illustrative' quotations in this
Epistle, particularly in the string of quotations in chap. i, to
show that the Christ is Creator and Lord and King, whereas
the angels are 'worshipping spirits'. Of these quotations, the last
('Sit thou on My right hand', Ps. cx, 1) is valid; the others apply
to the Son only if it is already admitted that He is far above the
angels; they do not prove it. The first two indeed ('Thou art
My Son', from Ps. ii, and 'I will be to him a Father', 2 Sam.
vii, 14), are scarcely illustrative in any true sense, for they could
be countered by other quotations which speak of angels also as
sons of God (such as Job i, 6) and they do not explain the difference between His Sonship and theirs. The argument is in no
way dependent on these Old Testament texts; they are being
used to illustrate a thesis which rests on the Wisdom Christology,
of which we shall speak later.

Imagery

4. Imagery

The distinction between the 'theological' and the 'illustrative' use of the Old Testament is in itself quite clear. But it is not always easy to trace its application in detail, and make a sharp dividing-line between the two, chiefly for this reason, that the theological principles of the Bible are most frequently set forth, not in 'exact' formulae, after the Greek manner, but in concrete imagery. The 'theological' use, in such cases, takes over some image directly, and applies it to Christ, as in the case of the 'homologies' of which we shall speak in the next section, in which some element in the Messianic Hope, such as the Second Exodus or the New Covenant, is seen as fulfilled in the saving work of Christ. The 'illustrative' use, on the other hand, finds some illuminating comparison in which there is not the same direct relation between prediction and fulfilment, as when St. Matthew in his manner of introducing the Sermon on the Mount ('Jesus went up into the mountain', v. 1) implies that He is the second Moses, or when He compares Himself with Jonah and Solomon (Luke xi, 29–32).

We will give first two instances in which theological and dogmatic facts are set forth with the help of Old Testament imagery: the vision of the Son of Man in Rev. i, in which the imagery is explicit, and the narratives of the Ascension, in which it is implicit.

In the midst of seven golden candlesticks St. John sees 'one like unto a son of man', and gives a detailed description in Rev. i, 13–18.[1] Are we to think of a figure vividly seen, and a description transcribed from a visual image? No, for in that case it would be possible to draw the figure; but a sword coming out from a mouth cannot be drawn; and further, the description is a cento of Old Testament quotations. Is it then a complex theological conception, first thought out as such, and then described in Old Testament language? No, for in that case the

---

[1] I owe the main idea of what follows to Carrington, *The Meaning of the Revelation*, 1931, pp. 83–6, and some of the details to Charles, *Revelation*, I.C.C., pp. 25–34.

theological meaning would have been given first, and then the quotations. But the one piece of theological explanation given, the identification of the candlesticks with the churches, comes at the end (v. 20). Also, he gives it as a vision: I saw. We ought then rather to take the description as a kind of intellectual vision, in which certain concrete images, belonging to the Old Testament, are successively recognized.

The meaning might then be rendered somewhat thus: 'I saw Him, and knew who He was. I knew Him to be the Highpriest in the sacerdotal vestment (ποδήρη, Exod. xxviii, 4): I saw in Him the Man whom Daniel saw, with a golden girdle, eyes like a flame of fire, and feet like glowing brass (Dan. x, 5, 6): and He was the Ancient of Days, with hair white as snow (Dan. vii, 9); and He was the God of Israel returning to Zion in His tabernacling Presence, His voice like the sound of many waters (Ezek. xliii, 2); in His hand were the seven stars, the angels of the seven churches; and He was the Servant of the Lord, whose mouth is as a sharp sword; and His countenance shone like the sun, as at His Transfiguration (Matt. xvii, 2). Like Ezekiel, like Daniel, I fell on my face; and He spoke to me as the Lord God, the First and the Last (Isa. xliv, 6), who was made man and died and rose victorious over Sheol and death. I knew Him as present in the midst of the Church, yet holding the Church in His hand; and He gave me a message to deliver to the Church.'[1]

The actual reality of our Lord's Ascension into heaven must of necessity transcend human experience; it is a fact belonging to the heavenly order of things. Physical movement up from the earth's surface does not actually bring a person nearer to 'heaven', or to God. Whatever, therefore, the Apostles saw could not be anything except a symbol of the theological fact of His session at the Father's right hand. We need not doubt that they

[1] Dr. Carrington says: 'An image which is a unity is created before us; and this creation is more powerful than any of the prophecies from which the separate quotations are made. . . . The spiritual truth enters the mind of the prophet, and organizes itself a body out of such material as is at hand; after finding union with that mind it collects and arranges the symbols in such a way that all are harmonious with the inward and spiritual unity. Nothing but symbols are presented to us; yet the symbols convey the unity.' —p. 83-4.

saw Him go up; but it is significant that the descriptions which they have left us are something more than mere reproductions of a visual image. The narratives are in Old Testament language. We need chiefly to attend to the verbs used for 'ascend'.

In Acts i, 1–11, the verb 'He was taken up' (ἀνελήμφθη) occurs three times, and once more in v. 22. It occurs also three times in the narrative of the Ascension of Elijah in 2 Kings ii. In both cases those who are left behind are looking steadfastly at him who ascends; in both cases, having done so, they receive the promised share of the Spirit which rested upon him.

The verb 'He was lifted up' (ἐπήρθη) was there for them to read in Ps. viii, 1 (*LXX*):

> '*O Lord our Lord, how wonderful is Thy Name in all the earth,*
> *For Thy majesty is lifted up above the heavens.*'

For the 'Cloud' that 'received Him out of their sight' the same word is used (νεφέλη) as for the Cloud which overshadowed them at the Transfiguration, Luke ix, 34, and for the Pillar of Cloud in the Wilderness throughout the Exodus-story, which also overshadowed the Tabernacle, Exod. xl, 34–35, whereas the other Greek word for cloud (νέφος) is never used in this sense.

St. Peter at Pentecost, speaking of the Ascension, quotes of course Ps. cx, 1, 'Sit Thou on My right hand'; he also uses the word 'being exalted' (ὑψωθείς), which occurs in Ps. xlvi, 10, 'Be still, and know that I am God; I will be exalted among the Gentiles, I will be exalted in the earth'; it occurs again in Ps. cx, 'Therefore shall He exalt His head' (v. 7); above all it occurs in the prophecy of the Suffering Servant: 'Behold My Servant shall understand, and shall be exalted, and shall be glorified, and shall be raised very high' (Isa. lii, 13, *LXX*).

St. John's word for 'ascend' (ἀναβαίνω, vi, 62; xx, 17), is used of Moses ascending to Mt. Sinai in Exod. xxiv, 1, etc.; but it is perhaps more significant that it is the word used in Ps. xxiv, 3, 'Who shall ascend into the hill of the Lord?' The fact that this psalm was used by the apostles with reference to the events of the Redemption is shown by the echo of 'the King of glory'

(v. 8) in 1 Cor. ii, 8, where St. Paul speaks of those who 'crucified the Lord of glory'.

Finally, our Lord's words to Caiaphas at His trial, 'Ye shall see the Son of Man sitting on the right hand of Power (i.e. of God) and coming with the clouds of heaven', consist of two quotations: from Ps. cx, 1, and from the vision in Dan. vii, 13–14, in which 'one like unto a son of man . . . came near to the Ancient of Days, and they brought him into His presence, and there was given to him power and honour and the kingdom'. This saying is therefore to be understood as referring to the Ascension rather than to the Advent.[1]

Thus the narratives of the Ascension and other early allusions to it are rich in imagery drawn from the Old Testament: partly liturgical phrases from psalms, and partly symbols drawn from pictures which can be visualized: the Ascension of Elijah, the Cloudy Pillar, the Son of Man vision. In these terms the writers represent the theological fact.

5. Homologies

In 1 Cor. x, 1 ff. and Heb. iii, 7 ff. the Christians are compared to the Israelites in the Wilderness, and are warned to beware lest they fall into the sins because of which that generation was not allowed to enter the Promised Land. St. Paul tells his Corinthians that they, too, have known the Cloud of the divine Presence, have passed through the Red Sea in their baptism, and in their eucharist have the Manna and the Water from the Rock. Therefore they must beware lest they lose their inheritance by lust, idolatry, fornication, tempting God, murmuring. In Hebrews Ps. xcv, the *Venite*, is used to make almost the same point.

They are examples of a very fundamental principle of Old Testament interpretation, which Dr. Phythian-Adams wishes us to call 'homology'[2]; and clearly some such name is needed to describe the parallel which is drawn between the divine operation in the First Redemption and in the second. The re-

---

[1] Lowther Clarke in *The Divine Humanity*, p. 12.
[2] Phythian-Adams, *The Way of At-one-ment*, p. 11.

lation is not one of 'analogy', since that word is used for a like-ness between things earthly and things heavenly, and here we have two corresponding series of earthly events. We have seen the beginnings of 'homology' in Jeremiah's prophecies of a New Exodus and a New Covenant, and again in the treatment of the Tabernacle in the Priestly Document, and in the view of the Conquest of Canaan which presented itself to the editors of the Book of Joshua.[1] But it is only in the New Testament that 'homology' comes fully into its own, and the thought is clearly worked out that the pattern of God's working, under two dis-pensations, is one and the same. Further, it becomes plain at certain crucial points that this conception also controlled the actual working-out of the events: it was not only used by the evangelists to interpret the events, but was in the mind of our Lord Himself.[2]

We meet at various points the idea that by His death and resurrection He has effected a New Exodus, redeeming His people this time not from a merely political enslavement, but from bondage to sin and to death. Once again God has called His Son out of Egypt (Matt. ii, 15; Hos. xi, 1). At the Trans-figuration, St. Luke shows Him speaking with Moses and Elijah of His Exodus which He is to accomplish at Jerusalem.[3] The idea of the Exodus may be further seen in the word 'ransom' or 'redemption' ($\lambda \acute{\upsilon} \tau \rho o \nu$ and derivatives), which occurs first in Mark x, 45; this word is regularly used of the Exodus in the Old Testament.[4] So again 'Christ our Passover is sacrificed for us' (1 Cor. v, 7–8). Part of the meaning of 'Behold the Lamb of God' in John i, 29, is that He is the Paschal Lamb provided by God Himself, of which not a bone is to be broken (xix, 36).

The New Covenant predicted by Jeremiah was explicitly in-augurated by Him at the Last Supper: 'this cup is the New Covenant in My blood' (1 Cor. xi, 25). Jeremiah's prophecy is quoted *in extenso* in Heb. viii; it is commented on at length in

[1] Pp. 146, 155, and 156 f. above.
[2] See pp. 122–6 above.
[3] Luke ix, 31. The rendering 'decease' in A.V. and R.V. is a bad mis-translation, and the 'departure' of the R.V. margin is rather worse.
[4] As in Exod. vi, 6; xv, 13; Deut. vii, 8; ix, 26; xv, 15; etc. See Westcott, *Hebrews*, pp. 295–7.

2 Cor. iii, 3–6; and it underlies every reference to the messianic gift of the Forgiveness of Sins, which in the synoptic gospels stands side by side with the healing of bodily disease as signifying the present operation of the powers of the New Order.[1]

Hence St. Paul, in comparing his Corinthians, surrounded by a corrupt pagan civilization, to Israel in the Wilderness, is not making a far-fetched and unreal comparison, but is following a broad high-road of Biblical interpretation. Indeed, the Church militant on earth is always in the Wilderness; and so was the Lord Himself in His earthly life, and above all in His Temptation in the Wilderness, the account of which is closely modelled on Deut. viii. It becomes further a question whether St. Mark's use of the same word (translated 'desert' in Mark i, 45; vi, 31 ff.) to describe the countryside of Galilee, is not intended to suggest the same thought; and certainly the idea is present in the comparison of the Crucified to the brazen serpent which Moses lifted up in the Wilderness (John iii, 14; Num. xxi, 9).

Connected with the thought of the Tabernacle in the Wilderness is that of the Presence, which late Judaism knew as the *Shekhinah*. St. Mark's gospel opens with a pair of quotations, 'Behold I send My messenger', Mal. iii, 1, and 'Make ye ready the way of the Lord', Isa. xl, 3, in order to indicate that in the advent of Jesus the promised Return of the Presence has taken place. St. John is explicit: 'the Word . . . tabernacled among us, and we beheld His glory' (i, 14).[2] Elsewhere the same thought is apparent in the use of the word 'glory' as meaning *'the Shekhinah'*; in Jas. ii, 1, the Christians meeting in their 'synagogue' are warned not to mix respect of persons with their faith in the 'Lord Jesus Christ the Shekhinah'.[3] It is apparent also in the designation of the Church as the true Temple, or rather Sanc-

---

[1] Cf. e.g. 'Thy sins be forgiven thee', Mark ii, 5, 10, with the description of the 'works of the Messiah' in Matt. xi, 5: 'the blind receive their sight', etc.; the similar quotation from Isa. lxi, 1 in the synagogue at Nazareth, Luke iv, 18–19; and the proof from the exorcisms that the Kingdom is present in the midst, Luke xi, 20.

[2] See Burney, *Aramaic Origin of the Fourth Gospel*, 1922, pp. 35–7, and the references there.

[3] Marshall, *H.D.B.*, vol. iv, p. 489, with the Talmudic references there given. He cites also Rom. vi, 4, Christ raised from the dead by the Glory of the Father, and 1 Pet. iv, 14, the Shekhinah resting on the martyrs.

tuary (*ναός*) in which a divine Presence dwells (1 Cor. iii, 16); and this thought may be present as an additional meaning in John i, 14, 'The Word . . . tabernacled in us'. So in 2 Cor. vi, 16, St. Paul takes a text from Leviticus where the preposition has meant 'among' and uses it to mean in: 'we are a sanctuary of the living God, as God said, I will dwell in them and walk in them'.[1]

In these homologies the events of the second Redemption are treated as corresponding to the events of the first. In doing so the writers are not merely drawing an interesting historical parallel. They need the Old Testament story in order to see in their true context the events which had lately happened; as they go over in their minds those recent events, they have floating in their minds the ancient story of the deliverance from Egypt and the Covenant. The terrible events of the passion, and the experience of the first Easter, were a Crossing of the Red Sea, in which the enemy had been overwhelmed in the waters, and the Pillar of Cloud had gone before, leading the Israel of God to salvation and freedom.

The same concrete imagery is seen also in the various descriptions which are given of the Christian community. These must be summarized very briefly. It is the Ecclesia, the *Qahal*, the Congregation of the Lord; hence in 1 Pet. ii, 9–10, it is the 'royal priesthood and holy nation' of Exod. xix, 6, and for it the *Lo-ammi* and *Lo-ruhumah* of Hosea are reversed, as in Hos. ii, 23. Here we are again on the line of the homology of the Exodu-. As Israel entered Palestine and in due course conquered Jerusalem, so the Church possesses, or rather *is* Jerusalem: not the earthly city, but the Jerusalem which is above and is free (Gal.

---

[1] Lev. xxvi, 12; see p. 201 above. We need both the meaning 'in' and that of 'among'. In John i, 14, the meaning 'among' is demanded, if the reference here is to the apostolic witness to the earthly life, as 1 John i, 1–3 seems to prove. Further, in Rev. vii, 15, 'He that sitteth on the throne shall tabernacle over them'; and in xxi, 3, the Presence is among the saints in heaven. For a right account of the Church as the true Temple, built of living stones, and the Presence in it, we need all these senses: Christ incarnate; Christ ascended, adored by the Church in its perfect condition in 'heaven', and in its incomplete condition on earth (where He is worshipped in the sacramental Presence, which is the liturgical counterpart of the Presence on the Sacred Ark); and His Real Presence in the hearts of the faithful.

The Old Testament in the New

iv, 26). The Lamb in Rev. xiv, 1, is seen 'on the mount Zion'.

The Church is the true Temple: not the temple made with hands, which the Lord said would be destroyed (Mark xiv, 58; xv, 29; John ii, 19), but the Temple which is His body, John ii, 21; built of living stones, a spiritual House for the true sacrificial worship, 1 Pet. ii, 5; built up, in the process of the building up of the body of Christ, on the foundation of apostles and prophets which in turn rests on the Christ who is the massive corner-stone, Eph. ii, 20–22.

It is the Bride of Christ, Old Israel had been chosen by Yahweh to be His Bride, Hos. i, ii, Jer. ii, 2 ff., Ezek. xvi, but had proved unfaithful; but in the messianic days Israel, penitent and restored, would be the Wife and Mother, Isa. lxii, 4–5, lxvi, 10 ff. Jesus had come as the Bridegroom, Matt. xxii, 2, xxv, 6; and the whole Fulfilment is seen in Eph. v, 23–30.[1]

It is the Flock of the Good Shepherd. In John x, the point is not so much that our Lord is compared to a shepherd in His care for the flock, but rather that all that is said of Yahweh as the Shepherd of Israel in Ps. lxxx, Isa. xl, 11, and above all in Ezek. xxxiv, is fulfilled in Him; the false shepherds are judged, and Yahweh Himself becomes the Shepherd of His people, seeking and saving that which was lost, and feeding them upon the mountains of Israel.

Once more, the Church is the New Creation. Here the great text is Isa. lxv, 17, 'Behold, I create new heavens and a new earth'; and this thought comes back repeatedly in St. Paul, where he speaks of the new creative work that has been accomplished, not for Israel only but for the human race, as in Gal. vi, 15; 2 Cor. v, 17; Eph. ii, 10, 15. Jesus is the 'second Adam', 1 Cor. xv, 45 ff.; Rom. v, 12–21. By His obedience He has reversed the disobedience of the first Adam, and is the Head of a regenerated human race.

6. Christ the Wisdom of God

The instances which we have seen of the 'theological' use of the Old Testament have so far mainly exhibited the meaning

[1] See Thornton, *The Common Life in the Body of Christ*, pp. 221–34.

of God's redemptive action through Christ. We come now to a different type of theological use, in which the doctrine of the Person of Christ is set forth in relation to the Creation, and to something approaching what we understand by a theological scheme. So long as the Gospel was being proclaimed on Palestinian soil, it was sufficient and fitting that the theology of the Incarnation should be expressed wholly in terms of Old Testament imagery. But a different treatment was needed as soon as the Church began to take root in the Graeco-Roman world. It was not, indeed, that the Greek-speaking converts should be allowed to drop the Old Testament; it was rather that the Old Testament imagery should be accompanied by a translation of it into the idiom of Greek thought, for the benefit of those who had been brought up on Greek philosophy, and were familiar with the Stoic doctrine of a *logos* or immanent rationality in the world of phenomena, and with the new Greek apologetic which Judaism had begun to undertake in Alexandria and Ephesus.

St. Paul's first taste of this was at Paphos in Cyprus, when in the drawing-room of Sergius Paulus he found himself confronted with Elymas, the local purveyor of the fashionable ideas of syncretistic Judaism. As he listened, there came over him an overpowering realization that the professor's discourse consisted of idle words signifying nothing, and that the Christian Gospel could go through such teaching like a knife through butter; and he turned on the man and denounced him as an impostor with such terrific force that they had to lead him helpless out of the room (Acts xiii, 6–12). St. Paul now understood that the Gospel of Jesus the Messiah must go on to conquer the world; if he had believed that before, now he knew it. This Gospel had the answer to all the Greek questions; there was no teaching in the Graeco-Roman world that could stand up to it. At least by the time that he wrote 1 Corinthians he was speaking of the Messiah as the Divine Wisdom and as the Last or Final Adam (1 Cor. i, 24, 30–1; xv, 45–9).

All this may have been implicit in the original Gospel; but it had certainly not been explicit. There is nothing in the tradition that comes to us in the synoptic gospels to connect Jesus with the creation of the world; the one clear allusion (Luke xi, 49) comes in an evangelist's editorial phrase, not in the Lord's own words.[1] Yet there was much that pointed in that direction. He was the Messiah of the Divine Kingdom, the Son of Man, the Servant of the Lord, the unique Son of God. In a very deep sense He *was* the Kingdom: He had come bringing it, and in His person and character its whole spiritual significance was gathered up. He was the Fulfiller: this Gospel of His gathered up in an extraordinary way the deepest truth of the Old Testament. The earliest Christians read in 'the Law of Moses, the Prophets and the Psalms' the things concerning Him.

There was then a theological question waiting to be asked: What was *ultimately* His personal relation to this Gospel of God? He was not its servant, its herald, as were His apostles who called themselves 'servants of the word' (Luke i, 2; Acts vi, 4). His phrase, 'for My sake and the Gospel's' (Mark viii, 35; x, 29) implied an intimate relationship; He was not the servant of the Gospel, but its Lord and its originator. Or, along another line: all Christians saw in Him the true pattern of human nature, and they knew in their own experience how through the messianic Salvation which had come to them they had found their true selves, they had become true men. In the earliest epistles the life of the Church and of its members is seen as being 'in Christ' (Gal. i, 22; iii, 28; 1 Thess. i, 1; ii, 14; iii, 8; v, 12, 19); and this thought of the membership of the Christians in the body of Christ runs through the Epistles. In 1 Cor. xv, He is the Final Adam; in what relation then does He stand to the original unfallen Adam, to man as he was created, to the primal pattern of human nature? With this thought we are back on synoptic ground: speaking of the true nature of Marriage, Jesus, in Mark x, speaks of the relation of the unfallen Adam and Eve, according to Gen. ii, 23-4, as revealing the true pattern of marriage and setting the standard which must be followed in the messianic order of things. It was therefore inevitable sooner or later that the 'new man' which Christians 'put on' at their baptism should be described in the terms used in Col. iii, 10: 'the new

[1] Yet He does in Matt. xii, 42 = Luke xi, 31, compare Himself to Solomon whose wisdom the Queen of Sheba came to hear.

man, which is being renewed unto knowledge after the image of Him that created him'.

This takes us one step further. In Him as man is the revelation of the true human nature: in Him as Son of God must be the beginning, the origin, of this pattern of human nature. He who as man is the Last Adam, as the Son of God is the Divine Wisdom; and by His Wisdom the Lord founded the earth, had her by Him as His master-workman in the act of creation, and she was daily His delight (Prov. iii, 19; viii, 30).[1] The name is given by St. Paul in 1 Cor. i, 24, 30; the idea is worked out with some fulness in Col. 1, 15–20, to which we will return in a moment. In Heb. i, 2, 3, He is described in phrases partly taken from Wisd. vii, 24–6, as the Agent of creation, and as Himself the radiance of God's glory and the Image of His person. The Prologue of St. John is mainly built up of phrases from the Wisdom-books: Prov. iii, 19–20; viii, 22–35; Ecclus. i, 1; xxiv; Wisd. vii, 30; ix, 1, 4, 9.[2]

The great Christological passage in Col. i, 13–20, begins with the statement that God has 'rescued us from the power of darkness and transferred us into the Kingdom of the Son of His love', and goes on to speak of Him as the Image of God (from Wisd. vii, 26), and the 'First-begotten before all creation' (perhaps from Ps. lxxxix, 28), and then goes on to what seems to be a commentary on the *Bere'shith*, 'In the beginning', of Gen. i, 1. Burney has suggested that his meaning is somewhat thus. First, he gives three meanings of the preposition '*b*':

Bere'shith: in *re'shith*: 'in Him were all things created', etc. (i, 16),
        by *re'shith*: 'all things have been created through Him' (16),
    unto *re'shith*: 'and unto Him' (16);

and then four meanings of *re'shith*:

---

[1] See the exposition of the praises of Wisdom in Hoskyns, *The Fourth Gospel*, pp. 152–3, quoted above, p. 195 f.

[2] See Hoskyns, *The Fourth Gospel*, 152–64, and Rendel Harris, *The Origin of the Prologue to St. John's Gospel*. For the connection of 'word' with 'Gospel', see pp. 79–80 above.

Re'shith means beginning: 'He is before all things' (17),
      means sum-total: 'and in Him all things consist'
          (συνέστηκεν, 17),
      means head: 'and He is the Head of the body, the
          Church' (18),
      means first-fruits: 'who is the Beginning, the first-born
          frcm the dead';

'that in all things He might have the pre-eminence', fulfilling
every meaning which can be extracted from *re'shith*. 'In every
possible sense of the word, Christ is the Fulfiller.'[1]

What is the meaning of all this? Is it that the New Testament
theologians are indulging in theological speculation, after Philo's
manner? But the teaching is not given in the tentative manner
proper to personal interpretations (cf. 1 Cor. vii, 25); it is given
as an exposition of the Christian Faith. Ought we not to say
rather that they have learnt so to interpret the cosmic function
of the Christ, through reading the Scripture with these questions
in mind? They were asking, somewhat in the words of the
Ethiopian Eunuch, Of whom speaketh the prophet this? Who
or what is this divine Wisdom which was with God in the creation of the world? The answer could not be doubtful. He, the
Saviour, was the Alpha as well as the Omega, the ἀρχή and λόγος
as well as the τέλος.[2] In Him was the answer to all the Greek
questions.

7. The Fulfilment of the Prophecies

One other aspect of the interpretation of the Old Testament
in the New remains to be considered: that of the Fulfilment of
the Prophecies. It has been commonly taken for granted that
the New Testament writers set forth an apologetic for the Christian Gospel based on the claim that the events of the history
have happened strictly according to a time-table drawn up
beforehand by the prophets, and that the hand of God is therefore to be seen both in the predictions and in the fulfilment.

---

[1] Burney, in *J.T.S.*, xxvii, pp. 160 ff.; Radford, *Colossians*, pp. 179–80.
[2] P. 52 f. above.

The Fulfilment of the Prophecies

'In the early church it was a leading conception, specially marked in the first and fourth gospels, that the whole of Christ's life was divinely ordered for the express purpose of fulfilling the Old Testament.'[1] It is possible to point to St. Matthew's formula of quotation, 'These things were done that it might be fulfilled which was spoken by the prophet ———, saying'; or to the opening words of St. Peter's address to the assembled disciples after the Ascension, 'Brethren, it was needful that the Scripture should be fulfilled which the Holy Ghost spake before by the mouth of David concerning Judas' (Acts i, 16). Yet what we have said about the principle of Homology may suggest that such a view is unjust to the New Testament writers.

To be sure, there were at certain points quite striking coincidences between prophecy and event; and where this was the case, it is not surprising that they should be pointed out. One such instance bears on its face every mark of primitiveness: in Acts iv. 25–7, the apostles, fresh from a moral victory in the Sanhedrin, recognize with wondering joy how literally 'the Gentiles have raged' and 'the kings of the earth set themselves in array against the Lord and against His Christ', in the persons of Herod and Pontius Pilate. Another is the prophecy of Zechariah about the potter's field and the thirty pieces of silver, fulfilled in the story of Judas Iscariot (Matt. xxvii, 9 f.). Here it appears that the narrative has been partly adjusted to suit the prophecy; for the exact sum which Judas received is mentioned in this gospel only (here and in xxvi, 15). The same has happened in the story of the Triumphal Entry, Matt. xxi, 2 ff., where two animals are brought to our Lord, as in Zech. ix, 9; and in the mention of the 'wine mingled with gall' (Matt. xxvii, 34), in place of St. Mark's 'medicated wine', to suit Ps. lxix, 21. It does not follow, however, that when a narrative shows the influence of an Old Testament passage, the points affected are necessarily unhistorical; of the three reminiscences of Ps. xxii in the narrative of the crucifixion in Mark xv, 25–39—the parting of His garments, v. 24, 'wagging their heads', v. 29, and the cry *Eloi*, v. 34—none need be questioned, and the last is authenticated by the fact that it is quoted in the original

[1] McNeile, *St. Matthew*, commentary on i, 22.

227

language, and the liturgical Hebrew at that, not the Aramaic which is reproduced elsewhere in this gospel.

But are the minds of the writers greatly occupied with the mere coincidences of detail? Clearly the appropriateness of Ps. xxii to the Passion of our Lord does not depend on these small points, but goes very deep indeed; for this poem is a rendering in psalm-form of Isa. liii, and it appears that He Himself had both scriptures in mind. We should notice also the texts that they refrain from quoting: the remarkable verse of Hosea vi, 2, about the resurrection, 'after two days will He revive us, and on the third day He will raise us up', or the text in Zech. vi, 11–12, which names Jesus as the Messiah: 'the man whose name is the Branch'.[1]

Let us now look in detail at St. Peter's address to the disciples in Acts i, 15 ff. He begins by saying that 'it was needful that the Scripture should be fulfilled'; and we read on with expectancy, to see what text it is to be. It turns out to be, not any remarkable coincidence of detail, such as that which we have noted in Matt. xxvii, 9, but a pair of texts from two 'imprecatory' passages in the Psalms: lxix, 25, 'Let his habitation be made desolate, and let no man dwell therein', and cix, 8, 'his office ($\epsilon\pi\iota\sigma\kappa\omega\pi\grave{\eta}\nu$) let another take'. The bearing of these quotations is, then, to identify the suffering and persecuted psalmist with Jesus, and the persecuting enemy, who falls under God's judgement, with the fallen apostle. We might then reconstruct the train of thought thus: 'The tragedy of the fall of Judas has been mysterious and perplexing; why has God allowed it to happen? But we have learnt that the supreme tragedy of the public branding of the Messiah as accursed of God by His death on the cross did not mean that the enemies of God were able to defeat His purpose of Salvation for Israel, but has been, on the contrary, the very means of God's supreme victory. This is

---

[1] There seems however to be an echo of the 'robe' and the 'crown' provided for Jesus the son of Josedech (Zech. ii, 5; vi, 11, *LXX*) in John xix, 5, 'Behold the Man', and 'wearing the crown of thorns and the purple robe', and in xix, 14, 'Behold your King'. Further, the *LXX* of Zech. vi, 12, which could be translated 'His name is Dayspring' ($\grave{\alpha}\nu\alpha\tau\omega\lambda\grave{\eta}$) is echoed in Luke i, 78, 'The Dayspring from on high shall visit (*or according to the variant reading,* hath visited) us'.

The Fulfilment of the Prophecies

shown by the fact that it was prophesied (as indeed He Himself taught us, Mark ix, 12, etc.); so that '*it was necessary* that the Messiah should suffer these things and enter into His glory' (Luke xxiv, 26, 46), and the crucifixion itself was 'by the determinate counsel and foreknowledge of God' (Acts ii, 23). In this same context we see the fall of Judas; it was all allowed for in the divine plan, for in the psalms also (such as lxix and cix, here quoted) the servant of God had to suffer in this way at the hands of treacherous enemies. God's purpose has not been frustrated, but is going forward; and we can take Ps. cix, 8, as authorizing us to find out the man whom our Lord has chosen to fill the vacant place in the Twelve' (v. 24).

We will turn next to the series of prophecies in St. Matthew's gospel which are introduced by the formula, 'that it might be fulfilled', etc. It is not to be denied that in certain cases at least these constitute striking coincidences; nevertheless, taken as a whole, they make up a magnificent scheme of Christology. It is likely that they existed as such, in a collection of *testimonia*, before the evangelist assigned them to their places in his gospel, to illustrate the meaning of the story which he has to tell.

Matt. i, 23—St. Matthew read the word 'virgin' in the *LXX* text, illustrating the tradition of the virgin-birth of Jesus; but the further point of his quotation is, 'They shall call His Name Immanuel', which means, God with us.

ii, 15—'Out of Egypt did I call My Son.' Behind the superficial coincidence between a story of the Infancy and a prophecy which referred originally to something quite different, lies the great Homology of the Exodus.[1]

ii, 18—'Rachel weeping for her children.' Deeper meanings are suggested here: Rachel is the *mater dolorosa* of the Old Testament, who dies in giving birth to Benjamin, and is pictured by Jeremiah as still weeping, over the sorrow of the exile. But the continuation of the passage is, that the children are to return from the land of the enemy; present sorrow is not the end of God's purpose. We can compare John xvi, 21: 'a woman when she is in travail hath sorrow', but sorrow leads to joy. It may

[1] See p. 219 above, and Hoskyns in *Mysterium Christi* (ed. Bell and Deissmann, 1930), p. 83 f.

be that thoughts such as these were in the evangelist's mind.

ii, 23—'He shall be called a Nazoraean.' It is not clear what prophecy the evangelist intends to quote. One of two interpretations is probably right—or rather, perhaps, *both* may be in mind.[1] (*a*) The meaning is that the name 'Nazoraeans' was coined by the Jewish Christians to turn the edge of the contemptuous designation of them as 'Nazarenes', and was derived by them from *nēṣer*, the Branch of Isa. xi, 1. 'If we can assume that the Jewish Christian developed from the technical Hebrew term *nēṣer*=Branch=Messiah an adjective *naṣôrai*, "Messianic One", and applied this to Jesus, this would account for the term Ναζωραῖος. They may indeed have derived this from the text of Isa. xlix, 6, where the word translated "preserved" in its unpointed form can be read *naṣôrai* and translated, "It is too light a thing that thou shouldest be . . . the Nazoraean (*naṣôrai*) to restore Israel".'[2] Or (*b*) as has lately been suggested, 'Nazoraean' is the same as 'Nazirite', and means 'separated', 'consecrated'. Thus it is a Messianic title, and connects up with the designation of Jesus as 'the Holy One', Mark i, 24=Luke iv, 34; Acts iii, 14; 1 John ii, 20; 'the Holy Thing', Luke i, 35, and many other passages.[3]

iv, 15–16—'Land of Zebulon, land of Naphtali.' This, from Isa. ix, 1, 2, illustrates the fact that the ministry of Jesus began in that part of Galilee. But it goes on to speak of Him as the Light of the World: 'the people which sat in darkness saw a great light'.

viii, 17—'Himself took our infirmities and bare our diseases.' This quotation comes in the middle of a collection of miracles, chiefly works of healing; but there is no record in the gospels of our Lord ever having been sick. It is taken from Isa. liii, 4: 'Surely he hath borne our griefs and carried our sorrows'; the suffering Servant is the sin-bearer. Without any doubt we must read this in the context in which the stories of the healings were told in the Church, in their application to the spiritual and

[1] It is a regular feature of the 'illustrative use' that alternative explanations are put side by side; cf. the instance from Origen, p. 274 below.

[2] G. H. Box, in *The People and the Book*, p. 440.

[3] T. Nicklin and R. O. P. Taylor in *C.Q.R.*, vol. cxl, July–Sept., 1945, art. 'Nazarene or Nazirite?'.

The Fulfilment of the Prophecies

bodily needs of each Christian coming to meet his Lord in the sacrament. He of whom the stories were told was the Saviour of every Christian soul; and each one could cast on the Lord all his troubles, and take to himself His word to the leper, 'I will: be thou made clean' (v. 3 *supra*), or to the centurion, 'Go thy way, and as thou hast believed, so be it done unto thee' (v. 13); for the Suffering Servant had on the cross 'borne his griefs and carried his sorrows'.

xii, 18–21—'Behold My Servant whom I have chosen.' Isa. xlii, 1–3, the first of the Servant-poems, quoted from the Hebrew, with the last clause from the *LXX*.[1] The appropriateness of this needs no comment.

xiii, 35—'I will open my mouth in parables.' This is far more than a mere illustration of the word 'parable'. Our Lord's parables were not, according to the superficial modern reading of them, mere 'earthly stories with a heavenly meaning', but *meshalim*, dark sayings, whose true significance the careless hearer would certainly miss, as has been explained in vv. 10–17. Those to whom it is given to know the mysteries of the Kingdom of heaven can begin to understand the parables; those to whom it is not will be found, as often to-day, praising the literary beauty of the Parable of the Prodigal Son, but not seeing that their own part in it is either that of the penitent son or that of the elder brother. The hiding of the meaning of the parables is the same as the hiding of divine truth from the wise and prudent and the revealing of it to babes (Matt. xi, 25). The parables declare 'things hidden from the foundation of the world': the saving work of God in Christ, which 'prophets and righteous men desired to see', which His disciples have the opportunity to see. But it is always, 'he that hath ears, let him hear'.[2]

xxi, 5—'Tell ye the daughter of Zion, Behold, thy King cometh unto thee.' This is interpolated into the narrative of the Triumphal Entry, derived from Mark; and it is generally agreed that it correctly gives the original intention of His action on that occasion. He had come as King of Israel, but not in the sense of Psalms of Solomon xvii; He was the King who would (as the

[1] See p. 205 above.
[2] Cf. T. W. Manson, *The Teaching of Jesus*, pp. 74–80.

passage from Zechariah goes on to say) 'cut off the chariot from Ephraim, and the horse from Jerusalem', and 'speak peace unto the nations' (Zech. ix, 10).

xxvii, 9—'And they took the thirty pieces of silver.' This quotation presents, as has been said, a coincidence between prophecy and event; in this one instance, it is hard to see any deeper meaning. But, taken as a whole, this series of ten quotations gives a splendid picture of the person and work of the Messiah, and fully justifies Canon Green in including as the frontispiece of his work of St. Matthew the figure of the reigning Christ (the *Pantokrator*) from the cathedral of Cefalu in Sicily.[1]

8. The Interpretation of the Old Testament in the New

This chapter must end with a summary of the conclusions which we have reached about the use of the Old Testament in the New, together with some estimate of the difference between the use of it there and in contemporary Judaism. This will lead up to the subject which will occupy the remaining chapters, the use of the Old Testament in the Church.

There are three principal ways in which the New Testament writers use the Old Testament; these, though in particular instances they sometimes merge into one another, are in themselves quite distinct.

(i) The Old Testament is most often quoted in the plain and literal sense, as when our Lord quotes the two commandments of love to God and love to neighbour, or St. Paul in Gal. iii, 8, cites the promise to Abraham, or in Rom. iii, 10–18, collects six texts from the Psalms to show how man is under sin. We are still on the ground of the literal sense when in Matt. v., 39–40, our Lord puts before His disciples the pattern of the Servant of Yahweh,[2] and when, explicitly in Luke xxii, 37, and implicitly elsewhere, He identifies Himself with the Servant; and again, when St. Paul, 'Hebrews' and St. John identify Him with the Divine Wisdom, since in doing so they are taking the concept of Wisdom in substantially the same sense which the writers

[1] F. W. Green, *St. Matthew*, Clarendon series.
[2] See p. 125 above.

of the Wisdom-books gave to it. Here the literal meaning is a theological meaning.

(ii) We took the word 'theological' in this chapter to describe that type of argument, based on the Old Testament texts, in which the incomplete accomplishment of the divine Purpose for man's Salvation in the Old Testament is shown to have been brought to completion in the New. Such is St. Paul's argument in Galatians; this, however, leads up to a 'spiritual' use of an Old Testament conception, when Gentile Christians are called 'Abraham's seed' and 'the Israel of God' (iii, 29; vi, 16). A whole series of other terms are similarly used in a 'transformed' sense: Christ is King, and Highpriest, and sacrificial Victim, and the Church is the new Israel, is Jerusalem, is the Temple of God. The fact that at the Last Supper He performed a sacrificial rite for the inauguration of the New Covenant links up this series of terms with the 'homologies' in which His saving work is described in terms of the Exodus, and the Christians are seen to be in the Wilderness, looking forward to their entry into the Promised Land. Such use of the Old Testament must be called truly 'theological', because it can be shown not to have been a series of devotional reflections imposed on the events thirty years after, but to have actually controlled the working-out of the events themselves.

(iii) The 'illustrative' use of the Old Testament is that in which it is used not to point out some necessary connection between the events of the Old Testament and those of the New, but merely to illustrate some point which is accepted as true on other grounds. It is difficult or impossible to draw a sharp line between the two classes, for the reason that the theological doctrine of the New Testament is largely given by means of imagery; yet the distinction is in itself quite clear. When our Lord is spoken of as the second Moses, this is something that relates itself to the Exodus-homology; when however He likens Himself to Jonah, this is a 'type', since what is here presented is a comparison which throws light on His mission and on the refusal of that generation to repent at His preaching, but not an argument that the working-out of the divine plan demands that there should be a second Jonah. When St. Paul illustrates the

position of the Christians and the unbelieving Jews by Isaac
and Ishmael respectively, he is using 'allegory'. The ambiguity
of this last word has been responsible for much confusion about
the 'spiritual interpretation' of Scripture, since 'the allegorical
sense' is often used also to cover 'theological' interpretations of
the Old Testament.[1] Allegory, in the strict sense, is not valid as
exegesis. Since it does not argue from the proper meaning of the
Old Testament texts as its basis, but imposes meanings on them,
the authority on which such teaching rests is not that of the
Old Testament text that is being used, but is some other. When
the teaching given is in accord with the general sense of Scripture and with the Catholic Faith, it is good teaching in itself;
and the allegorical use of the Old Testament can often illustrate
even the literal meaning of the text in a valuable way. Of this
we shall see instances in chap. ix.

Between the interpretation of Scripture given in the New
Testament and that of Judaism there are two outstanding
differences.

The first difference concerns the doctrine of the Spirit. In
this connection a passage from the Talmud is instructive, as
regards both its style of exegesis and its substance. 'In Hag.
i, 8, "And I will be glorified" (we'ekabdha) is written without the final he, and since the numerical value of he is 5, the
omission is taken to mean that five things—the Shekhinah, the
Ark, the Urim and Thummim, the sacred fire, and the Spirit of
prophecy, would be wanting in the Second Temple.'[2] In our
study of pre-Christian Judaism, we noticed the ugly phenomenon of Scribism appearing, from the time when it became the
accepted belief that prophecy was at an end. But the Christians
of the apostolic age shook themselves free from it at one bound.

St. Luke introduces the narrative of the ministry with the
sentence, 'The word of the Lord came unto John the Son of
Zachariah in the wilderness' (iii, 2); he uses the old Biblical
phrase in order to show that prophecy had begun again. Thereafter he repeatedly emphasizes the presence of the Spirit; after
John has declared that the coming Messiah will baptize with the

[1] For the Four Senses of Scripture, see p. 268 f. below.
[2] *Yoma* 21, 2; quotation from Farrar, *History of Interpretation*, 1886, p. 76.

Holy Spirit and with fire (iii, 16), Jesus is baptized, and the Spirit descends on Him (v. 22); 'full of the Holy Spirit', He is 'led by the Spirit in the wilderness' (iv, 1), and returns in the power of the Spirit to Galilee (v. 14), where at Nazareth He reads from Isa. lxi, 'The Spirit of the Lord is upon Me' (v. 18). Thereafter, in this and the other gospels, we hear Him criticize the formalism and externalism of the Scribes, who make the commandment of God of none effect by their tradition; what is lacking in them is a right sense of proportion between the reverence and fear due to the living God Himself, and the limited claim of the ecclesiastical system which exists for His glory. In John v, 39–47, He condemns the prevailing bibliolatry: 'Ye search the Scriptures, because ye think that in them ye have eternal life', yet though they testify of Me, 'ye will not come to Me that ye may have life'. If they had believed Moses, if they had shared the upward and forward-looking faith of Moses, they would have believed Jesus, and they would not have failed to recognize their own Messiah when He came. This passage is remarkably parallel, not in words but in sense, to Matt. xxiii, 29–31, where He says that they build the tombs of the prophets, saying that if they had lived in the days of the prophets they would (of course!) have been on the right side; but it is this very self-confidence of theirs that makes it certain that they would have been on the wrong side: 'Wherefore ye witness to yourselves that ye are the sons of them that slew the prophets' (v. 31).

The New Testament writers never criticize the accepted belief in the Inspiration of Scripture, interpreted as it was in the sense of Inerrancy. Yet they show a truly remarkable freedom from the limitations of view which usually associate themselves with the doctrine of Inerrancy; and this freedom is due to the fact that they are looking all the time for the great theological principles of God's work of salvation. Where the Scribes were looking for precise rules of religion and morality as laid down in the Law, and were interpreting it in the elaborate casuistry of the Tradition of the Elders, the Apostolic writers are tracing out the meaning of the Passion, of the divine love manifested in the Christ, of the gift to man of sonship, and of the fruit of the Spirit.

This difference of emphasis between the New Testament writers and the Rabbis makes it necessary to call in question the assertion commonly made, that because the apostolic writers assume the inerrancy of Scripture, they accept it in the rabbinic sense and take over unaltered the rabbinic notion of Inspiration. Such a view ignores the radical difference of outlook and mentality. In much the same way many in modern times have thought that the critical question of the authorship of Ps. cx is settled for all time by our Lord's citation of it as Davidic in Mark xii, 36. They need to be reminded that no statement can ever be rightly understood except in relation to the questions which were actually in the minds of those by whom and to whom the statement was made; and in this instance, the critical problem of the authorship of the Psalms simply did not exist in anything approaching the form in which it is asked by modern critical scholarship. The question which was actually being raised by Him was, as the context shows, whether the Scribes had rightly interpreted the messianic prophecies. He was proving that they had not considered the fact that a psalm admittedly messianic spoke of the Messiah as at once humanly born ('son of David') and seated at God's right hand (as David's Lord); thus the point which was really at issue is not in the least invalidated if David did not write the psalm.

Similarly we have seen that in their general treatment of the fulfilment of prophecy, the minds of the New Testament writers are set on something much wider than the exploitation of mere coincidences of fulfilment with prediction. With this goes, as we shall see in a moment, their uncommonly clear grasp of the importance of the Old Testament as history: as for instance when they record a saying of the Lord, 'The Law and the Prophets were until John; from that time the Kingdom of God is preached' (Luke xvi, 16).

In their application of these principles in detail we have seen that there is an imperfection, which is indeed allowed for in St. Paul's saying, 'We have this treasure in arthen vessels' (2 Cor. iv, 7). In the present connexion, perhaps the most notable fault is the quotation of texts out of their proper context, to illustrate some point quiet alien from the original meaning. It would be

surprising if they had not done so at all, for the Rabbis did it
regularly, habitually, and as a matter of course. We may, however, rightly point out that in most cases where a particular text
is thus misused, some other text might have been found which
would have served equally well, so that the argument is nevertheless true to the general sense of Scripture. The passages
where texts are taken out of their context are to be balanced by
the greater number of passages where the citation is deeply
faithful to the original sense.

The second outstanding difference between the New Testament and the Rabbis lies in the vivid sense which it has and
they lack, of God's action in history. It would indeed be absurd
to deny the plain fact that there was very much sincere piety
among the Jews of our Lord's day, especially the Pharisees.
The post-Christian Rabbinic literature, too, is full of true and
sincere godliness:[1] reverence for that which is holy, above all
for the sacred Name and the revelation in the Law of His ways
and of His will for man; respect for parents, neighbours, fellow-
men, even compassion on enemies; and a constant and faithful
waiting on God amidst long-continued oppression and persecution, often inflicted, as time went on, by a dominant Christian
power. But one does not find there any clear sense of God's
action in history, as similarly there is very little indeed about the
Spirit. The Rabbis have lost, all but completely, the first
Isaiah's grand sense of God's action in contemporary politics,
the constant appeal of Deuteronomy to God's action in the
Exodus, as the ground for hope in His future action for the
exiles,[2] or the looking forward to the messianic future which is
common to all the prophets who followed. Certainly there were
in the first century messianic hopes, and therewith an interpretation of God's purpose in history, though often conceived in a
narrowly nationalistic way. But a claimant to Messiahship was
crucified in the days of Pontius Pilate; and after that event, the
messianic programme of the Zealots led to the disaster of A.D.
70, and the renewed claim of Barcochba, encouraged by the
great Rabbi Aqiba himself, brought final disaster sixty years

[1] See for this Montefiore and Loewe, *A Rabbinic Anthology.*
[2] See the quotation from Deut. iv, p. 144 f. above.

later. It is true that Judaism has never wholly lost the messianic
hope; but very many centuries have passed since then, without
any sign of a movement in history towards its fulfilment. It is
not surprising if it has flickered. The loss by the Rabbis of the
sense of history is shown by the fact that in their interpretation
of the Exodus-story itself attention is regularly fixed not on the
divine act of deliverance, but on the giving of the Law.

When all irrelevances are cleared away, as they need to be,
there is one outstanding question, and one only, between Christians and Jews. It is the question whether God did or did not
accomplish in Jesus His purpose of Salvation for Israel: whether
we can truly say, 'Blessed be the Lord God of Israel, for He hath
redeemed and visited His people'. If He has not, then, as St.
Paul says, the Apostles were false witnesses of God, and we are
yet in our sins (1 Cor. xv, 15, 17); yet if that be so, neither the
Jews nor anyone else have any interpretation of the Old Testament to offer, which can vindicate the hopes raised by the
prophets as true. The Apostles, on the other hand, have a full,
many-sided, and satisfying interpretation of it, whereby it is
vindicated that the Holy Ghost really did speak by the prophets;
they have also their personal testimony to the events of the
ministry, the death, and the resurrection of Jesus, and the appeal
to history is fearlessly made. If the Gospel be not true, it is hard
to see any escape from the conclusion that the hopes raised by
the Old Testament, however noble and high-minded, are
illusory and false.

CHAPTER VIII

THE LITERAL INTERPRETATION OF
THE OLD TESTAMENT

We now come to study the use of the Bible in the Church for purposes of liturgy and teaching. We have seen how great a part the liturgical use of the sacred books played in their recognition as Scripture; indeed we may say that the authority which the books enjoy in being reckoned as Scripture is that which is acknowledged when they are solemnly read to the assembled congregation. So the books were read, from the first beginnings of the Synagogue, to the people in the Name of the Lord; and so they are read still. Likewise the Psalms have been and still are the primary expression of praise and supplication. Hence the study of the Christian liturgy is of the first importance for a right understanding of the authority of the Bible.

The acknowledgement of the authority of the Bible requires that it be interpreted in the first place in its plain and literal sense. Its authority is being truly respected only when it is taken as meaning what it says. Anyone who is content to accept false textual readings or false renderings of the words is not treating the authority of the text seriously, but is finding for himself a way to illustrate from it something which he wishes to believe on other grounds. On the primacy of the literal sense, Catholic tradition and modern criticism are in agreement. It is also true, as we have seen, in the case of both Testaments, that the literal meaning intended by the writer may be a 'spiritual' or 'mystical' meaning.

We shall then seek to cover in this chapter the use of the Bible in the Church according to its literal sense, following the three headings which we used in the second chapter, ἀρχή, λόγος and τέλος,[1] and then show how already in the Old Testament there is a movement towards the spiritual meanings which are taken up in the New Testament fulfilment.

1. The Bible as History

It is not necessary to repeat here what has been said in earlier chapters about the Christian appeal to history for the vindication of the historical truth of the Events of God's redeeming work, and about the tension, but not opposition, which must exist between Faith and Criticism. We are concerned here with the use of the Biblical narratives in the church lessons, and their place in our thinking. The discrepancies in the narratives are enough to show that their total inerrancy is impossible. If that is admitted, and it is seen that there are mythical and legendary elements in the Bible, does this effect the authority of the narratives for the ordinary Christian? No doubt the historical existence of Methuselah is of no great importance; but what about the stories of Abraham, of Moses, of David?

Perhaps this question is best approached, like many other Old Testament questions, by considering parallel instances from the New Testament. Let us take the miracle-stories in the Gospels. The assertion that a non-miraculous Christianity is impossible does not justify the claim that *every* recorded miracle must necessarily be accepted as historically true, and that to do so is essential to the Faith. In the Creed, only two miracles, one at the beginning of our Lord's earthly life and the other at the end, are treated as *de fide*. In the gospels the miracles are regarded as important for the sake of that which they signify, namely that our Lord is not 'a prophet, as one of the prophets', but is the Messiah and the Son of God, and has come bringing with Him the divine Kingdom in word and in power. Therefore that which, in the last resort, is crucial is not any particular miracle of the Ministry, but that of the Resurrection; for this is proclaimed by the Apostles to be the answer of God Himself to the rejection of our Lord by Caiaphas as a self-deluded impostor:

[1] See p. 52 above.

'this Jesus', they say, 'whom ye crucified . . . God hath made Him Lord and Christ' (Acts ii, 36). If, then, it is confessed that He is the Saviour, come from God to set up the divine Kingdom, He is not 'one of the sons of men' but a miraculous person; and that being so, the historicity of the particular miracles related of Him in the course of His ministry can be examined without fear or favour, and without any *a priori* prejudice against the stories on the ground of their miraculous character.

If we approach the Old Testament narratives in a similar way, we shall start, not with the examination of narratives about which no certain conclusions can be reached (how far are Ishmael and Esau personified tribes? how far, on the other hand, do the stories of Abraham appear to preserve authentic traditions?) but with the faith of the prophets, Amos, Hosea and their successors. Their fundamental faith is that Yahweh has chosen Israel for a position of special privilege; He has called His son out of Egypt; He has called Israel to be His people, that He may be their God. On the ground of this vocation, they accuse Israel of apostasy from Him, of taking His Name in vain by unreal worship, of going after other gods instead of Him, of oppressing His poor. On what does their faith rest? They say that it rests on certain events in the past, to which they constantly appeal, and to which the whole tradition of the Faith of Israel after them similarly appeals. The question then is, Were they right in so thinking? Or had God done nothing of the kind, and had an admittedly high religious experience succeeded in creating its own object?

There is no question of the value of the religious experience; the question is of the theological fact on which the religious experience believed itself to rest. If it can be proved that these prophets were wrong, and that the whole faith of Israel rested on a false foundation—then we had better know: just as, if Jesus did not rise from the dead, we had better know, and not continue to delude ourselves. For plainly we have here reached a point at which the substantial truth of certain historical facts is vital to the Faith.

It would indeed be a mis-statement of the question to say that the apologist must demonstrate *ab initio* that the events happened exactly so. He is not saddled with the *onus probandi*. The real issue is that we, Israel, the believing community, have been proclaiming for three thousand years that God has acted in certain events, and that we have held this tradition continuously from the times in which the events occurred. This is demonstrably true of the second Redemption; of the first it can be asserted so far back as the written records go. There exists, then, this tradition of the Faith, and it holds the field. By its very nature, this Faith must appeal to history, and must submit its records to examination. The result might be to show that the records are authentic in every possible detail—that, however, we know not to be the case. Or it might be to show that they are substantially trustworthy, with some errors of fact and some accretions of legend. Or it might be to show that they are self-contradictory and false; but in this case the false testimony will go back, as regards the Christian Faith, to the Apostles of our Lord, since the New Testament documents preserve to us their evidence.

But what is the meaning of 'substantially trustworthy', as applied to the Biblical narratives which we hear read in church? There is no doubt that the Church's use of the Bible depends on the belief that in the main it contains true history, and not a mere mythology like the tales of the Greek gods and heroes. David, for instance, is an important person in the story, and it is important to the Faith that he should really have existed, and that the portrait of him should be in its main outline true to fact. In 2 Sam. xxi, 19, we come across the statement that Goliath of Gath was killed by Elhanan the son of Jaare-oregim; this makes it not certain indeed, but probable, that the tale of the giant-killing has been transferred to the great popular hero. The question is, whether the knowledge of this fact will spoil for the ordinary Christian the splendidly told and deservedly popular story in 1 Sam. xvii. In such cases it is best to say that we need to take a middle line between a disregard for historical fact, and a scrupulosity which would demand a historical exactness that is actually unattainable.

We may reason the matter out as follows. In any historical narrative, from a Bible story to a newspaper report, there are two aspects to be taken into account. First, there is the factual accuracy of the story; and here we are aware that while no narrative can ever contain the whole of the facts with exhaustive completeness, yet there are certain facts of cardinal importance to the story: such facts as are determined in a court of law by the calling of witnesses. Second, there is the interpretation given of the story. The narrator of the story in 1 Sam. xvii has a vivid picture in his mind of God's blessing upon the youthful David, which is the real ground of his victory. It is plain that we do not read the Bible as a mere record of events; in that case we might replace parts of the Book of Kings by extracts from the Assyrian cuneiform inscriptions. Nor do we read it as a mere mythology. What is demanded is the union of the two. This point comes out with full clearness in the case of the gospels, which are not biographical memoirs after the modern style, nor yet mythological interpretations superimposed by the Church on the story of a Jewish prophet and reformer. If any of the first three gospels, or the fourth, were either a mere chronicle or religious fiction, it would not be a gospel. A gospel is a proclamation of the Gospel of Salvation as having been accomplished in certain events of history. The facts of cardinal importance in the story must be true facts, and the interpretation must be true to the facts. In the gospel story heavenly things are revealed by means of earthly things (John iii, 12), as the eternal love of God is revealed in the cross of Christ (ibid., vv. 16 and 14). Hence in the Bible story the events of the Redemption hold a key position; if these are not true, none of the rest of the story has any further interest, from the point of view of the Faith. If, however, these stand firm, then we can study the rest of the history at our leisure, and ask the historians to tell us what they can of its exact course.

It must not be forgotten, however, that Biblical writers are themselves, in a sense, part of the story. The Sacred History contains the record of the divine education of Israel in the knowledge of God and the way of His service; and in that process the narrators and editors of the Book of Kings are at least as important as the kings themselves. We read these stories in church not merely for the sake of the facts, but still more for what the narrators see in them, and wish to show us. It is impossible to be sure how much of the long story of Joseph is true as history; but one thing, at least, that was in the writer's mind was the over-ruling providence of God: 'Ye meant evil against me,' says Joseph to his brothers, 'but God meant it for good, to bring to pass as it is this day, to save much people alive' (Gen. l, 20).

It is such truths as these that the ordinary Christian can and does imbibe from the Bible stories as he hears them read. He knows, or ought to know, that the question whether David or Elhanan slew Goliath is one for the specialist historian to decide. But he himself is well able to appreciate the meaning of the divine blessing which is repeatedly said to rest on David; he is described as 'cunning in playing, and a mighty man of valour, and a man of war, and prudent in speech, and a comely person, and the Lord is with him' (1 Sam. xvi, 18). It is just at this point that the Responds in the Latin Breviary provide something which must always be understood when the lessons are read in church. In the weeks after Pentecost, when the story of David is read, we get the following Responds among others: 'The Lord heareth all men, He sent His angel and took me from my father's sheep, and anointed me with the oil of His mercy: the Lord who delivered me from the mouth of the lion, and saved me from the paw of the bear: and anointed me with the oil of His mercy.' 'I took thee from thy father's house, saith the Lord, and appointed thee to be the shepherd of My people: and I was with thee in all thy ways whithersoever thou wentest, establishing thy kingdom for ever: and I made thy name great, as one of the great ones of the earth: and I gave thee rest from all thy enemies: and I was with thee, etc. Glory be to the Father, etc. And I was with thee, etc.' The compilers of the Book of Common Prayer were losing something of great value when, in their zeal for simplicity, they dropped these Responds, which also bring out a further point, which we have not mentioned yet in this discussion. There is not only the truth of the narratives as history, nor only the truth of the narrator's interpretation, but also the personal relation that exists between the characters in the story and those who hear it. To us, David is not 'a Jewish boy', but *our* David; we read his story as being ourselves members of the Israel of God, and we accept him as being one of our heroes; we are asked in some measure to live through his experience, just as we live through the experience of the psalmists in reciting their psalms.

The liturgical use of the Old Testament involves the treatment of the Scriptures as in some sense contemporary to us. In this respect it falls for us into the two periods of pre-exilic and post-exilic. In the earlier period we have outlined for us the pattern of a Christian nation: a nation called to work out the way of its duty to God in the complex relations of a settled society, ordered on the basis of a national confession of faith in God and of obedience to His revealed will. Such is the outlook of Deuteronomy, and of the Deuteronomic editors of other books; and though the actual Israel always fell very far short of the realization of any such ideal, it is true to say that the unifying *motif* of the pre-exilic writers is that of Israel as the People of Yahweh, and that the Church in using these books transfers to each Christian nation this conception of the sanctification of a whole national life.

On the other hand, in the exile and to a large extent afterwards, Israel is a small believing and worshipping community in the midst of a pagan civilization. In the days of Ezekiel and Second Isaiah it is a small remnant, which through their ministry becomes intensely conscious of its faith and its vocation. Even after the Return, the same conditions still largely obtain; the Palestinian community is surrounded by pagan influences, and there is a Dispersion in Egypt, Babylonia, Egypt, and elsewhere. The nation, we say, has 'become a church', and the bond which unites it is already less a purely racial bond than that of the faith by which it lives and the law by which its life is ruled. It is needless to point out the close parallel with the life of the Church of to-day, not only in missionary countries but also in Europe.

'The ancient fathers', say the compilers of the Book of Common Prayer,[1] 'so ordered the matter that all the whole Bible (or the greatest part thereof) should be read over once every year

[1] In the Preface, 'Concerning the Service of the Church', dating from 1549.

intending thereby that the Clergy, and especially such as were Ministers in the Congregation, should (by often reading, and meditation in God's word) be stirred up to godliness themselves, and be more able to exhort others by wholesome doctrine, and to confute them that were adversaries to the truth; and further, that the people (by daily hearing of holy Scripture read in the Church) might continually profit more and more in the knowledge of God, and be the more inflamed with the love of his true religion.' It can well seem to us that they were over-zealous in 'cutting off Anthems, Responds, Invitatories, and such like things as did break the continual course of the reading of the Scripture', which had been introduced in order to indicate how the Scripture was to be understood. Yet the ancient principle of reading the Bible through is of permanent importance, just because of the historical character of the Bible. It is easy to complain that much of the history is dull and arid, and provides little matter for edification; this is constantly given in the Fathers as the reason for seeking allegorical interpretations, as we shall see. But these narratives need to be read in the context of the Sacred History as a whole.

This is just one of the points at which the Bible history gives us the key to all history. The world is full of innumerable 'uninteresting' lives, including (no doubt) our own; but those lives at once become interesting when they are seen in the light of the divine Purpose which gives them meaning. The key to the Old Testament is given in the genealogy at the beginning of St. Matthew's gospel, which shows how the generations of the Old Testament lead up to 'Jesus who is called Christ'; and it is profoundly impressive to view the Old Testament stories in the historical sequence which in the lectionary covers most of the year, and see the parts of the divine Purpose in relation to the whole. At the end of the Book of Ruth, after we have been told of the birth of a baby, we hear how 'they called his name Obed: he is the father of Jesse, the father of David' (Ruth iv, 17). This at once puts the story of Ruth in a wider context.

A similar whole view of the Bible history is taken in the historical psalms (lxxviii, cv, cvi) which lead up either to David or to the return from exile; when the former is the case, we are left asking ourselves whether in the writer's mind David is not typical of the Son of David, and his thought is fixed on the messianic climax of the Sacred History. Similarly in the great eucharistic prayer of Neh. ix, the history of God's mercy to Israel in the past is taken as the ground for the petition then made.[1]

While in the ferial course of lessons the story of Israel is told at length and in order, at the festivals we celebrate the Events of the Redemption itself, taking the events of the First Redemption, as we are taught to do in the New Testament, as typical of those of the Second. It is vital to the Faith that these are historical and not mythological commemorations.

Finally, every Eucharist is anchored to the Biblical history not only by the liturgical Gospel, in which we hear of some of the recorded acts or words of our Lord, but also and above all by the eucharistic action itself, whose whole meaning depends on the history of the night in which He was betrayed. That action of our Lord gathered up in itself the whole Biblical history—the Exodus commemorated at the Passover-season, the Covenant, the levitical sacrifices, the prophetic insights into the true meaning of sacrifice, and their predictions of the work of Salvation which He was to make complete—and its meaning for the Church of to-day rests on the historical truth of the commemorative action. Nothing perhaps is more fundamentally heretical than to make the meaning of the Eucharist depend on its 'numinous' quality, to the neglect of the matter-of-fact *Gegenwärtigsetzung*[2] of 'making-newly-present' of the messianic Sacrifice which was prepared for in the Old Testament and accomplished in the New.[3]

2. *The Bible Teaching about God*

No less fundamental than the authoritative testimony of the Bible to God's action in history is its function in transmitting

[1] P. 163 above.

[2] Cf. the quotation from Abbot Herwegen of Maria Laach in my *Liturgy and Society*, 1935, p. 64 f.

[3] There is a valuable section on 'Commemoration' in Brilioth, *Eucharistic Faith and Practice* (1929), pp. 34–41, cf. 280–2.

to us the truths about His nature and His will for man which Israel was set to learn in the course of the Sacred History. God the Holy Ghost spake by the Prophets; and the Inspiration of the Bible must denote the word which God has spoken to man by means of imperfect human instruments, till His final word was spoken in Jesus Christ. The Scripture is inspired because the Holy Ghost spoke through it; and that which He had to teach is seen in its completeness not in the words of the individual writers taken separately, but in the whole series of writings and the whole course of the Sacred History. Taken separately, the books are imperfect; but the imperfections of one writer are partly corrected by another, and the imperfections of all are corrected in the Son of God, who does not merely speak, but personally is, His Word.

The formal acknowledgement of these truths was made in the successive canonization of Deuteronomy, of the Law, of the Prophets, and of the Writings. The acceptance of the books as authoritative went hand in hand with their regular use in the temple liturgy and still more in the synagogue. The Church, from the very earliest days, carried on the same tradition; and the liturgy, as we use it to-day, has for one of its functions to preserve for us the Biblical conception of God and His ways, and to inculcate it continually upon us in Scripture lessons and recitation of psalms, and in responses and responds, introits and graduals, antiphons and anthems, which are with quite few exceptions taken directly from Scripture. The same is true of the traditional Christian forms of prayer, which are in the Biblical tradition and largely in Bible language; it is true also of the best of the hymns which are commonly in use.[1]

The conception of God presented to us by the Bible is marked by an extraordinary simplicity and directness, which makes it impossible for the writers to use the arts of rhetoric, as if their message needed to be prettily dressed up and given an attractive form. Here is God, they say, this is His will, and these are

[1] But it is one of the problems of modern liturgy that to a very serious extent many of the hymns fall far below the Biblical standard. Dissatisfaction with them seems to be widely felt; and a purge of the hymn-books must some day be undertaken.

His demands; before man lie the ways of the blessing and of the curse, of life and of death. But our modern world is engrossed in the study of phenomena, of natural science, of history, of psychology; it looks at religion itself from a psychological point of view, and is accustomed to study Christian doctrine itself historically, in the light of the development of ways of thinking about God and of human moral ideals.

The usual modern interpretation of the Bible is deeply coloured by this. It is common for admiration of the Hebrew prophets to be expressed because they echo the ideals of the modern Labour movement, or for the treatment of the Sabbath especially in Deuteronomy to be praised for its philanthropic character[1]—'that thy manservant and thy maidservant may rest as well as thou'—while its primary God-ward aspect[2] is left out of sight. Or again, the great advance of the New Testament on the Old is taken to lie above all in the conception of love: as though the God revealed in the New Testament were the loving Father, forgiving, tolerant, and easy-going, whereas the conception of His wrath belongs to the fierce and vindictive Yahweh-religion of the Old Testament. Needless to say, this is as outrageous a misrepresentation of the Old Testament as of the New.

It is indeed at this central point of its teaching, about what is called 'the character of God', that the Old Testament is most often criticized: why is God represented as savage and vindictive in His wrath against the enemies of Israel, and sometimes also as arbitrary and capricious in His dealings with individuals, in ways which are sharply at variance with the teaching of the New Testament? Without doubt this is a real difficulty; there are Old Testament texts which say unworthy things about God. We have said earlier in this book that this is not surprising, if God has revealed Himself through men, and put His chosen people through a process of spiritual education, so that there is clearly a development from the low cultural level of a primitive tribe to the high level of a civilized nation. It was impossible for the crude phrases about the wrath of Yahweh against Israel's enemies to be used after the prophets had accused Israel itself

---

[1] Cf. Driver, in *H.D.B.*, iv, 317 f.
[2] Cf. Ezek. xx, 12.

of sin, and had said that He Himself was sending its enemies against it for its chastisement.[1]

Our problem is, How can we at once be aware of the imperfections of the Old Testament, and obedient to its authority? How can we at once criticize it as human and reverence it as divine? Perhaps the word 'cultural' gives the needed clue. It is very much on the cultural level that the imperfections of the Old Testament lie; but behind and below this, there is a deeper level on which its teaching is profoundly right, above all, in its sense of the Reality of God, derived from Israel's experience of Him as the living God revealed in His redemptive action. It is just this side of the matter which our age, sensitive as it is to cultural values, is apt to miss. Some of the phrases used in the Old Testament about God's wrath may be crude; but the idea of His wrath comes again in the teaching of St. Paul and of our Lord Himself. Much that is said about the holy fear due to Yahweh in His tabernacling Presence in the midst of Israel does not come easily to an age from whose religion the very notion of holy fear is largely absent; and it may be that considerations such as this may give the key to so perplexing a passage as 2 Sam. vi, 6 ff., in which Yahweh breaks out upon Uzzah for his presumption in touching the Sacred Ark. When the teaching of the Old Testament about the sovereignty of the transcendent God is derided by moderns on the ground that God is being made into a sultan, it may be that those who make the criticism are precisely those who most need to defer to its authority.

There is the teaching of Ezekiel about the sanctification of God's Name. He speaks of this in chap. xxxvi, where he says that the House of Israel had defiled their land by their doings (v. 17), and Yahweh had punished them (18 f.); as exiles they had 'profaned' His Name, in causing it to be dishonoured in the eyes of the heathen (20); but He has pity for His holy Name, and, for His honour and not theirs, will bring them back, cleanse them, give them a new heart and a new spirit, and impart His Spirit that they may keep His statutes; seeing this, they will loathe themselves in their own sight for the evil that they have done (31). This thought of the sanctification and profanation of

[1] Cf. p. 72 above.

The Bible Teaching about God

God's Name occurs elsewhere, notably in Num. xx, 12, where sentence is passed on Moses and Aaron for losing their temper with the people who asked for water, in the words: 'Because ye believed not in Me, to sanctify Me in the eyes of the children of Israel, therefore ye shall not bring this Assembly into the land which I have given them.' It comes again in the Lord's prayer, of which the first petition is, 'Let Thy Name be sanctified'. The constant teaching is that as He alone is God and alone is truly good, the end for which the created universe exists is that He may be glorified; St. Paul in Eph. i, 14, speaks of this as the end for which the Church exists. Yet this Biblical view of the relation of God and man has quite dropped out of sight in much modern theology; and if the reader cares to turn up pages 283 and 284, of *The People and the Book*, he will find there an astonishing passage in which the late Dr. A. S. Peake, starting from the defective and limited outlook of Liberal Protestantism, altogether falls foul of the theological teaching of Ezekiel. In this, he is both sitting in judgement on a theology that is far better than his own, and is rejecting the authority of the Biblical teaching of both Testaments at a central point.

This Biblical doctrine of God is continually set before us in the liturgical use of the Scriptures. The Psalms, understood in their strictly literal sense, place us in the presence of God and confront us with our duty to Him, as creatures owing adoration and love to their Creator, as the people of His pasture and the sheep of His hand. It is not indeed that the psalmists find it easy to believe in God and cleave to Him amidst the troubles and contradictions of earthly life; they ask Him why He is absent from them so long, and how long He will forget them and hide His face from them. Yet, even so, they are sure that He only is their hope and their rock of defence. Job does not find it easy, as he cries to God out of his suffering; he is sometimes quite blasphemous in his impatience; yet the sincerity of his faith is shown in his rejection of the too easy answers which his friends give. If only God would let him alone! But God will not let him alone, because God is love. For the opposite of love is not hate; it is indifference. On the level of human love, it is an elementary fact of experience that love is liable to turn to anger and even to hate, just because

251

it cares intensely for the loved person. On the level of divine love, the Love of God demands as its correlative the Wrath of God, just because God does care, and because He is man's true Good, and He has called man to fellowship with Himself, and man's rejection of that fellowship is his ruin and perdition. Because the New Testament emphasizes the Love of God, it emphasizes His Wrath; the evangelists repeatedly show our Lord as righteously angry. Job, with all his impatience, stands on the same line. The trouble is that God is so persistent in His attentions to him, and the burden is more than he can bear. At least he knows that God is not indifferent.

This personal relation to God of man dominates the whole Old Testament; it can be seen, for instance, in the conception of the divine Grace and Blessing. It is a besetting fault of Christians to think of Grace as an impersonal influence or power, gained through prayer, bestowed by means of sacraments, and even to use in popular expositions of the doctrine of Grace the thoroughly misleading and harmful simile of an electric current. But this is to reject the authority of the New Testament, in which the Holy Spirit is personal, and of the Old Testament, in which the divine Blessing is always thought of in personal terms. The history begins with the Call of Abraham, in which Yahweh bestows His blessing on him; that is, He in whom resides the ulness and wholeness of life and power, imparts a share in it to His servant (Gen. xii, 2), so that Abraham prospers, and is saved out of dangers, and has peace. It is Abraham's blessing that is continued to Isaac and to Jacob (Gen. xxvi, 2–5; xxviii, 3–4). Saul began with His blessing; but he failed to retain it, and the time came when 'Yahweh was departed from Saul' (1 Sam. xviii, 12). But He was with David; He 'saved David whithersoever he went' (2 Sam. viii, 14), and even when Absalom rebelled and seemed to be carrying all before him, David's prayer that the counsel of Ahitophel might be defeated brought it about that Hushai's counsel was taken, and nothing could go right for Absalom and his cause.[1] This idea of God's blessing

[1] I owe the substance of this passage to the very valuable studies of Prof. Pedersen of Copenhagen, in *Israel I–II* (1926), esp. pp. 190 ff., 182 ff. See also the chapters on 'Peace and Covenant' and 'Peace and Salvation'.

occurs very often in the psalms, as in Ps. iv, 9, 'I will lay me down in peace and take my rest; for Thou O Lord only makest me dwell in safety'. Another psalm used at compline, xci, 'Whoso dwelleth under the defence of the most High', is wholly occupied with the thought of God's grace and blessing.[1] The 'blessing' is further seen as resting not only on a man as an individual, but also on his family, on the works of his hands, on the land and the crops. The classical text is Deut. xxviii, 1-14, where we have a picture of agricultural prosperity regarded as an integrity or wholeness of life, contingent on the faithfulness of the Israelites to God, on whom the 'blessing' depends.[1]

These points may illustrate what has been said above on the fundamental rightness of the Old Testament teaching about God.

A final word needs to be said about the early narratives of Genesis. Modern scholarship has rightly pointed out the close affinities of these stories with extant Babylonian literature; hence there has been a tendency on the one hand to overlook the extent to which the Hebrew writers may be consciously criticizing the Babylonian myths from the higher point of view of Israel's faith, and on the other to attribute to them 'a rudimentary, child-like conception of Deity',[3] overlooking the fact that they may be deliberately adopting the language of myth. This has been to some extent the case with regard to the great Creation-story of Gen. i, which should be seen in close relation with the prophecies of Second Isaiah, where there is a constant reference to the Creation.[4] It is less in evidence with regard to the story of the Garden of Eden in Gen. ii-iii, with which the commentators on the whole deal very well.[5] Here are set out the fundamental conditions of the life of man in relation to the earth on which he lives. 'The Lord God took Man (*Adam*), and put him into the Garden of Eden to dress it and to keep it' (ii, 15), giving him freedom to do as he would, subject always to the

---

[1] Pedersen, pp. 322, 333.

[2] See Pedersen, pp. 474-86. This is a point which is of special relevance to our circumstances to-day, and deserves to be fully worked out in relation to the modern agricultural revival.

[3] Driver, *Genesis*, p. 136, with reference to the dsee pp. Tower of Ba.bel.

[4] Isa xl, 28; xliv, 24; xlv, 12; xlviii, 13, etc.; and see pp. 159 f. above

[5] See e.g. Driver's good note on these chapters, *Genesis*, pp. 51-7.

restriction imposed by the Divine command; 'the acknowledgement and observance of a limitation imposed on his creaturely
freedom by his Creator and Lord, must be for man the starting-
point of everything else'.[1] Next comes the fundamental relation
of Man and Woman. Man needs a help meet for (answering to)
him (v. 18), and this the animals can never be (vv. 19–20). Then
Woman is formed; and at the first sight of her, the Man cries
out 'THIS is now bone of my bones and flesh of my flesh: THIS
shall be called Woman, because THIS was taken out of Man'
(v. 23).[2] After the Fall the Man forgets all that he said before
about the Woman as part of himself, and now regards her as a
separate individual, with whom he has got to live as best he can:
she is 'the Woman whom Thou gavest to be with me' (iii, 12).

The story of the Tower of Babel has, however, received far
less justice, though it comes from the same J.-narrative, and
perhaps from one and the same writer, one who, if only he were
to us a name and not merely a symbol, would be seen by all to
stand in the very front rank of the prophets, with the two
Isaiahs. But it seems that the purpose of the narrative has not
been grasped. It is commonly read as a piece of primitive folk-
lore, and Gunkel could even suggest that there may have been a
myth of the interruption by a Babylonian deity of the erection
of a *zikkurat* or pyramidal tower.[3] This must assuredly be very
wide of the mark. The seemingly 'child-like conception of Deity'
in the story can equally be explained if the writer is deliberately
adopting the language of myth; and since it was written within
Israel, we ought not to be surprised if its original motive was
to pass judgement on the pagan civilization of Babylon.[4]

[1] Dillman, quoted by Driver, ibid., p. 41.

[2] The point of the repeated pronoun is missed in the English versions: see
Coggin, *The Second Story of Genesis as Literature*, pp. 13, 18.

[3] Driver, *Genesis*, p. 137.

[4] The Bishop of Southwell (Dr. Barry) has kindly allowed me to make use
of the following note, from his letter in the *Southwell Diocesan Magazine* for
Feb. 1946: 'There is a strange old story in the Bible (Gen. xi) which describes
the failure of the first attempt to establish international "security".' They
said, 'Go to, let us build us a city and a tower whose top may reach unto
heaven, and let us make us a name. The tower was called Babel.' The story
came out of a 'time of trouble'—the break-up of the early Babylonian empire
which had been a kind of 'universal state'. One result of the disintegration

Is it possible that its meaning was somewhat as follows?

Some Israelites have been to splendid and fabulous Babylon, with its lofty temples of which their kings boasted that they had 'made their tops as high as heaven',[1] and had seen their sumptuous worship, which might well make Yahweh seem like a poor relation. But this was not their reaction, for they had mixed with the polyglot crowd in the great city, and learnt how crude their religious conceptions were. So the tale took shape. Yahweh, too, had been to see Babylon, and He had passed judgement on the overweening pride of man, seeking to exalt himself to the stars of God, and to 'be as God' according to the Serpent's promise. In result, the teeming population of Babylon did not understand one another's speech, and did not know one another's minds; the great Tower had been a failure. The meaning, then, of the tale is not unlike that of Mr. Eliot's *Waste Land*.

3. *The Predictions of the Future*

The acceptance of the Old Testament in its literal sense demands further that the predictive prophecies be taken seriously as predictions. In what sense and with what qualifications this is to be done, we must see in a moment. But they are not taken seriously when the sentiments which the prophets express are admired, and Second Isaiah is praised for his 'universalism', while the one fact that can be noted about his expectations of the course of future history is that they were mistaken. The

---

was that the language which had hitherto been the medium of a universal culture now became before long a 'dead' language, and the various succession-states, each of them with their own local dialect, could not communicate with one another. The 'confusion of tongues' in the myth of Genesis was the symbol of a world without unity. (See Toynbee, *A Study of History*, vol. v, pp. 484–6.) In all probability the Babel-story was included in the Bible for another reason. The narrator found in it a signal instance of God's judgement on the pride of man—on a world-state, organized apart from God and thinking itself permanently secure. In human affairs there is no such security. In any case, the 'gift of tongues' at Pentecost was obviously regarded by St. Luke as reversing the calamity of Babel. Here was the birth of a true world-society which was built on spiritual foundations. Here was a language which all could speak—"our own tongue in which we were born". The Gospel speaks in the language of man's home.'

[1] Driver, ibid., p. 135.

trouble is that the prophets are easily judged by a false standard of values, that belongs to our own day and not to theirs. In our day, when there is little sense among the general public of a duty of worship owed to God, or fear of His judgements, and a high sense of the human virtues of love to neighbour and broadly of philanthropy, it is tempting to isolate in the prophetic teaching such things as make an immediate appeal; the broad-minded outlook towards other nations, which we find in several exilic and post-exilic writers, seems to contrast very favourably with the narrow exclusiveness of Nehemiah and Ezra.

We have found, however, that this 'universalistic' interpretation is unhistorical, in that it drags the prophecies out of their historical context. Second Isaiah was 'universalist' not at all for the reasons which appeal to many of his modern admirers, but because he believed that Yahweh was the only God; he did not tolerate but bitterly derided the Babylonian religion; he looked forward to the vindication by Yahweh of Israel His chosen people, the return of the Presence of Yahweh to dwell in His Sanctuary, and—on this basis only—the eventual share of all nations in the knowledge of Him. Hence his 'universalism' has for its true basis a clear view of the special and exclusive vocation of Israel; and a truly historical view of the matter will trace the history of this hope, through the period after Ezra in which it seems to be lost, to the time when it emerges again as an element in the total fulfilment of the messianic hope in Jesus the Christ.

Thus we are compelled to return to the serious treatment of the prophecies as predictions, by seeing them in their true place in the course of the Sacred History. It is a false view of Prophecy to regard it as history written in advance. This is to neglect the truth that God has revealed Himself through imperfect human nature, and that the purpose which is fulfilled in the climax of the Sacred History is God's Purpose, of which its human interpreters can have had no complete apprehension. It was not given to the exilic prophets to 'know the times and seasons', and the fulfilment lay much further ahead in the future than they thought. Yet the truth of the prophets' insight into the principles of the future Divine Reign was shown by their endorsement by our Lord and His Apostles when the fulness of the times had come.

Therefore at each of the festivals which commemorate the cardinal events of the Fulfilment we read the relevant prophecies as lessons in church: not that we may note the mere correctness of the predictions, but that thereby the New Testament event may be related, as it needs to be, to the background of the whole Sacred History on which it stands.

4. *Literal and Spiritual Senses in the Old Testament*

We shall come in the next chapter to the consideration of the 'spiritual' or 'mystical' interpretation of the Old Testament in the Church, having already seen something of the spiritual interpretation of it given in the New Testament.[1] But we must first see how, already in the Old Testament itself, the principle of spiritual interpretation appears. This happens in three ways.

First, there are certain passages where a spiritual sense seems to have been intended by the original writers, or by the editors of the books. The earlier narratives of the Flood are more or less contemporaneous with the writing prophets; and such words as 'Yahweh saw that the wickedness of man was great in the earth, and that every imagination of the thoughts of his heart was only evil continually' (Gen. vi, 5), can hardly fail to bear some relation to the prophetic denunciations of the sin of Israel and her neighbours, as in Amos i–ii. A close parallel to the Flood-story comes in a prophet of the next century, Zephaniah, who threatens the total destruction of all things from the face of the ground (Zeph. i, 2 ff.).

A clearer instance still is that of Abraham's pleading for Sodom in Gen. xviii. It has been suggested that the latter part of this chapter, from v. 23 onwards, is contemporaneous with Isaiah; for Isaiah had called Jerusalem 'Sodom' (i, 9, 10). In this case the story expresses the anxious fears of the remnant in Jerusalem, as they saw how few there were in the city who truly feared God. Were there fifty, forty-five, forty, thirty, twenty?

[1] See esp. the summary, pp. 232–4.

Were there even ten? Was it even yet possible for the city to be spared?

Both the Flood-story and the Sodom-story are used by our Lord as types of the imminent eschatological Event: that is to say, with a spiritual meaning not unlike that of the original narrators. We may therefore digress for a moment to notice the interesting New Testament parallel which has been brought into prominence by the Form-critical school: that the gospel stories, as told by the evangelists, had a similar 'eschatological' reference to the ascended Lord, the Object of the worship of the community. They were not told merely as interesting memories of the Lord, as they would have been if He had been to them no more than 'a prophet as one of the prophets'; each Christian was to take to himself such an address to the Lord as 'Lord, if thou wilt, thou canst make me clean', or 'Lord, that I may receive my sight'. The healings were thus interpreted spiritually as types of the healing of the soul; in Matt. viii, 17, the evangelist applies to them the words of Isa. liii, 4, 'Surely He hath borne our griefs and carried our sorrows.' This spiritual interpretation of the gospel narratives has lasted on in the Church by a continuous tradition; and when Tertullian says of the story of the Stilling of the Storm, that 'this boat presented a type of the Church, which in the sea (this world) is distressed with the waves (persecutions and temptations), while the Lord in His patience seems to be sleeping, till aroused at last by the prayers of His saints, He restrains the world and restores quietness to His own',[1] he is giving an exposition such as might be paralleled from almost any of the patristic homilies on the Sunday Gospels in the third Nocturn at Mattins in the Roman Breviary.

Further Old Testament instances of spiritual interpretation are seen in the pattern of the Messianic Hope, as it took shape in the exilic prophets, who looked for a second Exodus, a new Covenant, an outpouring of the Spirit, the return of the Presence, the re-possession of Canaan; this thought was certainly present in the minds of the editors of the Hexateuch. Further, it dominated the minds of the 'Priestly' authors of the descriptions of the Tabernacle in the Wilderness; they were

---

[1] Tertullian, *De Bapt.* xii.

plainly thinking of the restored Temple and of the ideal future when its sanctuary would be filled with the adorable presence of their God. We have also seen how when they speak of 'David', some of the psalmists and the author of Chronicles are clearly thinking of the 'Son of David'. Finally, Hosea saw a 'spiritual' meaning in the unhappy story of his own relations with Gomer, as typifying the spiritual marriage of Yahweh with Israel. This conception is not only developed in later prophets, notably Jeremiah and Third Isaiah; it also seems to give the reason why the Song of Songs was finally accepted as canonical, if we may judge by the description of it by Rabbi Aqiba at the Council of Jamnia: 'The whole world is not worth the day in which the Song was given to Israel. For all the writings are holy, but the Song of Songs is a holy of the holies.'[1] This quite plainly implies that the book then received a 'spiritual' interpretation.

A second sense in which 'spiritual' interpretation appears in the Old Testament depends on the fact that, as the conception of Yahweh as the Spouse of Israel shows, the relation of the unseen God to mortal man cannot be otherwise described than in such 'spiritual' language: 'The Lord is my Light'; 'the Lord is my Shepherd'; 'as a father pitieth his children, so is He merciful to them that fear Him'. There is further a spiritual interpretation of ritual practices: of circumcision, especially in Deuteronomy and Jeremiah: 'Circumcise therefore the foreskin of your heart, and be no more still-necked', Deut. x, 16; of ritual ablutions, in Isa. i, 16, 'Wash you, make you clean, put away the evil of your doings from before Mine eyes', or in Ps. li, 2, 'Wash me thoroughly from my wickedness, and cleanse me from my sin'; of fasting, 'Is not this the fast that I have chosen? to loose the bonds of wickedness, to undo the bands of the yoke, and to let the oppressed go free, and that ye break every yoke?' (Isa. lviii, 6). Above all, there is the spiritual interpretation of the sacrifices. At the highest points of insight in the Old Testament, it is seen not only that the sacrifices are profaned when they are treated as a species of commercial transaction; and not only that He has no need of material offerings, and desires above all the love and obedience of His people; for there is a further in-

[1] *H.D.B.*, iv, p. 589, art. 'Song of Songs'.

sight yet. It is that the material sacrifice is the type or symbol of 'the sacrifice of God', which is 'a broken spirit, a broken and a contrite heart' (Ps. li, 17). That is to say, there is a *reality* of spiritual sacrifice lying behind the material action and symbolized by it; it is a mystery of humble penitence, offered to God on a spiritual altar. This thought reappears in one other place in the Old Testament, where the martyrdom of the Suffering Servant is declared to be such a sacrifice: 'When Thou shalt make his soul a guilt-offering' (*'asham*, Isa. liii, 10). This spiritual interpretation of Sacrifice is not a mere approach towards the New Testament conception, but a clear expression of its essential idea.[1]

A third way in which a 'spiritual' interpretation of the texts appears within the Old Testament period arises out of their liturgical use in the Synagogue. The Old Testament books were not only written within Israel, but were also used by Israel as the vehicle of man's approach to God in worship, and for instruction and edification. In being so used, texts which originally applied to some particular situation were in a manner universalized by being understood with reference to the lives of those who used them. Already in the Synagogue the words of Ps. lx, 8 (cf. cviii, 9) must have received a spiritual reinterpretation (unless indeed such a spiritual sense were the meaning given to them by the original writer): 'Moab is my wash-pot; upon Edom will I cast out my shoe: Philistia, shout thou because of me.' Moab, Edom, Philistia were the traditional enemies of Israel; those who used the psalm in the synagogue must have referred the words to the conflict with the Lord's enemies in their own day, whatever the precise form which that conflict took for them.

When Ps. xxii ('My God, my God, why hast Thou forsaken me'), which the evangelist refers to our Lord's crucifixion, was used in the synagogue, it must have been interpreted of the sufferings of Israel. Of this psalm a modern writer says: 'To suppose that such a psalm as the twenty-second had no reference at all in the first instance to any person but our Lord, deprives it of all significance for the time to which it originally belonged.

[1] Cf. my book *The Throne of David*, pp. 120–2.

Literal and Spiritual Senses in the Old Testament

It would in such a case have been a mere enigma till the Coming of the Christ. But if we take it as the outpouring of a faithful soul in sore distress and persecution, and yet confident that out of his trouble a future glory would come, we see at once its significance and value for the Jewish Church. And at the same time we can see how it is that the Psalm contains expressions inapplicable to the actual circumstances of the Psalmist. For it seems clear that the writer was led beyond himself to anticipate the Sorrows of a more tragic Sufferer, out of whose woe a more complete triumph should spring.'[1]

When this psalm, or Isa. liii, is applied to our Lord, we are still on the ground of the 'literal sense'; for His passion, considered from the human side, is an instance of the same sort of suffering as is depicted in the martyrdom of the Sufferer in the psalm, or of the Servant of the Lord. Hence it is only the prevalent confusion on the whole subject of the spiritual interpretation of the Bible that can explain the strange passage in Abrahams' essay in *The People and the Book*, where we read: 'At all events, in so far as there was at all a Jewish interpretation of the Suffering Servant, it passed through three stages: the Messianic, the Personal, the Communal. All that Jews were agreed upon was the dogmatic negative that whoever was meant it was not Jesus. ... The real marvel is that Christian expositors have come to accept this negative as emphatically as Jews ever did' (instances, Mowinckel and König). 'This retreat, however, by no means implies a surrender of the "typical" application by Christians of Isa. liii.'[2]

Really, however, Dr. Abrahams' words belong to the literature of the Jewish and Christian controversy; he can well remark that 'The marvel is a most honourable testimony to that love of truth, which has not precluded theologians from receding from a strongly entrenched position in the polemic field',[3]

---

[1] 'The Mystical Interpretation of Holy Scripture' (anonymous) in the *Church Quarterly Review*, vol. xxii (1886), p. 48. We shall refer to this article later: see p. 267 *n*. below.

[2] In *The People and the Book*, p. 410. See however W. Manson, *Jesus the Messiah*, pp. 168–71, for the paraphrase of Isa. liii in the Targum, and his comments upon it.

[3] *Ibidem.*

for he has scored a controversial victory over the Christians, and he is right in thinking it to be a marvel that they have abandoned the properly Christian position. Why did the Christian scholars make this admission? There is no doubt of the answer. They felt constrained to say that the true meaning of every passage is that which the author intended, and that no one could hold that the prophecy in question was intended by its author to refer to a person who would live six centuries later and be called Jesus. So far, so good; but a false doctrine of the Inspiration of Scripture led them to attach that Inspiration exclusively to each author considered in isolation, and prevented them from seeing that the word which God has spoken in the Bible must be sought by Christians in the Bible as a whole, and that when the Bible is read as the Book of the divine Kingdom, this prophecy must refer above all to Jesus, not by way of type, but of direct application.

While therefore Christians ought to feel bound to say that Isaiah liii does apply supremely to our Lord, it is not wise, as Dr. Lowe warns us, to base this on the ground that 'the meaning of a text may be more than the author is conscious of at the time'; for this is to provide no criterion of the true meaning, and to open the door, perhaps, to that type of interpretation in which, as he says, 'anything can mean anything'.[1] It is necessary to start from the literal meaning of what the prophet wrote, and then to show how, when his prophecy is used in the Church, and particularly in the Christian liturgy, it necessarily gains a wider application and a fuller meaning; a meaning which is fixed by the place which the prophecy takes in the context of the whole Sacred History, and which it is the business of theological exposition to draw out. It is in this sense, which indeed we can confidently assert to have been that in which our Lord Himself used it, that it is seen to apply in fullest measure to Him.

---

[1] In the *Interpretation of the Bible*, ed. Dugmore, pp. 120–1.

CHAPTER IX

THE SPIRITUAL INTERPRETATION OF
THE OLD TESTAMENT

1. The Problem

It is common to find no distinction made between various kinds of 'spiritual' or 'mystical interpretation'; all are classed indiscriminately as 'allegorical', and such a passage as the following is taken as a normal type of such interpretation: 'Abraham seeking a bride for his son is a type of God the Father, who also seeks a Bride (the Church) for His Son. Eliezer, who is sent on this errand is the representative of the Twelve Apostles. The well at which Rebecca is found corresponds to the water of baptism, and the presents brought by Eliezer are the divine word and the good works of the servants. Jacob's words, "I am Esau, thy first-born", cannot be called a lie—they are a *mysterium*—in a tropical sense they are true. Jacob, in using them, is a type of the Gentiles, who claim them and receive the adoption and blessing belonging to the chosen people. Jacob had two wives. So Christ calls the Jew and the Gentile. Leah, the tender-eyed, is the blinded Israel . . . Deborah (the synagogue) incites Barak (Israel) to battle against Sisera (Satan) and routs his forces. Jael (the Church) meets him, stupefies him with milk (prayer) and slays him with a nail (the Cross).'[1]

Every reader of the Fathers will recognize some at least of these interpretations, and acknowledge that they are such as the

---

[1] Zchokke, *Biblische Frauen des A.T.*, Freiburg, 1882: quoted by Henry P. Smith in *Inspiration and Inerrancy*, by Briggs, Evans and Smith; a book of American essays published with an Introduction by Prof. A. B. Bruce, London, 1891, p. 218.

Fathers habitually give. It would be rash to condemn them all as valueless; but at least it is clear that whatever it is that is being given here, it is not exegesis of the Old Testament. It will be necessary for us to try to find some criterion for judging such interpretations. But we have already seen enough to know that not all spiritual interpretation is of this type. We have also made what seems to be a useful distinction between the 'theological' and the 'illustrative' use of the Old Testament.

Some such distinction appears to underlie the wise words of guidance recently given by Pope Pius XII on this subject, in a context in which he has just been stressing the primary importance of the literal sense:[1]

'It is true that not every spiritual sense is excluded from Sacred Scripture; what was said and done in the Old Testament was wisely so ordained and disposed by God that the past would spiritually foreshadow what was to happen in the new covenant of grace. It is therefore the duty of the exegete to discover and expound not only the proper or "literal" meaning of the words which the sacred writer intended and expressed, but also their spiritual significance, on condition of its being established that such meaning has been given to them by God. For God alone was able to know this spiritual significance, and He alone could reveal it to us. And, in fact, this sense is declared and taught to us by the divine Saviour himself in the Holy Gospels; the Apostles, following the example of the Master, exhibit it both in speech and in writing; and it is shown in the perpetual and traditional teaching of the Church, as well as in the most ancient liturgical usage, according to the well-known adage: the norm of prayer is the norm of belief.

'This spiritual sense, therefore, intended and ordained by God himself, must be shown forth and explained by Catholic commentators with the diligence which the dignity of the word of God demands; but they must be scrupulously careful not to propound other metaphorical meanings as though they were the genuine sense of Holy Scripture. For although, especially in preaching, a somewhat wider use of the Sacred Text in a meta-

[1] In the Encyclical *Divino afflante*, 10th Oct. 1943, E.T. by Canon G. D. Smith, p. 20. Cf. the earlier quotation from this Encyclical, p. 111 above.

phorical sense may be profitable, if kept within reasonable bounds, for illustrating doctrines of faith and commending moral truths, yet it must never be forgotten that such a use of the words of Sacred Scripture is, as it were, extrinsic and adventitious to Holy Writ.

'Moreover, the practice is not without its dangers, especially to-day, since the faithful, and particularly those who are learned in both sacred and profane sciences, want to know what it is that God Himself means to say to us in the Sacred Scriptures, rather than what some eloquent speaker or writer is propounding with a dexterous use of the words of the Bible. "The word of God . . . living and effectual, and more piercing than any two-edged sword, and reaching unto the division of the soul and the spirit, of the joints also and the marrow . . . a discerner of the thoughts and intents of the heart' (Heb. iv, 12), certainly needs no human artifice or manipulation in order to move and stir the soul. The Sacred Pages themselves, written under the inspiration of the Holy Ghost, abound in their own intrinsic meaning; enriched by divine virtue, they have their own power; graced with supernatural beauty, they shine with their own bright splendour—if only their interpreter explains them so completely and exactly as to bring to light all the treasures of wisdom and prudence latent within them.'

One more quotation, from Prof. C. H. Dodd, will be of value: 'The essence of historical criticism is that it aims at understanding precisely what the biblical writers meant, at the moment when they wrote, for their particular public at the time; not as though this were the end of biblical interpretation, but insisting that this is the indispensable beginning. In pursuing this aim as objectively as possible, without trying to save the credit of the biblical writers by showing them to be in harmony with "modern thought" (a phrase of unstable meaning), the most recent critics are putting us in the way of rediscovering the apprehension of God's self-revelation in history which emerges from the Bible itself, and provides the only really valid framework or *schema* within which its interpretation must be essayed. The striking thing is that this *schema* is now seen to be substantially that which is implied in the Liturgy and pre-supposed

The Spiritual Interpretation of the Old Testament

(though with some measure of dislocation) in patristic and medieval interpretation at its best. There is within this *schema* a place for the method of symbol and allegory, rightly used; some biblical writings deliberately invite it; but it cannot be safely practised except by those who have the humility to allow the writers first to speak for themselves, and patience and courage to face all the difficulties of the primary or "literal" meaning, instead of flying away upon the wings of fantasy.'[1]

In dealing with the interpretation of the Old Testament in the New we treated the 'theological' use first before passing to the 'illustrative'. But in this chapter it will be best if we go straight to the central point of difficulty and speak first of the 'allegorical' interpretation, primarily of the Old Testament stories, but also of the gospel narratives,[2] which occur in the Fathers and in the Church tradition generally. There is great need here of a sound criterion by which to judge between that which is justifiable and that which is not. Very much in the traditional interpretation rests on a sound 'theological' basis; we shall leave that till later. We are concerned first with the 'illustrative' use, in which the interpretations given do not rest on the exegesis of the literal sense. Of these interpretations, some consist of teaching which is in itself both interesting and valuable; others are in various degrees trivial and unilluminating. We would then suggest this as a criterion: That in every instance where the use made of a text cannot be taken as the original and proper meaning, or a legitimate development or fulfilment of it, we should ask *on what authority the interpretation rests*. It does not rest on the proper meaning of the text quoted, but it may nevertheless be soundly based on the general sense of Scripture; and it may, or may not, usefully illustrate the idea expressed in the original text.

Much that from our point of view seems to be a perverse mishandling of the texts, really has its basis in a deep sense of what we may call the 'catholicity' of our Lord.[3] The Fathers confess Him to be the universal Saviour and the appointed Judge of all

---

[1] C. H. Dodd, in *J.T.S.*, xlvi (July–Oct., 1945), pp. 208–9.
[2] Pp. 230–1 and 258 above.
[3] Cf. p. 291 f. below.

mankind; by Him in the beginning the world and all men had
been created; He had been present with Israel throughout the
Sacred History, so that the Scriptures not only contained the
prophecies of His coming, but also spoke of Him from end to end.
St. Irenaeus, commenting on 'Moses wrote of Me' (John v, 46),
says that this is 'no doubt because the Son of God is implanted
everywhere throughout his writings; at one time indeed speaking with Abraham, when about to eat with him; at another
time with Noah, giving him the dimensions (of the ark); at
another, inquiring after Adam; at another, bringing down
judgement upon the Sodomites; and again, when He becomes
visible, and directs Jacob on his journey, and speaks with Moses
from the bush'.[1] The interpretations given by the Fathers suffer,
without doubt, from their ignorance of the literal meaning, and
their lack of all that equipment which the modern exegete has
within easy reach. But the advantage does not all lie with us.

A proper account of this subject needs for its basis a trustworthy history of the interpretation of the Bible in the Church;
but it is a mark of the low ebb to which Biblical studies have
fallen in our day, at least in this respect, that such a history does
not exist.[2] All that we can do, therefore, is to attempt with imperfect equipment to set out the chief principles which emerge.

[1] St. Irenaeus, *Contra Haereses*, IV, x, 1.
[2] F. W. Farrar's Bampton Lectures on *The History of Interpretation* (1886)
ought to have provided what is needed; but though they cover the ground
and display much learning, in everything that matters they are a model of
what such a work ought not to be. The title of the book had better have been
'A History of Misinterpretation', for Jewish and Christian exegetes from the
beginning onwards receive with a few partial exceptions one undiscriminat-
ing condemnation, from an extremely limited mid-Victorian point of view.
The work needs to be done all over again. On mystical interpretation generally, there is Darwell Stone in the *New Commentary* (O.T., pp. 688–97); he
gives many useful quotations, but he is at a loss for the needed criteria. In
The Interpretation of the Bible, ed. Dugmore, there is the valuable first lecture
by H. J. Carpenter, but it is all too brief. The best that I have found is the
article in *C.Q.R.*, vol. xxii (1886), pp. 22–64, on 'The Mystical Interpretation of Holy Scripture'; its anonymity is tantalizing, for this is a first-rate
article of high theological value. I learn that it may perhaps be by W.
Bellars. G. D. Barry's *The Inspiration and Authority of Holy Scripture* (S.P.C.K.,
1919) consists of a useful series of introductions to the chief writers on the
subject from Philo to St. Augustine. In this chapter I owe much to help given
by Fr. Bertram Lester, S.S.M.

The Spiritual Interpretation of the Old Testament

2. The Four Senses of Scripture

There is no difference of principle between the classification of the senses in which Scripture is to be interpreted,[1] as given by Clement of Alexandria (the literal, mystical, moral and prophetical senses), that of Origen (the literal, the moral and the spiritual), and the medieval distinction of the literal, allegorical, moral and anagogical senses, as given in the couplet:

> *Littera scripta docet: quid credas, allegoria:*
> *Quid speres, anagoge: quid agas, tropologia.*

The principle is thus stated by St. Thomas:[2] 'The author of Holy Scripture is God, in whose power it lies not only to fit words to a meaning, which man also can do, but also the things themselves. Therefore, while in all sciences words have meanings, the property of this science (theology) is that the things signified by the words receive a meaning. The first mode in which words show the meaning of things belongs to the first sense, which is the *historical* or *literal* sense. The mode by which the things signified by the words further signify other things is called the *spiritual* sense, which is founded upon the literal sense and presupposes it; and this spiritual sense has a threefold division. As the Apostle says (Heb. vii), 'the ancient law is a figure of the new law; and the new law itself, as Dionysius says, is a figure of the future glory; also in the new law the things which were done in the person of our Head, are signs of what we ought to do. Hence, in so far as the things of the ancient law signify those of the new, we have the *allegorical* sense; in so far as the things done in Christ, or the things which signify Christ, signify the things which we ought to do, we have the *moral* sense; while according as they signify the things which belong to eternal glory, we have the *anagogical* sense'. He adds further: 'Thus there is no confusion in Holy Scripture, since all the senses are founded upon one, the literal sense, from which alone

---

[1] For a precise account, see Darwell Stone, *New Comm.* (O.T.), pp. 689–94.

[2] *Summa Theologica*, I, i, x, *in corp. art.*

The Four Senses of Scripture

an argument can be drawn, and not from those which are spoken allegorically.'[1]

The illustration commonly given is that of Durandus of Mende (*ob.* 1296): 'Jerusalem is understood historically of that earthly city to which pilgrims go; allegorically of the Church militant; tropologically of every faithful soul; anagogically of the heavenly Jerusalem which is our country.'[2] 'Or again, Manna may be taken *literally*, for the food miraculously given to the Israelites in the wilderness; *allegorically*, for the Blessed Sacrament in the Eucharist; *tropologically*, for the spiritual sustenance of the soul day by day through the power of the indwelling Spirit of God; and *anagogically*, for the food of blessed souls in heaven—the Beatific Vision and perfected union with Christ.'[3] From this it is clear that the Moral sense does not denote the practical lessons to be drawn from the narrative (for these belong to the literal sense), but 'from a figurative treatment of the passage, as affording a type of the Christian soul'.[4]

On this traditional classification of the four senses, a number of comments need to be made.

(*i*) This distinction cuts across that which we have given above, of the 'theological' and the 'illustrative' use of the Old Testament. An 'allegorical' meaning can belong to the former class, when it derives directly from the fulfilment of the Old Covenant in the New, as when our Lord at the Last Supper speaks of the New Covenant in His blood, or when St. Paul speaks of 'Christ our Passover', and signifies the theological completion of the divine acts of the first redemption in the

---

[1] Ibid., *resp. ad primum.*

[2] Darwell Stone, *art. cit.*, p. 694.

[3] *C.Q.R.*, *art. cit.*, p. 33. For the second of these, the author refers to John vi, 31–5; for the third, he refers later in the article (p. 51) to Deut. viii, 3, where we are told that the reason for the gift of Manna was 'that they might discern a great principle of God's dealings with men—viz. that man doth not live by bread alone; that the mere material food would in no case convey or support *life*, but that it is God's Divine energy which works by means of food, as by a sacrament, and that man in truth lives by every word of God'. For the fourth, he cites the reference to the 'hidden Manna' in Rev. ii, 17.

[4] Ibid., p. 34.

second; or it can be a quite fanciful illustration of it, as in the case of the favourite patristic use of the red cord hanging from Rahab's window on the wall of Jericho to signify the blood of Christ.[1] The moral sense is always 'illustrative', except indeed where the literal meaning is moral, as in Isa. i, 22, 'Thy silver is become dross, thy wine mixed with water'.

(*ii*) The distinction between the allegorical and anagogical senses is one which the New Testament writers would scarcely recognize, or at least would not press to the point to which the later expositors press it. In their view, the visible Church on earth is the projection into time to a divine and heavenly reality; but the sharp medieval distinction between the two anticipates the Protestant distinction of the 'visible' and the 'invisible' church, and tends to force apart two things which in the New Testament and in the authentic tradition of Catholic sacramentalism are essentially one. The office for the Dedication of a Church, which speaks throughout in terms of 'Blessed city, heavenly Salem', is here true to St. Paul's teaching that 'our citizenship is in heaven'. Origen, too, runs these two senses into one, as 'the spiritual sense'.

(*iii*) In some of the many places in which Origen rejects the 'literal sense' in favour of the spiritual sense he is taking the 'literal sense' in a curiously materialistic, almost a fundamentalist way, which was certainly not the meaning intended by the original writer. Thus he writes about the Creation-story: 'Will any sensible man suppose that there was a first day, and a second, and a third, evening and morning, without sun and moon and stars, and the first day even without a heaven? And who is so silly as to imagine that God, like a husbandman, planted a garden eastward in Eden, and put in it a visible and tangible tree of life, so that whoever tasted of the fruit with his bodily teeth received the gift of life, and further that anyone who ate of the fruit of that other tree became partaker of good and evil? And if God is also said to walk in the garden in the evening, and Adam to hide himself under a tree, I do not sup-

---

[1] As in Clement *ad Cor.* xii; Justin, *Dial.* iii; Origen *In lib. Jesu Nave homilia* iii, 3–5; Ambrose *de Fide* iv; Augustine, in Ps. lxxxvi (lxxxvii) §6, on v. 4.

pose that anyone will doubt that these passages by means of seeming history, though the incidents never occurred, figuratively reveal certain mysteries. Moreover, Cain's going out from the presence of God, if we give heed, is a distinct inducement to inquire what is meant by "the presence of God", and by a man "going out" from it. Why say more? Those who are not quite blind can collect many similar instances of things recorded as actual occurrences but not literally true'.[1] St. Chrysostom, commenting on the text quoted above from Isa. i, 22, 'Thy silver is become dross', says that some give a mystical interpretation, that the silver signifies words of God and the wine His teaching; but that he himself holds to the literal view, that the prophet is thinking of the frauds of money-changers and traders' tricks.[2] Here the 'literal sense' is not being used, as we are accustomed to use it, of the original meaning of the writer, but rather as meaning 'literalistic'.

3. Homiletic Allegory

The allegorical interpretation of Scripture had for Origen two main purposes: the one negative and apologetic, the other positive and didactic.[3] We have seen some of his criticisms of the literal sense of the Book of Genesis; but he found many other stumbling-blocks, both historical and moral, in the literal sense of the Old Testament and of the New, which were forced on him by Gnostic and pagan adversaries. 'His fearless logic saw but one way of escape. These passages, he admitted, in their literal sense are not true. Why then, urged the adversary, are they found in what you Christians call the Word of God? To this he replied that, though in one sense untrue, they are in another the highest, the only valuable truth. They are permitted for an object. These impossibilities, trivialities, ineptitudes, are wires stretched across our path by the Holy Spirit, to warn us that we are not in the right way. We must not leap over them; we must go beneath, piercing down to the smooth broad road

---

[1] Origen, *de princ*, IV, iii, 1.
[2] *In Es.*, ad loc. Quoted by Darwell Stone, *art. cit.*, p. 692.
[3] Bigg, *The Christian Platonists of Alexandria*, 1886, p. 137.

of the spiritual intelligence. They are the rough outer husk, which repels the ignorant and unfit reader, but stimulates the true child of God to increased exertion. The letter is the external garb, often sordid and torn; but "the king's daughter is all glorious within". It is as if the sunlight streamed in through the crannies of a ruinous wall; the wall is ruinous that the sunlight may stream in.'[1]

But Origen makes a positive use of Allegory for homiletic purposes; and it will be worth while to give an extended paraphrase of one of his Homilies on the Book of Numbers, as an illuminating instance of his method.[2]

'Thence was the well; this was the well of which the Lord said to Moses, Gather the people, and I will give them water to drink. Then sang Israel this song upon the well, Begin ye unto it; as for the well, the princes dug it, the kings of the nations hewed it out, in their kingdom, in their dominion' (Num. xxi, 16–18, *LXX*). He says how strange it seems that the people should have to be brought together to drink, and not come of their own accord; this is a case in which 'the meanness of the literal sense drives us back to the richness of the spiritual interpretation. And so I think it convenient to collect from other parts of Scripture the mysteries of the wells, that by comparison of several texts the obscurities of this passage may be made plain.' He then quotes Prov. v, 20: 'Drink the water of thine own vessels, and of the fountain of thine own wells; let not the waters be poured out outside thy fountain' (but he notes that other copies omit the 'not'); 'let thy waters be for thee alone, and let no stranger share in them'. Each of us, he says, has a well in himself, not one well or one vessel only, but several wells and several vessels. The patriarchs all had their wells; go then through the Bible looking for the wells, till you come to St. John iv, where it is said that he who drinks of the earthly well shall thirst again, but he who drinks of the water which Jesus will give him, shall have in him 'a fountain of water leaping up to eternal life'; and later (vii, 38) that he that believeth in Him,

---

[1] Ibid., p. 138. Dr. Bigg gives a general reference to *De Princ.* iv and the *Philocalia*.

Homily on Numbers, xii; Migne, *P.G.*, xii, pp. 656 ff.

as the Scripture saith, out of his belly shall flow rivers of living water. 'You see then that he who believes in Him has in himself not only a well but wells, and not only fountains but also rivers, and moreover not the fountains and rivers which minister to this mortal life, but those which bestow life eternal.'

We should think, then, of a well as deep, covering some profound mystery, but of a fountain as overflowing for the life of the people; we should notice further that in Prov. v, 'wells' are spoken of, in the plural. Such 'wells' are the knowledge of the several Persons of the Trinity. Yet again, each of the natural sciences is a well—here he quotes Wisd. vii, 17–20, where various sciences are enumerated. When Christ came and the Spirit was given, the 'wells' became fountains and rivers; hence our Lord's words, that in the man who believes in Him there should be fountains of living water. 'As that one well which is the Word of God becomes wells and fountains and rivers innumerable, so man's soul which is made in God's image can have in itself and produce from itself wells and fountains and rivers.'

The wells in Genesis needed to be cleared, after the Philistines had filled them up; this clearing is necessary, that the rational meanings which God has put there may produce clear streams. The Philistines dared not do this while Abraham lived; when he died, the Philistines choked them, for jealousy. Afterwards Isaac dug them again.

Abraham's servant, when he went to get a wife for Isaac, found Rebecca (that is to say, Patience) at the wells. Similarly Jacob found Rachel and Moses Zipporah by the wells. So, if thou wouldest take Patience for thy bride, or Wisdom, or the other virtues of the soul, be always at thy wells; 'for by the living waters, by the streams of the living word, it is certain that all the virtues of the soul dwell'.

In the present text (Num. xxi, 16) it is said that those who digged the wells were kings and princes, and a hymn was sung to God at the wells, and Moses gathered the people to the wells. Moses signifies the Law; and the true Well is Jesus the Son of God. 'To this well, to the faith of Christ, the Law bids us come; for He said, Moses spake of Me.' The Law calls us to Christ, to drink the water and sing to it a song: that is, with the heart to believe unto righteousness, and with the mouth to make confession unto salvation.

When it says, Begin ye unto it, the meaning is, to place as the beginning of all things this Well; for He is the Beginning, the First-begotten before all creation, in whom all things were created. Or,[1] let your heart begin to understand what is this Well of which spiritual waters are to be drunk and the faithful refreshed; open to Israel this well, that whoever beholds God with his heart may drink of the spiritual sense. And it must be this Well, the Well to which Moses points us: not that of Marcion, or of Valentinus or Basilides, who came not through Moses, for those are the wells in the Valley of Salt, where are slime-pits. In the Valley of Salt, and bitter, is every heretical opinion, and every act of sin.

'That which we now have in our hands, which has been read to us, is a well, and so are all the Scriptures of the Law and the Prophets; so all the evangelical and apostolic writings are one well, which none can dig or delve except they be kings and princes. Truly kings and princes are they who remove the earth from the well, remove the surface-meaning of the letter, and from the rock within, from where Christ is, bring forth the spiritual meanings as living water.'

This is beautiful teaching; but whatever it is, it is not an exposition of the Book of Numbers. On what then is it based? Primarily on St. John's gospel, and the spiritual meanings there given to Jacob's well and the living water; using this as his real basis, Origen finds spiritual meanings in the Old Testament texts about the wells. Taken as a whole, the matter of this Homily is sound and scriptural. He lost much, no doubt, by neglecting the literal sense to the extent that he did. Yet underlying all there is a constant awareness that the revelation of God has been given through history. In all these respects Origen stands in marked contrast with Philo, who was the fountainhead of this allegorical interpretation, and exercised great influence on the Fathers and on the Church tradition of exegesis generally. Philo's mystical interpretation was an instrument by which he found in the Scriptures not the authentic teaching of

[1] Note the alternative explanation; cf. p. 230 above.

the Scriptures, but notions taken from the Greek philosophers; he had almost no conception of the action of God in history, which dominates the Old Testament itself, and he had strayed much farther away from the faith of his fathers than he ever knew.[1] Where the Church fathers have behind them a doctrine based on the theological fulfilment of the historical revelation of God in the Old Testament by the history of the New Testament, Philo was a heretical Jew, and to a large extent the basis of his teaching did not lie in the Old Testament at all.

A very large part of the Scriptural interpretation in the Fathers is directly homiletic in its scope. So, for instance, St. Hilary's purpose in his commentary on Ps. cxix is homiletic throughout; he interprets it in the light of the knowledge which he assumes in his hearers of the Faith of the Gospel. It is the same with Ambrose and Augustine, with Athanasius and Cyprian; and so it is, back to the Roman Clement. In their comments on the Old Testament the Fathers' primary purpose is to arouse awareness of the revelation of God in Christ. They and their hearers are living in the Christian tradition of faith, which had its historical origin in the revelation which unfolded itself in the experience of the Old Testament saints, and reached its completeness in Christ.

While however the Fathers had this general sense of a Revelation given in history, they did not know how to interpret the Bible historically. They were liable to read into this or that passage from the Old Testament—in fact into almost any phrase in it, without regard to its proper context—the full revelation of the things of God which Christ gave. They read the Bible as it were backwards. This method of interpretation became a tradition. Abel is found offering to God the Christ whom the firstling of his flock typifies. Abraham believes in God and knows Him; and since God is always the same and Christ is God, Abraham believes in and knows Christ. In the three travellers whom he

---

[1] 'The philosopher of Alexandria saw no *historical* bearing in the career of Abraham. As he was severed from the heart of the nation, so the pulses of the national life had ceased to beat in him. The idea of a chosen nation retained scarcely the faintest hold upon his thoughts. Hence the only lesson which he drew from the patriarch's life had reference to himself. Abraham was but a type, a symbol of the individual man.'—Lightfoot, *Galatians*, p. 163.

welcomes to his tent he discerns the Holy Trinity, and in saluting one of them as 'My Lord' shows that he knows the Second Person as He was to be incarnate. Old Testament types and New Testament antitypes meet and converse together in protean confusion. Thus patristic tradition presents a fascinating but unreal and unconvincing picture of the meaning of the Bible, because of the absence of a right historical perspective.

There is further a tendency in some of the Fathers[1] (to which parallels can be found in recent devotional literature) in speaking of the life of our Lord to pass straight from the events of His nativity to those of His death and resurrection, neglecting the intervening record of His ministry and His teaching. This is due, no doubt, to the tradition which began in the apostolic age itself of interpreting the miracles of healing as types of the salvation of the soul. But whereas for the gospel-writers such interpretation presupposes the truth of the history, in the later expositions this is less prominent; here perhaps we can see a result of the habit of interpreting the Old Testament incidents purely as types, to the neglect of their historical actuality.

Another feature of patristic interpretation is the mystical significance assigned to numbers. Numbers seem to have a strange fascination for the human mind; among logicians, from the Greek philosophers onwards, the queer tendency has persisted of treating mathematical propositions, such as $2+2=4$, as the normal type of a 'true' proposition, and we have seen in an earlier chapter how John Locke thought that the evidence for the existence of God was 'equal to mathematical certainty'. Perhaps the notion of the mystical significance of numbers is not altogether unrelated to this. This notion is found even in the Fourth Gospel, and more markedly in the Book of the Revelation; but it reaches its most fantastic heights in the Rabbinic Gematria, which trades largely on the numerical value of letters. Thus there was a popular explanation of the 318 members of Abraham's household, in Gen. xiv, 14, which occurs first in the Epistle of Barnabas: in the 300, represented by the Greek letter τ, we are to recognize the cross, and in the ι (for 10) and the η (for 8) the first two letters of the name of

---

[1] This would be notably untrue of the Antiochene School.

Jesus. 'Of course it is quite *possible* that God should have caused this household to be 318 in number, because He foreknew that the Greek letters by which this number would be represented in a future translation of the narrative, would be thought by some persons to have a hidden reference to our Saviour. But for our part we can only say that such a conception of God's purposes does not seem to us to be a worthy one, or to be in accordance with what we know of His mode of dealing with men.'[1]

There is an interesting passage in St. Augustine where he asks himself why mystical interpretations are as attractive to him as they are. Speaking of the effect of divine grace in implanting in men love to God and to their neighbour, he says: 'How is it, I ask, that if a man makes this plain statement he does not please the hearer so much as when he draws its content from that passage in the Song of Songs where the Church is praised under the figure of a beautiful woman, and it is said of her, "Thy teeth are like a flock of sheep that are shorn, which come up from the washing, whereof every one bears twins, and none is barren among them" (Cant. iv, 2). Does the hearer learn anything more than when he heard the fact expressed in plain statement without the help of the figure? And yet, I know not why, I feel greater pleasure in contemplating holy men when I view them as the teeth of the Church, disengaging people from their errors and bringing them into the body of the Church with their rudeness softened down, as if torn off and masticated by the teeth. With the greatest pleasure, too, I recognize them under the figure of sheep that have been shorn, having put off the burdens of the world like fleeces, and coming up from the washing—that is, from the waters of baptism—and all bearing twins—that is, the twin commandments of love—and not one of them barren in that holy fruit. . . . No one has any doubt that it is pleasanter sometimes to have knowledge communicated through figures, and that knowledge gained with difficulty by searching gives greater pleasure in the finding. He who seeks without finding suffers hunger; he who seeks not at all, because he has what he requires at hand, grows languid from satiety.

[1] *C.Q.R., art. cit.,* p. 38 and note.

The Spiritual Interpretation of the Old Testament

Weakness from either of these causes is to be provided against; and therefore the Holy Spirit, with admirable wisdom and care for our well-being, has so arranged the Holy Scriptures as by the plainer passages to provide against under-nourishment, and by the more obscure to stimulate our appetite. For there is scarcely anything dug out of those obscure passages which may not be found elsewhere set forth in the plainest language.'[1]

Tastes differ; and certainly most modern readers would find this particular illustration decidedly unpleasing. But St. Augustine liked it; and he has given us in this passage a clear statement that the authority of these allegorical interpretations does not rest on the texts themselves, but on the truths which they illustrate, and which can equally well be expressed in a quite different way. It was these truths, depending on the tradition of the Faith, and thus on the general sense of Scripture, that the Fathers were seeking to convey to their readers, in what was to them an attractive form. Their allegorical exegesis provided a means whereby these truths could be clothed in concrete imagery; and if we are to do justice to them, we must look always for the positive meanings which they were expressing. At the same time we are bound to recognize that their failure to grasp the literal and historical meaning of the texts which they allegorized obscured for them, so far, an important element of the truth of the Old Testament.

This, however, is not the whole story. The patristic tradition and that of the Church generally shows in other respects a remarkable fidelity to the intrinsic authority of the Scriptures themselves, and presents us with spiritual interpretations of the Old Testament which are directly in line with those given by the New Testament writers.

4. The Theological Use: Christian Dogma

It is frequently assumed that there is no difference in principle between Justin Martyr's interpretation of Moses' outstretched hands upheld by Aaron and Hur during the battle against Amalek, as typical of our Lord's hands stretched out on the

[1] Augustine, *De doct. Christi*, II, vi.

cross,[1] and St. Paul's comparison of the situation of the
Corinthian Christians in 1 Cor. x, to that of Israel in the wilderness. That assumption must be called simply erroneous. The
former is an illustrative comparison, which is up to a point
interesting and suggestive, but entirely lacks any exegetical
foundation. The latter belongs to the Exodus-homology which
formed the classical pattern of Israel's messianic hope, and
which was not only applied by the Apostles to the fulfilment of
the messianic hope in Christ, but actually provided the form
which that fulfilment followed; not only did St. Paul speak of
Christ as 'our Passover', but He Himself at the Last Supper in-
augurated the New Covenant of God with Israel to take the
place of the Covenant of Horeb. Here, then, there is a direct and
essential connection, along the line of the 'theological' use of the
Old Testament in the New. We shall trace it out along two lines:
first, the properly theological development of Christian dogma,
and second, the use of the corresponding imagery, chiefly in the
Christian Liturgy.

St. Irenaeus has in the fourth book of the *contra Haereses*
(chaps. xvii, xviii) an excellent theological argument, in which
he seeks to establish the Christian doctrine of sacrifice on the
basis of a series of Old Testament passages quoted in their
original and literal sense to prove that God wanted something
better than the animal sacrifices of the Jews; and though he has
not fully seen the point expressed in the theological argument of
Hebrews, that the Law and the Prophets are fulfilled in the
Sacrifice of Christ, he has quoted the right texts, and has clearly
shown the spiritual interpretation of Sacrifice which those texts
contain.

Such a spiritual interpretation, both of sacrifice and of other
God-ward actions, had become necessary as soon as, and in proportion as, it was grasped that Yahweh the God of Israel was
different from all other gods; that He was no mere personifica-
tion of the genius of the nation, but was the true and living God,
was holy, was righteous. This meant at once that His relation
to Israel was a 'spiritual' relation, which could be infringed as
directly by oppressing His poor as by breaking the taboos of

---

[1] Exod. xvii, 11–12; Justin, *c. Tryph.* xcvii.

uncleanness; and it made it impossible to think of sacrifice as a quasi-commercial transaction. The real circumcision was that of the heart; the true uncleanness was sin; and the sacrifices of God were a troubled spirit.

But there remained a tension between the two, which was not resolved till the New Covenant was given. The Old Testament grasped the spiritual principles, but was impotent to fulfil them. The sacrifices were ordinances, similar in general to those of the pagan religions, but capable also of a spiritual interpretation as symbols of a future reconciliation of man with God, in which man's sin should actually be done away. The New Testament announced that just such a reconciliation, following the lines of the spiritual interpretation of these ordinances, had been effected in certain historical events. It, too, had ordinances; but they were sacraments which symbolized and mediated the reconciliation that had been carried out. Thus it is that the spiritual interpretation of the Old Testament ordinances became a primary basis of Christian dogma.

Of this re-interpretation of concepts belonging to the world of experience to serve as symbols of the realities which are not seen, there are many instances; and it will be best to begin with the expression of the spiritual relation of man to God in His Kingdom, or Kingly Rule, which was the main theme of the Gospel which our Lord proclaimed, with Himself as the central figure.[1] It was a spiritual interpretation of the idea of the 'King' and the 'Kingdom'. On the Mount He refused 'the kingdoms of this world and the glory of them', and thereafter appears to have discouraged the use of the title 'Christ', with its associations of temporal power as expressed in *Psalms of Solomon* xvii; and in the one synoptic passage where He claims by implication the title of King, He explicitly distinguishes this royalty from that of the kings of this world, who exercise domination over their subjects (Mark x, 42). 'But it shall not be so', He says, 'among you', since in the truth of things he who rules is the servant of all and the bearer of the burdens of all; 'as the Son of Man came not to be served but to serve, and to give Himself as a ransom-price on

[1] For a fuller treatment of the office of Christ as king, see my essay in *The Apostolic Ministry*, pp. 506–9, cf. pp. 523–7.

The Theological Use: Christian Dogma

behalf of many'. Here He equates supreme royalty and kingliness with supreme self-giving on behalf of man; it follows that He who is supremely the Servant is in truth the King of kings.

The Old Testament had not lacked a spiritual conception of the meaning of kingship. Behind the earthly king is the overlordship of the divine King, as when David confesses 'I have sinned against Yahweh'; and the office of the earthly king is constantly described in terms of that of a shepherd, as when David is appointed to 'feed My people Israel' (2 Sam. v, 2). God Himself is directly addressed as King: 'I will magnify Thee, O God, my King' (Ps. cxlv, 1). When, therefore, in the passion-narrative of St. John the Jews cry out 'We have no king but Caesar' (xix, 15), they are categorically denying a spiritual truth to which their whole national existence had borne witness, and there was no alternative open to Pilate but to deliver up Jesus to be crucified. It would appear that St. John is correctly rendering the situation as described in all the gospels, and involved in the action of the Jews in bringing a claimant to Messiahsihip before a pagan judge. Either they needed the pagan offic al to tell them who was their true Messiah, or it was treasonabler for any man to claim to be Messiah. Hence in the very act of b inging Jesus to be judged by Pilate at all, they were shirking and thereby abjuring the spiritual office of the People of God. Therefore He is crucified, with the title of King over His head, and the title is written in the three languages which matter in the ancient world (John xix, 19–20). The evangelist's meaning is, not that in spite of His crucifixion He is nevertheless King, but that in His crucifixion itself He is seen to be most truly royal; for from the cross above all He exercises that spiritual authority which He bears, as having come into the world to bear witness unto the Truth (xviii, 37). In being lifted up from the earth He draws all men unto Him (xii, 32), and commands their absolute allegiance, to the point of their bearing the cross themselves:

He that loveth his life loseth it:
And he that hateth his life in this world shall keep it unto life eternal:
If any man serve Me, let him follow Me.

(xii, 25–6.)

The Spiritual Interpretation of the Old Testament

The sense in which our Lord regarded Himself as the Davidic King was shaped by the interaction of the three concepts of the Messiah, the Son of Man, and the Servant of the Lord. The last two are brought together in the Markan predictions of the passion, where in every instance 'the Son of Man' is the subject of the sentence. Perhaps in interpreting these we should not forget that even in the primary Son of Man passage—Dan. vii —it is implied that 'the son of man must suffer', since the 'son of man' is identified with 'the people of the saints of the Most High', and they are told that they are to suffer cruelly at the hands of the Fourth Beast (vii, 21, 25).

It is, then, altogether in line with the gospel conception of His kingly office that He should at the Last Supper interpret His death as the Sacrifice whereby the New Covenant is inaugurated (1 Cor. xi, 25), looking back to the corresponding sacrifice of the Old Covenant at Sinai and superseding it (Mark xiv, 24, where His words 'This is My blood of the Covenant' are an echo of Exod. xxiv, 8), and as the guilt-offering of Isa. liii, 10 (hence the Matthaean addition, xxvi, 27, 'for the remission of sins').[1]

The spiritual meaning of Sacrifice is thus identified, in its last fulfilment, with the completeness of self-giving love. This identification is introduced, as generally understood and needing no further explanation, in Eph. v, 2, where the Christians are bidden to 'walk in love, as Christ also loved us, and gave Himself up for us an oblation and sacrifice to God for a savour of a sweet smell' (i.e. as a burnt-offering). St. John introduces his passion-narrative (xiii, 1) with the words 'Jesus . . . having loved His own which were in the world, loved them to the uttermost': as the Good Shepherd gives his life for the sheep, and as no man has greater love than this, that he lay down his life for his friends. Here is the final meaning of Sacrifice.

All this is set forth in quasi-liturgical imagery in Rev. xix, 11–19, where the King is seen riding forth to judge and make war; yet He is completely unarmed, having no weapons of offence or defence, except for the sharp sword which proceeds

---

[1] The allusion to Isa. liii appears in any case to be fixed by the words 'for many' in the Mark-Matt. account, which are in themselves so strange that we are compelled to see in them the influence of Isa. liii, 11, 12.

out of His mouth, that is the sword of the word, to which the mouth of the Servant of the Lord is likened in Isa. xlix, 2. Again in Rev. v, 5 ff., there is the Lion of the tribe of Judah, who is also the Lamb that is seen, not lying dead, but standing, living through sacrifice, and receiving the adoration of the four living creatures, and the elders, and the angels, and every created thing.

Thus, behind the teachings of Christian doctrine lie 'spiritual interpretations' of Old Testament words. The doctrine of the eucharistic sacrifice is not the perpetuation in the Church of an oblation external to the offerer; for it is first the performance of the Lord's command, Do this for My *anamnesis* (that is, for the making-newly-present of My Sacrifice), and then the offering up of the worshippers themselves, in Him and through Him, as is attested by a collect from the Leonine Sacramentary which defies translation: 'Propitius quaesumus Domine haec dona sanctifica: et hostiae spiritualis oblatione suscepta, nosmet ipsos tibi perfice munus aeternum';[1] or by the famous words of St. Augustine, 'The whole redeemed City itself—that is, the congregation and society of the saints—is offered as a universal sacrfiice to God by the High Priest, who offered even Himself in suffering for us in the form of a servant, that we might be the body of so great a Head. . . . So when the Apostle exhorted us that we should present our bodies as a living sacrifice, holy, pleasing to God . . . which whole sacrifice we ourselves are, this is the sacrifice of Christians: the many one body in Christ. Which also the Church celebrates in the Sacrament of the Altar, familiar to the faithful, wherein it is shown to her that in this thing which she offers she herself is offered to God.'[2]

5. The Theological Use: Liturgy

It is a central point in the use of the Old Testament in the New, that the course of the messianic fulfilment in Jesus Christ is shown to have followed the pattern of the messianic hope as given in the prophets; and everyone who is familiar with the

[1] Secret for Whit Monday in the Roman Missal.
[2] Augustine, *City of God*, ix, 6.

The Spiritual Interpretation of the Old Testament

traditional liturgy of the Church can testify how faithfully the New Testament interpretation of the Old is there reproduced. The compilers of the Book of Common Prayer, in spite of their over-drastic pruning of valuable elements in the old rites, made it their aim to restore their original idea, and so preserve, most markedly at the points of central importance, namely the great festivals of the Redemption, the essential Scriptures and Psalms. In the Roman Breviary and Missal the classical tradition in this matter has been preserved through many revisions. The services date from the patristic period; it was in the fourth, fifth and sixth centuries that they were settling down into something recognizably like their final shape.[1] The way in which the Scriptures are there used shows how well the compilers knew them and how deeply they loved them. In consequence the Christian liturgy is the best of all schools for the study of the theological unity of the Bible.

We will then go straight to the liturgy of the seasons of the liturgical year. In Advent we are given the key to a right understanding of the complex problem of Biblical eschatology. We hear the New Testament prophecies of the Second Advent, which is the consummation of all things in the completion of the messianic Kingdom, and therewith of the divine Purpose for the world and for man—and in connection with this, the eschatological crisis of death and judgement which awaits each individual. But also, against the background of the Last Judgement, our attention is directed to the many judgements of God in the course of history: those predicted by the Hebrew prophets, the Fall of Jerusalem which our Lord foresaw, the ruin of the commercial civilization of Rome proclaimed by the Seer of the Revelation; and here the fact that this judgement took effect some three hundred years later than the Seer expected indicates that the prophecy in question is dealing with principles which are repeatedly exemplified in history. Thirdly, the association of Judgement with Salvation in the divine Purpose is illustrated by the fact that Advent is the preparation for Christmas, which

---

[1] Among liturgical books, the most useful for the present purpose is Batiffol, *History of the Roman Breviary* (E.T. from the 3rd French ed., by A. M. Y. Baylay, 1912).

is the eschatological irruption of the Divine into history by the human birth of the Son of God; this is the 'realized' eschatology, wherein the Age-to-Come projects itself into this world, and man on earth is new-born to eternal life. Hence in the Sarum compline for Christmas Eve the antiphon upon *Nunc Dimittis* is: 'Take ye heed, watch ye all and pray, for ye know not when the time is; watch ye therefore, because ye know not when the Master of the house cometh, at even, or at midnight, or at cock-crow, or in the morning: lest coming suddenly peradventure He should find you sleeping.' On the same night the angels, who are none other than the angels of the Parousia, are heard singing Glory to God in the highest.

It would take far too long to go through the choice of psalms and scriptures at all the festivals, and show how fundamentally right is the choice in almost every case; for indeed, this is a point which can only be verified by actual use. The scripture lessons from the Old Testament are those which directly apply to the subject, whether as messianic prophecies, or as belonging to some point in the great Exodus-homology; whereas the psalms that are sung come sometimes under the 'theological', sometimes the 'illustrative' use. Thus, one of the Christmas office hymns (*English Hymnal*, 14) picks up two psalms which occur in the services: Ps. xix, in which Christ, the Light of the world, is compared to the sun rejoicing to run his course:

> *Forth from his chamber goeth he,*
> *That royal home of purity,*
> *A giant in twofold substance one*
> *Rejoicing now his course to run.*

> *From God the Father he proceeds,*
> *To God the Father back he speeds;*
> *His course he runs to death and hell,*
> *Returning on God's throne to dwell.*

This belongs, of course, to the 'illustrative' use; it is a fine poetical comparison of the Redeemer's progress to that of the sun in the heavens. The next verse alludes to Ps. xciii,[1] in which the

---

[1] This psalm occurs in the introits for the second mass of Christmas, and for the Sunday after Christmas.

Lord, the King, puts on glorious apparel and girds Himself with strength; but the 'apparel' is frail human flesh, and the 'strength' is perfected in weakness:

O equal to thy Father, thou,
Gird on thy fleshly mantle now;
The weakness of our mortal state
With deathless might invigorate.

This is as plainly the 'theological' use, since the original reference in the psalm is to that divine work of Salvation, which at Christmas comes into effect.

In Holy Week we have among the lessons that are read, Lamentations, the Servant-poems, the figure of the Brazen Serpent, certain passages about sacrifice. If our Lord's death is the true Fulfilment of Sacrifice, the connection thereby established between the Old and the New Testaments must throw light on both, illuminating not only the meaning of His death, but also that of the old sacrifices. Hence it is deeply suggestive when at evensong on Wednesday in Holy Week we read, from the rubrics of the Day of Atonement: 'Then shall he kill the goat of the sin-offering which is for the people, and bring his blood within the veil . . . and sprinkle it upon the mercy-seat and before the mercy-seat . . . and there shall be no man in the tent of meeting when he goeth in to make atonement in the holy place, until he come out and have made atonement for himself, for his household, and for all the assembly (*qahal*) of Israel' (Lev. xvi, 15, 17).

A word needs, however, to be said about the story of the Sacrifice of Isaac, Gen. xxii, which is read on Good Friday, but is difficult for the modern student, because the commentaries chiefly dwell on the connections of the story with the practice of human sacrifice, which in the days of the original writer was being unhappily revived. 'The history', says an author whom we have already quoted,[1] 'tells us that Abraham was moved by an instinct which he recognized as the voice of God, to sacrifice his son, the laughter of his heart, the heir of the promises. And our faith, too, must learn to sacrifice to God's glory even that

[1] *C.Q.R.*, vol. xxii, 1886, *art. cit.*, p. 51.

spiritual fruit which it counts most dear, accounting that He is able to raise it up to us again. But this spirit of absolute surrender of that which we count most precious, as an offering of love, is but a faint reflection of the spirit which God Himself has manifested towards us, in that He spared not His own Son, but delivered Him up for us all. And if so, if the spirit of such a sacrifice is in fact Divine, it is no mere casual analogy which has prompted the Church to direct this narrative to be read as a lesson for Good Friday. The sacrifice of Isaac was a type of the Sacrifice of Jesus Christ, not because of a certain chance similarity in the external details, but because in the inner heart of it it was the manifestation in a dim, imperfect way of that spirit of self-abnegation which is the fundamental characteristic of Love, and therefore eternally characteristic of God, who is Love, and who commended His love towards us in that while we were yet sinners, Christ died for us.'

At Easter the glorious paschal *praeconium*, during which the paschal candle is blessed, is wholly based on the Exodus-homology, which indeed occurs as the constant refrain throughout—'Christ our Passover is sacrificed for us'—and reappears, as a matter of course, in the hymn: God has 'loosed from Pharaoh's bitter yoke, Jacob's sons and daughters; Led them with unmoistened foot Through the Red Sea waters'.

Among other specially notable instances of the use of the Scriptures in the liturgy we may note the Mattins and Lauds for the Departed, and for the Conversion of St. Paul, and the very interesting series of Masses for the four Ember seasons, which still retain in some instances as many as five Old Testament lessons, besides the Epistle and Gospel. The following series of notes, made for personal use on the proper for the Ember Saturday in Lent, may give some idea of the sequence of thought in this 'liturgy of the word':

The Introit: Prayer is not in vain—'O let my prayer enter into Thy presence: incline Thine ear unto my calling' (Ps. lxxxviii). *First Lesson:* God's purpose for His people—'The Lord hath chosen thee that He might be thy God, and that thou shouldest walk in His ways . . . and be to Him a peculiar people . . . for His praise, and name, and glory' (Deut. xxvi). *Second Lesson:*

The Spiritual Interpretation of the Old Testament

God's grace—'There shall no man stand against you' (Deut. xi). *Third Lesson:* Temptation—'O Lord God, who deliverest Israel from all evil' (2 Macc. i). *Fourth Lesson:* The conversion of the Gentiles—'As Thou hast been sanctified in us in their sight, so shalt Thou be magnified in them in our sight, that they may know Thee as we have known Thee, because there is no other God beside Thee, O Lord' (Ecclus. xxxvi). *Fifth Lesson:* This comes to pass through suffering—'The Angel of the Lord went down with Azariah and his companions into the furnace . . . and those three with one accord praised and glorified and blessed God in the furnace, and said: Blessed be Thou, O Lord God of our fathers: and to be praised and magnified for ever'— and the rest of the Song of the Three Children. *The Epistle:* written to those who have passed through the passion, and are living in the power of the Resurrection—'Rejoice always. Pray without ceasing. In everything give thanks. . . . And the God of peace Himself sanctify you wholly, that your spirit, soul and body may be preserved whole and without fault at the Coming of our Lord Jesus Christ' (1 Thess. v). *The Gospel:* The glory of the Lord—'And Jesus took Peter and James and John his brother and led them to a high mountain apart; and He was transfigured before them . . . and behold, a voice out of the Cloud, This is My beloved Son, in whom I am well pleased; hear ye Him' (Matt. xvii).

As for the Anglican rite, perhaps its chief original contribution lies in the admirable series of proper lessons for Apostles' and other similar days in the 1922–8 lectionary, which was here in most but not all respects a marked improvement on that of 1871.

Are there any points open to criticism? Certainly some of the homilies on the Sunday Gospels in the Breviary, particularly certain of those from St. Ambrose, St. Gregory the Great, and the Venerable Bede, can occasion a certain lifting of the eyebrows; but these are patristic expositions of Scripture, and we are concerned with the selection of lessons. Legitimate questions can however be raised by the use of texts from the Wisdom-literature on the feasts of our Lord's Mother; for the suggestion, at least, is that the texts relating to the Divine Wisdom are to be applied to her. But in the New Testament, as we have seen, Wisdom is plainly identified with our Lord, and used to explain His relation to the world which He created. It is interesting therefore to note that in the Mass for the Assumption, the earliest of the festivals of our Lady, a verse and a half from Ecclus. xxiv is omitted, lest it should seem that pre-cosmic existence was predicated of her.[1] This reserve, however is not followed in some of the other masses for her festivals, and their vigils; on 8th September and 8th December the Lesson in the mass is from Prov. viii, 22 ff.: 'The Lord possessed me in the beginning of His way, etc.' Yet there is no obligation for anyone to take these Wisdom-texts as applying to her; they can always be read in their plain and literal sense, as referring to the Divine Wisdom, who is the Son of God.[2]

A further word needs to be said about the use of the Psalms in Christian worship. Whenever the psalms are used liturgically, whether in synagogue or in church, they are at once taken out

---

[1] The text is as follows (in A.V.)—the words in brackets are omitted in the Roman Missal: 'With all these I sought rest: and in whose inheritance shall I abide? So the Creator of all things gave me a commandment, and He that made me caused my tabernacle to rest, saying, Let thy dwelling be in Jacob, and thine inheritance in Israel. [He created me from the beginning before the world, and I shall never fall. In the holy tabernacle I served before Him;] and so was I established in Zion. Likewise in the beloved city He gave me rest, and in Jerusalem was my power', etc.

[2] This raises the problem of the Sophiology of Fr. Sergius Boulgakov, in his book *The Wisdom of God*, which to most of us Westerners has been a morsel exceedingly hard to digest; it is so hard to see why these things are said and what they mean, that one is tempted to suspect that the whole is a construction based on two assumptions: that *Ecclesiasticus* and *Wisdom* are to be accepted without qualification as inspired Scripture, and that Inspiration means Inerrancy. But such a judgement would certainly be unjust. Fr. Boulgakov was a convert from Marxist materialism, and his real aim (we are told) was to work out a profound answer to that attitude of mind. He put forward the idea of the Divine Wisdom—the first apologetic effort of Judaism when it was confronted with the Greek mind—in order to present the modern mind with a doctrine of the divine Immanence in the created order, and thereby, perhaps, to give a more satisfying answer to the modern problem than our Western theology, which tends to accept too fully certain presuppositions which it shares with materialism; it shows a certain bias towards a deistic conception of God, and a universe regarded as controlled by natural law rather than by the personal action of the Creator. If that be so, the sophiological riddle is worth reading.

of any individual reference they may originally have had, and are universalized in being applied to the experience of Israel as a whole. But that means that in Christian use they must at once be referred to Christ, since the whole life of the Christian is lived 'in Christ', as a member of His body. The church tradition has therefore always understood the psalms as the prayer of Christ and of His members.[1]

Psalm cxxviii, 'Blessed are all they that fear the Lord. . . . Thy wife shall be as a fruitful vine, upon the walls of thine house; thy children like the olive-branches,' is rightly used in the Marriage Service in the literal sense, as a benediction on the natural family. But there is also a spiritual Family, that Family which was taught by our Lord to pray, Our Father, that Family in which Christ is the Bridegroom and the Church His bride; rightly therefore in the First Vespers of Corpus Christi the antiphon to the psalm is, 'Like the olive branches shall the children of the Church be round about the Table of the Lord'.

Psalm cxxxix, 'O Lord, Thou hast searched me out and known me,' expressed the psalmist's wonder at the formation of the natural human body and its growth. But if St. Paul is right in speaking of the Church as Christ's body, then it is right to use the words 'In Thy book were all my members written, which day by day were fashioned, when as yet there was none of them' (v. 16), to illustrate the wonder of the ever fresh growth of new members of the body of Christ.[2]

Psalm cxii, 'Blessed is the man that feareth the Lord: he hath great delight in His commandments', is a picture of the godly Israelite ordering his household; this and other verses of the psalm have too often appeared on tombstones in English churches to extol the virtues of some respected squire. It is better to reflect on Fr. Benson's title: 'The offspring of the Covenant of Righteousness.'

This last instance brings up a point which can be a danger in the use of the psalms; often it seems that the psalmist is a little too satisfied with his own godliness. There is little danger that

---

[1] See esp. E. Mersch, S.J., *Le Corps mystique du Christ* (Louvain, 1933), vol. ii, ch. iv, pp. 80–131.

[2] R. M. Benson, *War Songs of the Prince of Peace*, ad loc.

the worshipper will take harm from the imprecatory psalms; but the danger of self-complacency is more subtle. St. Augustine has some valuable comments on Ps. lxxxvi (lxxxv) 2: 'Preserve Thou my soul, for I am holy.' He doubts if anyone could say these words but He who alone was without sin, who came not to commit sins but to take them away. In them we therefore recognize His voice. But He is also Head of the Church; if then His members cannot be separate from Him, then 'for I am holy' must apply to me also. But how can I dare say this? If I mean that I have a holiness derived from myself, and that I do not need Another to sanctify me, then they are words of pride and of falsehood; but if I mean 'holy' in the sense of 'sanctified'— in the sense of 'Ye shall be holy, for I am holy'—they express not the pride of a vain man, but the confession of a thankful man, who has received the grace of holiness, the grace of baptism and of the remission of sins. For 'what hast thou that thou didst not receive'? Say then to God, I am holy, because thou hast made me holy; because I received it, not because I had it; because Thou gavest it me, not because I deserve it. You have been baptized into Christ, and have put on Christ; those who have been made members of His body and say they are not holy, are doing an injury to their Head. 'Ye were once darkness, but now are ye light in the Lord.' Therefore let every Christian, and the whole body of Christ, cry in every place while suffering tribulations, temptations, scandals innumerable, 'Preserve Thou my soul, for I am holy; my God, save Thy servant, which putteth his trust in Thee'.[1]

The essential basis of this use of the Psalter as applying to Christ is that sense of His 'catholicity' of which both the New Testament writers and the Fathers are firmly persuaded. He is the Beginning, in whom all things consist; He who in the Incarnation revealed the true pattern of human nature was He who at the first made man in His image. He was present with Israel His people throughout its long conflict; He is to be found everywhere in the Old Testament; in Him all the sufferings of prophets and wise men and scribes are gathered up. He gathers into one those who follow after as well as those who go before.

---

[1] Augustine, *Enarr. in Ps. lxxxv*, §4 (paraphrase).

The Spiritual Interpretation of the Old Testament

In Him, in membership of His body, the life of salvation consists; all true prayer is that which is offered in Christ and
through Christ. Christ is not, in the first place, an ideal for us
to imitate, but the living and reigning Lord and Saviour; hence
the true way of prayer is not that each Christian, as an individual, should pray in a Christ-like spirit, but that all should
pray in unity, as members of Him, their prayer being taken up
into that prayer which Christ makes.

Thoughts such as these explain the use of the psalms as the
prayer of Christ and of His members; and they explain the
endeavours of the Fathers to find Him everywhere in the Old
Testament. The Fathers made mistakes, no doubt, in their fanciful allegorical interpretations. But they were right in seeking
Him in the Old Testament, for He is to be found there. We too
have not understood our Old Testament aright, if we have not
at least begun to find Him in it; for without this we shall have
missed the theological unity of the Bible.

CHAPTER X

SCRIPTURE AND TRADITION

The last chapter of this book must draw the various threads together in a study of the relation of the Bible to the Tradition of the Church. With one element in that tradition we have been occupied in the last two chapters, where we have seen how faithfully the classical tradition of the liturgy has preserved the interpretation of the Old Testament which is given in the New. A large and important place in the Tradition has been taken by the interpretation of the Bible. But with the divisions of Christendom the Tradition itself has become divided; the division has involved some measure of faultiness; and the faulty views of the Inspiration of the Bible with which we started, those of Inerrancy on the one side and of 'degrees of inspiration' on the other, have their historical place and their explanation in the traditions out of which they sprang. In the same way the history of the Tradition of the Faith provides the explanation of the various views which have been taken of the relation of the Bible to Tradition. Sometimes it has seemed that the Bible has become almost submerged in the Tradition, as though the fact that the Church decided which books were to be counted as canonical proved that the Church in the last resort has an authority superior to that of Scripture. Or it has seemed that the function of Scripture is to provide proof-texts for the church doctrine, as in the slogan 'The Church to teach, the Bible to prove'. On the other side it has been held that the Bible is so completely the standard by which everything else in the Church is to be judged that nothing can be allowed to come between it and the individual Christian, and it must be regarded as wholly committed to the individual to exercise his private judgement upon it.

Scripture and Tradition

All these views about the Bible, including the last, have their explanation in some degree of faultiness in various forms of the tradition. Only some such faultiness can explain either this or the anomalous phenomenon of divisions within the body of Christendom, since it is part of the essence of the Church that it should be one, and the Church exists in order to gather men into unity with one another through bringing them first into communion with God. The permanent schisms which have broken the visible unity of Christendom have come into being as a result of spiritual loss of unity in the Tradition.

On the other hand, the appeal which all Christians make to the New Testament is really an appeal back to the primitive wholeness or integrity of the Tradition, as it came from the Apostles of our Lord. Certainly that appeal has often been made with the object of justifying some imperfect or partial view. But the appeal itself is to the original Tradition itself, at the point where it is acknowledged to be whole and integral.

1. The Biblical Tradition

The central point in our whole study has been that the Israel of God, the *qahal* or *ecclesia*, has had a continuous history, under two Covenants, and a continuous tradition. The history has been the Sacred History of God's Purpose of salvation for mankind, and of the establishment of the divine Kingdom. The Church, therefore, is not 1,900 but 3,400 years old; and the Bible is the book which tells of the foundation of the divine Kingdom, declares its character, and announces the end to which it is moving. The Bible takes up the story at the beginning, and leaves it at the point at which the Purpose of God with the one nation of Israel has been completed, and all nations are called in to be incorporated into the Israel of God and receive His gift of salvation.

From the point at which the Bible as such begins to exist, it stands in the closest relation to the tradition of Israel. The 'canonization' of Deuteronomy, the first book to become 'scripture', marks a decisive point in the history of the tradition, the point at which the victory of the faith of Yahweh over the nature-religions of Canaan was finally won; the history shows what this new idea of 'holy scripture' meant. Or rather we should say, the thing itself came first, before a name was found to describe it; the essential point was that Israel, under its king, had solemnly confessed itself to be the People of Yahweh, had pledged itself to believe in and to serve Him alone, and had accepted the Book as defining the terms of its faith in the God who had redeemed it out of Egypt, and of the spiritual service which He had imposed upon it.

Israel took Deuteronomy into exile, and other writings also; and in exile it set itself to learn the meaning of God's dealings with it. The focus of Israel's tradition now became the Synagogue. Of the actual origin of the synagogue there is no record; we have to argue back to its origins from its effects in creating a believing and worshipping community, firm in faith and disciplined in the way of the divine service. The Pentateuch, which, as it seems, was canonized in 397 B.C., was essentially a revised and enlarged Deuteronomy; and it remained always the core of the Bible, holding the place of honour in the synagogue tradition. There seems to be no doubt that the canonization of the Prophets first, and later of the Writings, as authoritative books side by side with the Law, was closely associated with their use in the synagogue; and with the liturgical reading of the Law went the exposition of it which we meet in the gospels as the Tradition of the Elders, and which was later written down in the Mishna and the Talmud.

The Biblical Tradition is characterized throughout by a many-sidedness in which a variety of contrasted aspects is gathered up in a single whole. We have seen how Deuteronomy drew out a scheme in which the whole life of Israel should be unified under the rubric of faith in Yahweh and obedience to His commandments. Ignorant of our division of 'sacred' and 'secular', it assigned their respective parts to king and judges, to priests and prophets, and to the ordinary Israelite at his worship and in his home, in his commercial dealings and his relations with his neighbour. Again, there is the duality of Creation and Redemption. The prophets set forth Israel's faith in Yahweh primarily as the Redeemer and the God of the Covenant, who would also in His future messianic action bring to pass a second and greater Redemption, and a New Covenant. But concurrently with this went the proclamation of Him as the Creator of heaven and earth; the Babylonian gods were vanity, and He was the universal King to whom at last every knee shall bow and every tongue shall swear. The doctrine of creation received further exposition in the Wisdom-literature, when the Jew came to be confronted with the Greek; and it called forth the psalmists' constant appeal to all created things to join with man in praising their Maker. It demanded also that man should be regarded as composed of body and soul, and not as a soul temporarily housed in a body. When therefore the doctrine of the future life appeared, it envisaged a resurrection of the body, not an immortality of a disembodied spirit.

This many-sided fulness in the religion of the Old Testament is nevertheless incomplete. It suffers from a certain defectiveness due to immaturity, when pre-exilic Israel hates its enemies with a lusty hatred. Graver defects appear in the post-exilic period, when the balance of the tradition is damaged by the cessation of prophecy; the necessary emphasis on Israel's preservation from pagan defilement involves the temporary loss of the prophetic desire for the coming in of the Gentiles; and the building of the walls of the sanctuary symbolizes a narrowly religious outlook on the part of the godly, and a divorce between 'religion' and 'life'. In the days of our Lord the publican and the sinner are outsiders.

All these defects and limitations are swept away when He comes. The sinners find their Saviour: the Spirit is poured out: the Gospel is preached to all nations: love is seen to be the fulfilment of the Law. In the apostolic Church there is a truly astonishing wholeness and fulness. The Gospel is a message of Redemption; but it is the redemption of the world which God has created, and is itself presented as a 'new creation'. Man is seen as belonging at once to eternity and to time. In the advent of the Son of Man, the Day of the Lord, the promised divine Reign, has arrived, and the Christian is confronted with the eternal issues of Salvation and Judgment; yet at the same time he has his daily life to live in this world, and the daily task is to be consecrated to God's glory. The Church is at once divine and human; those who are 'sanctified' are nevertheless subject to temptation, and in danger of losing their inheritance through sin. They have been brought into union with Christ and made members of His body, that the sin which is also in them may be fought and conquered in detail. This demands an entirely whole-hearted effort and endeavour ('Work out your own salvation with fear and trembling'); yet the victory is wholly the work of the Holy Ghost ('for it is God that worketh in you').[1] They are already risen with Christ, and the truth about them will be manifested when He shall appear; yet they have to be warned to mortify their members which are on the earth and put off the sins of the flesh, the world and the devil.[2]

This many-sided fulness comes as the result of the fulfilment of the messianic promises of the Old Testament, by the impact on human life of the eschatological reality of the divine Kingdom, in the life, death and resurrection of Jesus and the gift of the Spirit. If the Revelation had consisted primarily in a making-known of truths about God in a scheme of doctrine, all would have no doubt been consistent and clear. As it is, to give a fully articulated and consistent system of Christian doctrine is a task which theologians must always attempt but can never fully achieve. There is no Christian 'doctrine' of the Atonement:[3] there is a Gospel of the reconciliation of man with God which must and can be proclaimed, described and expounded in human words, as a divine act of redemption, or deliverance, of man from bondage to sin and death, and of sacrifice in bringing him into communion with God, through the human obedience of Jesus the Son of God to the divine will and His vindication by God in the resurrection. But it demands to be expressed in paradoxes: man in being brought into slavery to Christ is thereby set free; by the fact that he is not his own, but has been bought with a price, he becomes truly himself; in losing his life he finds it. Similarly therefore in the Eucharist,

---

[1] Phil. ii, 12, 13.

[2] Col. iii, 1–7.

[3] Gustaf Aulen is therefore entirely justified in his distinction between the classical 'idea' of the Atonement in the Christian tradition and the 'doctrines' or 'theories' of it: *Christus Victor*, pp. 174–5.

which from the Last Supper onwards has been understood in the Tradition as a sacrificial action, there is the one and all-sufficient Sacrifice of Christ, and yet every Eucharist is a sacrifice. Christ has offered Himself once for all, yet man also makes his oblation of bread and wine, the symbol of his offering of himself, though he has nothing to offer of his own but his unworthiness; he must offer his all, yet he comes to receive all; Christ is at once Priest and Victim, the *victor victima*, the Lion of the tribe of Judah, the Lamb of sacrifice, and the Bread of life.

In the liturgy as in the New Testament these seeming contradictions lie side by side; in the Sacrament as in the written Word they are seen to be necessary to one another, and to explain one another. The Christian at the Eucharist knows what it is to be brought into the presence of these overpowering realities, which defy rational formulation and demand to be expressed as Scripture expresses them, by means of imagery. Yet there is no place here for irrationalism; on the contrary, rational understanding and explanation of the mystery is demanded to the limit of what is possible, for the safeguarding of the mind from error. The same St. Thomas who works out with theological subtlety the doctrine of the Real Presence in terms of the philosophy of substance and accident is also the author of the *Adoro te devote*. In the liturgical tradition, as in the New Testament, man is confronted with the reality of the Transcendent God, his Creator, Saviour and Judge. The mystery of the divine revelation in Christ surpasses his power of comprehension; yet to apprehend it is to have eternal life. In the 'eschatological' reality of the coming of God to man lies the root of the wholeness and fulness of the apostolic Tradition of which the New Testament is the primary document.

2. The Tradition in Church History

The continual effort of the Church throughout the centuries has been to maintain the integrity of the Tradition, as against the divisive forces which have attacked it. Yet the effort itself depends on the fact that this wholeness has been once for all given, in the very constitution of the Church as one, holy, catholic and apostolic, by the advent of the Messiah and His redemptive work and the gift of the Spirit. The Church is divine and it is human; its unity, holiness, catholicity and apostolicity stand as the basis of its existence, and yet have to be unceasingly fought for and maintained. All Christians are one in Christ, and His body is indivisible; yet every sin against charity is a breach of Christian unity.[1] The Church is holy, because Christ is holy and the Holy Ghost is the Sanctifier; yet every sin that its members commit is a breach of that holiness.[2] The Church is Catholic, in the four 'dimensions' of catholicity, in being extended throughout the world, in possessing the wholeness of truth, in embracing all sorts and conditions of men, and in providing healing for all sins; yet every heresy and schism is an infringement of that catholicity.[3] The Church is Apostolic in possessing the apostolic tradition of faith and order; but history has shown how endless have been the possibilities of damaging that apostolic inheritance.[4]

The dangers to the Tradition which were involved in the Church's mission to all nations may be compared to those which confronted Israel in Canaan, when its faith in Yahweh was in peril of becoming swamped by the Canaanite nature-religions. Yet the true answer to the problem was not that given by such stubborn Yahwists as the Rechabites, who never accepted the conditions of agricultural life, still less those of life in cities: 'Jonadab the son of Rechab our father commanded us, saying, Ye shall drink no wine, neither ye nor your sons for ever, neither shall ye build house, nor sow seed, nor plant vineyard, nor have any: but all your days shall ye dwell in tents; that ye may live many days in the land wherein ye sojourn' (Jer. xxxv, 6–7). The true answer was given not by these 'true believers', but by men such as Jehoiada, Hosea or Isaiah, who belonged to the cities and fully shared in the education and civilization of their day, and yet lived by their faith in Yahweh, and while in

[1] See, for this, my *Form of the Church*, pp. 61 ff.
[2] Ibid., pp. 74 ff.
[3] Ibid., pp. 90 ff.
[4] Ibid., pp. 106 ff.

the world were not of it. Several codes of law claimed the agricultural festivals for Yahweh, and by Deuteronomy the process was complete; all that could be assimilated of the Canaanite culture was taken up into the new synthesis of the whole life of the nation round the one Sanctuary of the one God.

A similar synthesis was necessary when the Church went out into the Graeco-Roman world. It is the same to-day when the Church goes out to win for Christ the national cultures of India, China, Africa, and every nation of the world; it is the same in contemporary Europe. Each nation must hear the Gospel, 'every man in our own tongue wherein we were born': yet in such a way that each several culture is incorporated into the body of Christ, and the apostolic tradition of the Catholic (whole or universal) faith and way of life dominates the particular form of life which each nation and culture represents. The peril always is that the Tradition should be allowed to become assimilated to the contemporary form of Baal-worship, and a syncretistic product emerge: as if, for instance, in India the images of the Christ and the Buddha should stand side by side. True Catholicity means that all the nations bring their glory and honour into the City of God, and the Magi of every nation lay their gold, incense and myrrh at the feet of Christ the King.

In one sense, of course, no national culture can be Catholic or universal; there are diversities of gifts, and no particular culture can possess them all. Yet there is one Spirit, as there is one Lord, one Faith, one Baptism; and there is a wholeness or catholicity of the Tradition which needs to be maintained unimpaired by each and every christianized culture. This is the meaning of the fact that everywhere and in all ages the Church must have the Bible, the Creeds, the Sacraments, and the Apostolic Ministry; for all these are the essential forms of its Catholicity, which need in all places and at all times to be kept intact. But this Catholicity is threatened by the limited and partial character of each and every element which the various cultures bring to be integrated into the Church's fulness, as well as by every sin and act of rebellion against the divine will and the divine Reign.

Hence the Church, when it went into the Graeco-Roman world, was beset on every side by new dangers, of which we are made aware in all the later books of the New Testament: thus for instance Ephesians and Colossians, the First Epistle of St. John, and the Revelation all speak of the deadly perils against which they uphold the catholicity of the Tradition. The peril becomes fully developed in the Gnostic heresies of the second century, in which the Biblical wholeness of the Tradition is threatened by the denial that the world has been created by the good God, that His Son was incarnate in the flesh, and that the body has been redeemed. The Church confronted the peril by appealing to the integrity of the Tradition as attested by the Scriptures of the Old Testament and the New (which now became canonical), by the traditional teaching of the apostolic sees, and by the living voice of the episcopal successors of the Apostles.

In the great Irenaeus and in Tertullian we see how acute the conflict was. Marcion brought up against the Old Testament some of the same difficulties which are felt by many to-day, objecting to the Old Testament teaching about the character of God.[1] It was such objections as these that Origen had to meet; the pressure of these difficulties drove him to take flight from a truly historical exposition of the Old Testament narratives in an allegorism which was indeed good and valuable in itself, because it was based on the orthodox tradition of the Faith, but was defective in so far as it failed to give an exegesis of the books according to the literal sense.[2] Yet, though the Fathers abandoned to a large extent the historical exegesis of particular texts, they did uphold that historical view of the Old Testament as leading up to Christ, which is indeed essential to the Christian view of history; their allegorism never even remotely suggests that the whole Old Testament is being dissolved into fable. We may remind ourselves further how continually they appeal to the fulfilment in Christ of prophecies which had actually been made; or again, how admirable a summary of the Old Testament history appears in the anaphora of the *Liturgy of St. Basil*.

The Tradition succeeded in taking up into itself from Greek thought the two allied but distinct elements of rationalism and

---

[1] See Tertullian, *c. Marcionem*, bk. II (throughout).
[2] See pp. 274-5 above.

mysticism. Rational theology has been indispensable to the Church for the purpose of clarifying and reducing to order the dogma derived from the Hebrew eschatology, formulating the metaphysical ideas present therein, and thus distinguishing the Biblical and Christian doctrine of God from paganizing distortions of it. Thus in the Trinitarian and Christological controversies, the ultimate reason for the rejection of Arianism was that the conception of God which it implied was not that of the personal God whom to know is to have eternal life, but that of the remote and unknowable Absolute; phrases were therefore embodied in the Creed to bar the road to this error. While, then, it is the function of rational theology to reduce to order the uncouth eschatological imagery of Scripture, that of liturgy is to maintain within the Tradition the dominance of the Hebrew element and the authority of the Scriptures.

Mysticism, too, has been taken up into the Tradition, and has helped to shape ascetical practice and ways of prayer. Here, too, the necessary safeguard of the Christian Tradition lies in the witness of the Bible and the liturgy to the facts of the Redemption effected in history through the Incarnation of God in true human flesh, and thereby to the sanctification of the life of the common Christian, who is called to glorify God primarily in his daily work. Apart from this, a mysticism learnt from the Neoplatonists could lead to a false identification of the spiritual with the non-material, and thereby to the denial of the sacredness of common life, and that divorce between 'religion' and 'life' which interprets devotion as devoutness, and makes religion the preserve of the religiously gifted individual.

But have the elements of rationalism and mysticism been properly assimilated by the Tradition? This question brings us to the central point at which Protestantism challenged the medieval Catholic system. Dr. Nygren of Lund has posed the problem for us in terms of the way of *agape*, which is the properly Christian way of salvation, and that of *eros*, which is the fundamental *motif* of Greek religion. He shows with admirable clearness that what he calls Luther's 'Copernican Revolution'[1] was an assault upon the medieval synthesis itself and the Augus-

[1] A. Nygren, *Agape and Eros*, Pt. II, p. 463, title.

tinian foundation on which it rested; and he proves that Luther himself was fully conscious of this. In Nygren's terminology, *agape* is God's own love, spontaneous and uncaused, poured out on sinful man not because of any worthiness in its object, but because God is Love; whereas *eros* is man's desire and effort to attain to that true Good which alone can satisfy his longing.[1] Luther intended, and Dr. Nygren thinks that he was right in intending to dissociate *agape* from *eros*, and thereby set free the purely Christian element from its pagan accretions, return to the pure teaching of Scripture, and in effect wipe out the intervening centuries which had made a false compromise with paganism.

It is plainly impossible within the limits of this chapter to give any adequate or satisfying account of the theological issues which were thus raised, or of the three streams into which western Christendom then became divided: orthodox Protestantism, the Renaissance and the Liberalism which succeeded it, and the Catholicism of the counter-Reformation.[2] We are concerned here only with the relation of the divided traditions to

[1] In my Translator's Preface to the first volume of Dr. Nygren's *Agape and Eros*, published in 1932, I gave the following theological statement of the meaning of the two terms: That *agape* is the name for God's love, and describes a divine fact, but *eros* is the name for human love, and therefore describes a human and a psychological fact. God alone can save man (by *agape*); man cannot save himself (by his *eros*). In the Incarnation of the Son, God's *agape* came down from heaven to take to Itself our human nature whose motive-power is *eros*. In Him, *eros* is seen perfectly controlled by *agape*; in us, too, when we become His members by the grace of the Holy Ghost, *eros* becomes the instrument of *agape*, in so far as our life becomes harmonized and unified in following the Christian way.

Such, I believe, is the true account of the matter; but it now appears that I was misrepresenting Dr. Nygren's own view. The reason was that the first volume of his work was purely descriptive of the New Testament doctrine of *agape* and of the idea of *eros* in Plato, Aristotle and Plotinus, and the author nowhere showed what his own view was. It was only in the second part, which deals with the two *motifs* in Church History down to Luther, that his position was made unambiguously clear; and this was not published in Swedish till 1936. My preface to the first volume did, however, state the theological assumptions with which I undertook the translation.

[2] For this the reader is referred to pp. 11–45 of *Catholicity: A Study in the Conflict of Christian Traditions in the West* (Dacre Press, 1947), which is a Report presented to the Archbishop of Canterbury by 'a group of Anglicans of the "Catholic" school of thought', of which I was a member.

the interpretation of the Bible, and with the fact that it is by an enfeebled and divided Christendom that the Bible has been interpreted.

The aim of the Reformers was to return from the corrupt state of religion which they saw around them to the purity of the Gospel; in other words, they desired to recover the integrity of the apostolic Tradition. The fact that the schisms took place and have never yet been healed indicates that the solution of the problem was not then found. Luther believed, indeed, that he had found at any rate the all-important key to the problem, in the proclamation of the direct action of God in saving sinful man, and of the paramount need of the personal response of faith. Calvin believed that he had recovered the true system of Christian faith and order, according to the divine plan laid down in the New Testament. That both Luther and Calvin made contributions of the highest importance towards the solution of the problem is not to be denied. But if we believe that the Christian faith is true, we must believe that it contains the divine answer not only to the need of the individual soul for reconciliation with God, but also to the need of men for unity one with another, in the Israel of God opened to all nations by the Sacrifice of the Messiah; we are bound to think, therefore, that if any of the Reformers had succeeded in restoring the apostolic Tradition in its wholeness and fulness, the unity of Christendom would never have been lost, or would soon have been restored.

The result, however, has been not unity but schism; and in fact the Reformers were themselves children of the late Middle Ages, and were necessarily unable to view the primitive Gospel except through spectacles derived from their own time. At one point after another it is possible to see how their teaching reflects habits of thought derived from later periods of history, as for instance from the Augustinian doctrines of predestination and election, the medieval nominalism, or the medieval formulations of eucharistic doctrine, while the religion of the Reformed Churches reflects the individualism and pietism of the later Middle Ages. It is never possible simply to put the clock back and return to a previous period.

The Distorted Traditions and the Bible

It is one of the great tragedies of history that the endeavour of those men to return to the pure Gospel and the simplicity of the Apostolic Age should have had as its immediate result the disruption of Christendom by schisms on a scale hitherto not imagined to be possible. But, in fact, the schisms were caused, not by the truths which Luther and Calvin were raised up to proclaim, but by the fact that the Tradition of Christendom, to which the Reformers also belonged, had become seriously damaged and distorted in the course of the assimilation of Graeco-Roman culture, particularly as it had been developed by the Western Church in isolation from the East, and as it had been influenced by the incorporation into it of the rude and half-converted Teutonic races. In our own day the weakness of Christendom is due far less to the loss of efficiency caused by division of forces, than to the enfeeblement of the Tradition which originally caused the schisms and has been perpetuated by them. In Dr. Demant's words, 'It is an illusion to think that we are weak because we are divided. We are divided because we are weak. Matters of order and jurisdiction loom large because we are weak in matters of faith, doctrine and liturgy.'[1]

3. The Distorted Traditions and the Bible

The internal division within the Christian Tradition, which is the prior fact underlying the loss of outward and visible unity, provides the explanation of the various faulty conceptions about the Bible and its Inspiration with which we have been confronted in the course of our study. In the ideal condition of things, when the Tradition is preserved in a state of wholeness, the Faith is proclaimed as the Gospel or Glad Tidings of a divine work of salvation wrought out in the history of Israel, made complete in Christ, and available for all nations in the visible Church; and the Bible falls naturally into its place as the Book of the divine Kingdom, which tells the story of the events of the Redemption and sets forth the Christian way of life, and as the handmaid of the liturgical action in which the whole

---

[1] V. A. Demant in *Union of Christendom* (ed. Mackenzie, 1938), p. 57.

mystery of the divine work of salvation is recapitulated and made present, and the Church is truly seen for what it is: as the Israel of God, with the Lord present in its midst.

But when the balance has been so far lost that the Faith is presented to men not as a Gospel, explained and applied in a moral teaching and a liturgical practice, but as an articulated system of doctrines, to be assented to by faith, on the authority of a hierarchical Church administered on juridical lines, the Bible immediately loses its central place. It is even argued that the Church is proved to have authority superior to Scripture, by the fact that it decided which writings were canonical; this however is fallacious, because the witnesses whom a counsel calls do not derive their testimony from him, nor do the sayings of our Lord related in the gospels owe their authority to the evangelists who record them. A somewhat higher place is given to the Bible when it is used to provide proof-texts for the church doctrine; but there the Bible is being maltreated, when its texts are interpreted as if they were oracles possessing a timeless and infallible truth, and are not viewed in the first place historically, in the light of their original meaning and of their place in the Sacred History. It is true that when thus interpreted historically, they do in fact provide the basis of the Christian doctrine; but the Gospel itself is then seen as primary, and the doctrine as the necessary formulation of it. But when the doctrinal formulation is treated as primary, the interpretation of the Bible is cramped by the treatment of its texts in isolation from their context and as *ex hypothesi* free from error.

Yet the doctrine of Inerrancy was not very harmful in an age which thought of 'truth' primarily as belonging to the revelation of God and of the eternal meaning of man's life. The Bible was regarded as teaching chiefly spiritual truths about God and man. It was otherwise when the 'scientific age' had begun; truth was now commonly understood as the matter-of-fact truth of observable phenomena, and so great a man as Locke could make the outrageous statement that the existence of God was as certain as the propositions of geometry.[1] The Inerrancy of the Bible was understood as guaranteeing the literal exactness of its

[1] P. 96 above.

every statement. This is the Fundamentalism which has been a potent cause of modern unbelief. This materialistic Inerrancy needs to be carefully distinguished from the theological and religious Inerrancy in which earlier ages believed.

The Protestant revolt against the scholasticism and the juridical ecclesiasticism of the Middle Ages set up the Bible as the sole authority. No Church Tradition might be allowed to come between it and the individual believer. We get on the one hand the Calvinistic system of belief and church order, rigorously deduced by him from his interpretation of Scripture, and on the other the assertion of the right of each believer to make his own interpretation. In this last assertion the Tradition has reached its lowest limit of dissociation. Yet in practice the Protestant communities had their traditions of interpretation, by which men's beliefs and their lives were guided.

There is truth, of course, in the principle of Private Judgement. No man can be justified, on any authority, in declaring that to be false which he thinks to be true; every man has the responsibility of forming his judgement. In the field of Biblical interpretation, the scholar has the duty of using his expert knowledge to say what the text means, and he is bound by the truth as he sees it. A right doctrine of Authority must leave this principle intact, just as the true ideal of Democracy is that of the co-operative action of free men; and we have seen that where the Faith is held in its wholeness, it can make a creative synthesis of such apparently incompatible opposites.[1] It is the dismembered state of the Tradition that has produced on the one side a totalitarian notion of church authority, and on the other the corresponding idea of an unqualified Private Judgement.

Finally, the Liberal Protestant doctrine of 'degrees of inspiration' erred, as we have seen, by considering the various Biblical writings in isolation from the Bible as a whole and from the Tradition to which they belonged. This view of the Scriptures seems to connect itself directly with the individualistic religion which Protestantism inherited from the personal piety of the later Middle Ages, which had lost the ancient wholeness of the common life of the body of Christ.

[1] See pp. 297–8 above,

Scripture and Tradition

4. Re-integration and Reunion

As when a human body is diseased, nature herself seeks to counteract the mischief and recover health and wholeness, so in the body of Christendom movements of re-integration have for a long time past been taking place, in which there has been a reaching out, in many directions, to regain that which has been lost. The most notable instance is perhaps that of the Catholic revival in the English Church, of which the main objective has been the recovery of lost traditions of the idea of the Church and its worship. In the Roman Church the liturgical movement refuses to let the liturgy be regarded as the province of the clergy only, and insists on the exercise by the laity of the priesthood which is proper to them. Protestants of a zealously orthodox type, whose whole outlook had been concentrated on the Gospel of Redemption, are now found to be turning to see what is to be made of Natural Theology. Others seek to learn from Catholic ascetical practice, and study methods of prayer and the use of retreats. A Protestant religious community exists at Iona, and there is another at Cluny in France.

With this movement towards re-integration there goes a new attitude towards the Bible. Probably we shall hear no more of the opposition between Scripture and Tradition. It is now being understood that the Bible is the Book of the Israel of God, and that its several books must be read in the light of the development of the Tradition; it is further being understood that the Church is directly continuous with the Israel of the Bible. The Bible therefore falls naturally into its proper place, not as merely one among several elements in the life of the Church, nor as an infallible oracle to be distinguished as sharply as possible from Church Tradition, but as that element in the life of the Israel of God whose function it is to regulate the Tradition and to keep it sound.

The internal division within the Tradition has been the prior fact which underlies and has caused the ecclesiastical schisms. Reunion, therefore, must be expected to come, not by clever schemes for amalgamating the several denominational administrations, while leaving the inner dissociations unhealed, but rather by the spiritual process of re-integration and recovery of the wholeness of the Tradition; this will lead in due course to the recovery of visible unity. Nothing, perhaps, is more important than that this order should be observed: first the spiritual, then the outward; first unity in faith, then the solution of the problems of church order.

If this be so, the interpretation of the Bible is of central importance for the reunion of Christendom. About all the other Forms of the Church there has been bitter controversy: we have argued over the use of the Creeds, we have had bitter controversies about Baptism, Confirmation and the Holy Eucharist, and the problem of the Ministry has seemed humanly insoluble. The Bible alone has been accepted by all the various confessions, and the misinterpretations of it and the controversies about it have gone on within the various denominations, mostly on parallel lines. There are no memories of inter-confessional strife to prevent it from being a centre of unity; and a centre of unity it is bound to be in increasing measure, when it is understood as the Book of the Faith in which the Tradition is found expressed in its primitive wholeness.

The condition of this coming-together is the same which was imposed on the remnant of Israel in exile in the sixth century: that of penitence. The whole possibility of the future development of Israel's faith rested then on the sincerity of their confession, 'We have sinned'.[1] Because they truly repented, all things became possible. We too to-day are in exile on Babylon's strand, and we long to be at peace in our own Jerusalem, not only in the life of the World to come, but also in this—O that the Church might truly *be* the Church, and possess its spiritual inheritance! Once again, the condition is penitence; and it is that Christians of all confessions should acknowledge the fragmentariness of their respective traditions, as seen in the light of some apprehension of the meaning of the true Catholicity, which is the authentic wholeness of the Christian Tradition. With that, all things are possible; but nothing is possible so long as the representatives of the various traditions either maintain

[1] See p. 147 above.

the sufficiency each of his own tradition, or on the other hand declare that only pragmatic considerations need be taken into account, and that the organizations must be amalgamated for the sake of efficiency.

It is then necessary to analyse rigorously and thoroughly the divisions within the tradition: to assess the positive truths proclaimed by orthodox Protestantism, and also its defect and failure; to see in the same way what has been the truth and the error of Liberalism; then to trace the roots of both in the Middle Ages, and the extent to which the Roman Catholic Church has perpetuated the medieval system, and how far it has gone beyond it; and then to see the place of the Church of England in all this, combining in a queer way the virtues and faults of all three. It desired certainly to return to the wholeness of the Tradition, by reasserting the authority of the Scriptures and of the Church of the early centuries: why has it failed? Was it that the imposition of an order on the Church by state authority created an organization within which various parties could jostle about unreconciled? Has the fault been that of a 'comprehensiveness' which misses true Catholicity by failure to seek and find a theological unity? But the repossession of the wholeness of the Tradition implies a theological unity—not indeed an agreed formulation of all Christian doctrine, but a unity of faith and of theological understanding—and this means a unity based on the scriptures.

But there is one more group of people which must not be left out of account. In the prayers for the Unity of all Christians which are made year by year from 18th—25th January, it is customary to devote one day to prayer for the Jews. The Christian mind can never think of classing the Jews with the pagan world; for they are 'the Israelites, whose is the adoption, and the glory, and the covenants, and the giving of the Law, and the service of God, and the promises; whose are the fathers, and of whom is Christ concerning the flesh' (Rom. ix, 4–5). The division of Jews and Christians is a division within Israel.

That division began very far back; it began when the scribes who had come down from Jerusalem were found saying that Jesus was casting out devils through Beelzebub. From that point the rejection of Jesus by Judaism runs through the New Testament and all subsequent history. It is fatally wrong to forget that in the controversy between the Jews and the Christians this is the one point that matters: whether in the coming of Jesus the Lord God of Israel was not or was redeeming His people. That is absolutely primary. But however deep the gulf between the two sides, there is a certain relief in recognizing that *all* other causes of division are secondary—the persecution of Christians by Jews in the first century, and of Jews by Christians in most centuries since; the isolation of the oppressed race, the herding of them into ghettos, the jealousy of their industry and ability, the cringing to their financial superiority, the racial dislike, the anti-Semitism—all this is ultimately irrelevant to the central issue, however much penitence it ought to call forth on both sides, but chiefly on ours.

For neglect of this, there has been in recent years a false rapprochement of liberal Christians and liberal Jews. To a limited extent, indeed, this mutual approach has rested on truth; Jewish liberals, such as Israel Abrahams and Claude Montefiore, have helped Christian students to study the documents with more sympathetic eyes, to discern the Semitic background of the gospels, to become more conversant with the Rabbinic tradition. Yet the rapprochement has been fundamentally false; primarily on the part of the liberal Christians, who were false to their principles (as their Jewish friends were not false to theirs), in regarding their Lord as in effect one of the Jewish prophets. But it is impossible to read very far in the writings of these Jewish scholars without becoming aware that their standard of judgement was liberal rather than Biblical; the exclusive claim which is a permanent element in the Faith of Israel is found to have given way to a liberal undenominationalism.[1]

It is the orthodox Jew, after all, with whom the orthodox Christian must ultimately find the deepest affinity; and new hope is suggested by a book that has recently appeared, *Communion in the Messiah*, by an Orthodox priest, Fr. Lev Gillet.[2]

[1] Witness the quotation from Abrahams on p. 111 f. above.
[2] Lutterworth Press, 1942.

Scripture and Tradition

In this book two main ideas are advocated. 'One is the idea of a "dialogue" substituted for the idea of a one-sided mission to Israel. By dialogue I mean that if Christianity has a definite message to bring to Judaism, Judaism has also a message to bring to Christianity.'[1] 'The other is the "communion" of Jews and Christians either in the same personal Messiah (this total communion is a distant goal rather than an immediate possibility) or in messianic values common to both of them (this partial communion can be reached to-day and progressively enlarged). It does not mean that the differences between Judaism and Christianity should be obliterated or minimized. Egerton Swann is perfectly right in saying, "Judaism and Christianity are nearest to an agreement when Judaism is most unambiguously Jewish and Christianity most unambiguously Christian". But Jews and Christians have to acknowledge and even to experience in their spiritual life the immanence of Judaism in Christianity. A new and fruitful meeting between Judaism and Christianity implies a certain Judaization of the Christians as well as a certain completion of the Jews' Judaism.'[2]

This is the right way. It is to accept the actuality of the conflict: Jews deny and Christians affirm that Jesus is God's Messiah. But both accept as essential to their traditions the messianic hope announced by the Prophets. There let them meet; and while we Christians are sure that the most needful thing of all is that which we have to teach them, we must confess also that they have very much to teach us with regard to the manner of apprehending it. There is no greater need to-day

[1] *Communion in the Messiah*, p. x. That is, the Christian's understanding of his own faith needs to be more Biblical, more Hebraic. But I feel unhappy, in many passages, with Fr. Gillet's phrases, as when he says (p. 192): 'The deposit of the Old Testament has been entrusted to Israel, and Israel is still the keeper of the Scriptures. We mean that the ancient rabbinical interpretation of the Old Testament is a very positive contribution of Judaism to Christianity—we would say more: it is the right approach to the understanding of the Old Testament. Like Jerome, the Christian Church should learn the Old Testament from the Rabbis (we do not mean modern rabbinism, but the old masters of Israel).' I have sought to show earlier (pp. 237–8 above) that the Rabbis' interpretation of the O.T. falls far short of the true meaning, through their defective sense of the divine action in history.

[2] Ibid., p. x–xi.

than that we should go back to the Bible and learn far more fully that we do to see the Christian dogma in terms of the Biblical imagery. The contemporary Church suffers through the weakness of its grasp of its rich Hebrew inheritance and of those Biblical ways of thinking which have moulded the traditional forms of its liturgical life. It is just these which Israel according to the flesh can help it to recover. 'If the casting away of them is the reconciling of the world, what shall the receiving of them be, but life from the dead?' (Rom. xi, 15).

The reunion of Christendom will not be complete, and possibly it will not be effected at all, without the return of the Jews to believe in their own Messiah.

5. *The Kingdom of God*

The Bible is the Book of the divine Kingdom. F. D. Maurice once called it 'The Book of the Wars of the Lord'; there runs through it from start to finish the theme of His conflict with all that militates against His glory and constitutes a denial of His kingly rule. Israel is called to be His witness and to fight His battle. Often in the Old Testament there is a too simple identification of the cause of Israel with the cause of the Lord; but already before the Exile it has become clear that there is also a conflict within Israel itself, between the claim of the Lord God and the selfish heart of man.

So to-day in the world the Church stands as God's witness against the secular forces with which it is confronted. There has been the Renaissance denial of Original Sin; Humanism has built up the modern European civilization on the basis of faith in man and his power to progress from good to better: and the final term of this development is seen in a technocratic industrialism which creates a new slavery, and fierce nationalisms in which patriotism becomes the idolatry of a corporate Ego. To these ideals the Church is consciously opposed. Yet at the same time it is immersed in the civilization which is controlled by them; in the midst of that civilization it is set to proclaim the present fact of the Kingdom and Reign of God, and it must seek always to achieve in terms of the current civilization some incomplete yet real expression of the divine Reign. There is further the conflict that is being fought out in every human soul, which the Church sees not only as a human agent in the drama of world affairs, but also as a soul undergoing its probation for Eternity, and faced at every moment with the choice between Heaven and Hell.

The Church, living by the wholeness of the Tradition, knows itself to belong to two worlds at once. But it is able to find a meaning in this world, because it believes that God Himself has set up His Kingdom in this world, and is fighting His own battle in it. The nature of that conflict is set out once for all in the Preface to the Bible:

In the beginning God created the heaven and the earth. And God created man in His own image, in the image of God created He him; male and female created He them. And God saw everything that He had m ade, and, behold, it was very good.

And the Lord God took Man, and put him into the Garden of Eden to dress it and to keep it. And God commanded Man, saying, Of every tree of the Garden thou mayest freely eat: but of the tree of the knowledge of good and evil, thou shalt not eat of it: for in the day that thou eatest thereof thou shalt surely die.

And the Serpent said unto the Woman, In the day that ye eat thereof, ye shall be as God, knowing good and evil. And when the Woman saw that the tree was good for food, and that it was a delight to the eyes, and that the tree was to be desired to make one wise, she took of the fruit thereof, and did eat, and she gave also to her Husband with her, and he did eat.

And God saw the earth, and, behold, it was corrupt; for all flesh had corrupted His way upon the earth.

What, then, did the Lord God do with His world? The Sacred History gives the answer.

INDEX

Index

Index

Index

Index

Index

INDEX OF SCRIPTURE REFERENCES

Index

Index

Index

Index

Index

Index